"A brilliant historian of modern Germany, Childers is also a masterful Tennessee storyteller. He has often made me laugh and think. *Wings of Morning* made me weep and wonder. As a fifty-year old family mystery slowly yields to a professor's detective skills, we learn anew that war is less about causes than about brothers and sons who die far away, and the sisters and mothers who mourn them."
> —Walter A. McDougall, Pulitzer Prize-winning historian, and author of *Let the Sea Make a Noise: A History of the North Pacific from Magellan to MacArthur*

"The best book ever written about the air war over Germany. *Wings of Morning* is a 'must read' for the half million airmen who flew the heavies in that great struggle over fifty years ago."
> —Leslie J. Tyler, B-17 navigator in the E.T.O.

"A labor of love. . . . A remarkable effort. . . ."
> —*Chattanooga Free Press*

"*Wings of Morning* is a fitting tribute to the crew of the *Black Cat* and the families who waited in vain for these men to return home. Even readers not especially attuned to military history will find this a moving story. I cannot recommend it too highly."
> —*The Richmond Times-Dispatch*

"This book is a joy to read. . . ."
> —*General Aviation News & Flyer*

"Childers tells his true and tragic story with both the narrative flow of fiction and a you-are-there immediacy. A fitting memorial to the crew of the *Black Cat*."
> —*Kirkus Reviews*

"A remarkable addition to our understanding of the life of airmen during the dawn of the Air Force. It is a beautiful example of what good history should be: evocative, descriptive, detailed, and thoroughly researched."
> —*The Stars and Stripes*

"[Childers] has done as good a job as anyone in conveying both how the air war was fought and how men got through it."
> —*The Chicago Tribune*

"This is a truly extraordinary book. Thomas Childers is an accomplished professional historian—whence the carefulness and the accuracy of the myriad detail; but here he shows a mastery of narrative craft that is rare nowadays. *Wings of Morning* is full of imagination, compassion, and suffused with a sense of participation that elevates it above the often unsatisfactory categories of 'objective' and 'subjective' writing. The life and death of an American airman—I am conversant with much of the literature of W.W.II, and I make bold to say that there is no other book such as this." —John Lukacs

"The strengths of *Wings of Morning* lie in its detailed picture of daily life in the Army Air Corps, with its insane mixture of boredom and terror, and the vivid recounting of the anguish of the loved ones at home. . . ."
    —*The Cleveland Plain Dealer*

"A powerful, poignant saga. . . ."
    —*The Philadelphia Daily News*

"Quite a literary feat. . . . Imaginative and emotive, and factually unerring, this outstanding remembrance is possibly the most original title among [1995's] anniversary works." —*Booklist*

"If Childers is as good a teacher as he is a historian, his classes must be sellouts."
    —*Grand Rapids Press*

"This work, a poignant tale of the airmen who almost made it home and those who waited for and loved them, is a heartfelt story. [I]t captures the intense feelings of wartime and, as such, deserves to be read."
    —*Library Journal*

"*Wings* is an intricately reported and superbly evocative rendering of the life of a Liberator crew." —*Orange County Register*

"A model work of history [and] a monument of familial love and memory more lasting than granite."
    —*Greensburg Tribune-Review*

WINGS OF MORNING

OTHER BOOKS BY THOMAS CHILDERS

The Nazi Voter

The Formation of the Nazi Constituency (editor)

Reevaluating the Third Reich (editor)

WINGS OF
MORNING

THE STORY OF THE LAST
AMERICAN BOMBER SHOT DOWN
OVER GERMANY IN WORLD WAR II

Thomas Childers

DA CAPO PRESS
A Member of the Perseus Books Group

Many of the designations used by manufacturers and sellers to distinguish their products are claimed as trademarks. Where those designations appear in this book and Perseus Books was aware of a trademark claim, the designations have been printed in initial capital letters.

Grateful acknowledgment is made to the following people for use of family photographs that appear in the insert:
Arthur Peterson, for the photograph of the Peterson family; Bill Deal, for the photograph of himself in England; Earl Beitler, for the photographs of the men inside the officer's hut, of the crews awaiting call, and of the Farrington crew en route to the flight line; Mrs. Josephine Graegin, for the photograph of Louis Wieser and his father; and the 466th Bomb Group Association Archive, for the photographs of the 466th en route to target and over target, and of the *Black Cat*. The diagram of the B-24 Liberator is taken from *Bombenkrieg gegen Deutschland* by Olaf Groehler and appears with kind permission of Akademie Verlag, Berlin. All other photographs are from the author's collection.

Excerpt from *The Things They Carried*, copyright © 1990 by Tim O'Brien. Reprinted by permission of Houghton Mifflin Company/Seymour Lawrence. All rights reserved.

Library of Congress Cataloging-in-Publication Data

Childers, Thomas, 1946–
    Wings of morning: the story of the last American bomber shot down over Germany in World War II / Thomas Childers.
        p.   cm.
    Includes bibliographical references.
    ISBN 0-201-48310-6
    ISBN 0-201-40722-1 (pbk.)
    1. World War, 1939–1945—Aerial operations, American. 2. Flight crews—United States.   3. World War, 1939–1945—Campaigns—Germany. 4. Bombing, Aerial—Germany.   5. B-24 bomber.   I. Title.
D790.C466   1995
940.54′213′092273—dc20
[B]   94-24296
                                                                          CIP

Cover design by Suzanne Heiser
Text design by Richard Oriolo
Set in 10-point Bodoni Book by Pagesetters

Perseus Books is a member of the Perseus Books Group

Find us on the World Wide Web at http://www.perseusbooksgroup.com

For all those who
did not come back,
and those who
miss them still.

If I take the wings of the morning, and dwell in the uttermost parts of
the sea;
Even there shall thy hand lead me, and thy right hand shall hold me.
If I say, surely the darkness shall cover me, even the night shall be
light about me.
Yea, the darkness hideth not from thee, but the night shineth as the
day. . . .

Psalm 139

And in the end, of course, a true war story is never about war. . . .
It's about love and memory. It's about sorrow.

Tim O'Brien, *The Things They Carried*

CONTENTS

PROLOGUE

A ROOM FILLED WITH COLOR

They sold my grandmother's house that summer. She had been ill for some time, living in a nursing home, and the house had sat empty for months. The furniture remained in place, exactly as she had left it, but she was gone and would not be coming back. In the early spring—it was three years ago now—she died quietly in her sleep. I flew down for the funeral, to say my last good-byes. We buried her in Hillcrest Cemetery, beside my granddaddy and my uncle Howard, and afterward, amid the cakes and casseroles people had sent over, we wandered around the rooms of the house, talking, reminiscing. I think we were looking for her. Later it was decided to sell the house, and in May, with the yard in full bloom, a buyer came forward, and my mother called to tell me that the deal had been made. My grandmother's things would have to go, and if I wanted anything of hers from the house I should come down.

In June my wife and I packed a suitcase, loaded our two small children into the car, and drove from Philadelphia to East Tennessee. The house sits in a small town just northeast of Chattanooga, on the old Lee Highway that runs up through Knoxville and into Virginia. I grew up there, and though I have not lived in the town for more than twenty years, it is still home. Like almost everywhere else in America the old downtown has dried up and died, and the landmarks on the compass of my childhood—Central Drug Store, the Princess Theater, Cooper's Book Store, the courthouse (torn down and replaced by a squat modern structure with no windows), and even the post office (moved out of town to the bypass)—have all vanished. The town has grown and is by most standards even prosperous, but with its shopping malls and WalMarts and Pizza Huts and cable TV, it bears no resemblance to the magical if insular place where I grew up.

But my grandmother's house had not changed. Here and there you could find the nightclub ashtrays and Swiss clocks and hand-painted Italian china my uncle Jim brought back from his trips to New York and Europe—all tasteful, even elegant, items—but most of the furniture, the pictures on the walls, the pie plates and cast-iron skillets in the kitchen dated from an earlier time. They had remained in place for years and years, permanent points in the topography of my memory.

Although I had visited often through the years I had not slept in the house since I was a child, and never without grandparents or aunts and uncles and cousins. On that first night sleep came hard. For what seemed like hours I tossed restlessly under the light sheet, listening to the occasional car rumble down Georgetown Pike toward the interstate. I checked on the kids in the guest room. I had a drink from the tap in the kitchen. But I could not settle down. Around two in the morning I gave up. With the central air-conditioning murmuring and the house as quiet and cool as a tomb, I got up and wandered into the living room.

Everything there was so familiar I hardly needed the light. The heavy chairs flanking the fireplace, the divan just opposite, and the oil portrait of Howard above the mantel—the only painting in the house—were in their customary places. My eyes took them all in, but I was drawn to the ancient secretary that stood in the corner, just before the entrance hall. With its glass-encased china vases, the wooden shoes Howard had sent home from Belgium during the war, the collection of college textbooks and condensed novels from the *Reader's Digest*, it was what I had come to find.

I decided to open the drawers. Swollen shut in the air-conditioned dampness, they had been closed for years, sealed tight as a grave. I knew vaguely what they contained, and although they resisted, groaning and creaking so loudly I thought they would wake up the children, I finally pried them open one by one. They gave off the musty odor of old paper and cloth, and in them were the things I knew would be there. My mother's diploma from the McKenzie School of Business in Chattanooga, dated 1941, a scrapbook of Howard's sports career at the high school and another one of mine. Another drawer held photographs, some sepia and brittle and curling at the edges, of my daddy in his army uniform, just back from Europe, of Uncle Jim in cap and gown at the university, of Aunt Sibyle, only a child, perched on a pony at the side of the house, and of my granddaddy standing proudly beside the old Chrysler.

In the third and largest drawer I found what had drawn me to the secretary in the first place. In carefully packed paper bags and gift boxes from Miller's Department Store were bundles of letters, still neatly folded in their envelopes. They carried postmarks from 1943 and '44 and '45, and their return addresses bore names, eerily familiar, from St. Louis and Chicago and Brooklyn. Another box yielded up a series of small envelopes with tiny microfilmed lettering and APO numbers, V-mails from overseas during the war. Among the letters were a handful of photographs, tiny, wallet-sized snapshots, formal portraits, and picture postcards, all of men in uniform. One, I realized, was Howard's bomber crew. They were posed beneath the wing of a great silver plane, the blade of its giant propeller just behind them. I turned it over. In a clear, precise hand Howard had written their names and positions—pilot, copilot, and so on. Eleven names. I studied the photograph, trying to match names and faces. Peterson, Perella, Brennan, Barrett, and on across the rows. A pleasant-faced, dark-haired boy, maybe nineteen, knelt in the front row beside Howard. Albert Seraydarian. Why did I know that name?

As I shuffled through the snapshots, flashes of an old image—was it a memory? a dream? I didn't know—came back to me, an image that had been with me all my life. I stand in a room filled with color. Splashes of brilliant red, tangents of blue and white, bundles of green rise, kaleidoscopic, from the floor to the ceiling, blotting out the windows, hiding the walls. I am a small boy and in the room filled with color voices come like whispers. The image had come to me now and then at odd moments over the years, at work or driving the car, sitting at home with the children. It was not dramatic or unsettling. It was not a nightmare, this room filled with color. It was, I had come to believe, my first conscious memory—could that be?—but of what I could not say.

It was then, as I sorted through the V-mails and the faded photographs, that I saw it. It was tucked into a large bundle of 8 X 10 glossies, portraits of Howard in high school, at college, during air force training. And in the time it took for the photograph to slide from the bundle onto my lap, the room filled with color leapt up at me from a shadowy black-and-white image and the years fell away and the memory hit me with the force of a blow.

I am a historian by trade, a professor at an Ivy League university where I have taught European, but especially German, history for almost twenty years. When asked by colleagues or students how Germany came to occupy the center of my professional life, I had a standard answer I would give. It was couched in appropriately intellectual terms and it was compelling, scholarly, respectable. Until that night in my grandmother's living room, I think I even believed it myself.

It is three years now since I opened the drawer in the secretary. In those three years I have completely put aside my other work, and I have followed the trail of the letters and photographs all across the United States, to New York and Illinois and Florida, to Maine and Mississippi and California. They led to other letters in other houses, buried in the vaults of memory for almost fifty years, and to sheaves of documents in Washington and St. Louis and Montgomery. They led to a deserted air base in England. They led to a field in Germany.

I did not understand what drew me to the secretary in my grandmother's house that night three years ago. I do now.

In the cool living room I began to arrange the letters. I began to read.

CHAPTER 1

[★]

GONE FOR A SOLDIER

He was eighteen and the world was at war and they would get him soon. For weeks he waited, sitting in his cluttered dorm room, following the war news on the radio, watching his classmates disappear. Buddy McLeod, who had roomed with him during the fall semester, was gone, enlisting in the Air Corps before he could be drafted. His brother-in-law Tom was gone, and his friends Pokey Schultz and Dee Gibson and C. L. Bivens were gone, and he knew that his number would be up soon and he would be gone too.

He started college at Western Kentucky in the fall of 1942, playing football, writing home to Nancy, trying to study. He thought about engineering or law, but he wasn't sure. It was hard to concentrate. At the college movie theater he watched the newsreels of the war—marines wading ashore at Guadalcanal, GIs slogging through the desert in North Africa, acrobatic P-38s slicing through the clouds over France. It hardly seemed real. But when he returned to Bowling Green after Christmas vacation he found among the postcards and letters a short notice from the Selective Service. "Well, I got back to school okay," he wrote to his parents in early

January. "I went to the post office and I had the card for my blood test. It had
been there for seven days. I went down to the draft board and they told me to
come . . . Tuesday for my examination."

He had thought about enlisting, picking his branch of the service, but
wasn't sure just what he wanted. "I went down to see the navy yesterday and
they said they weren't taking anyone, only through your draft board. I think
I'll see the marines tomorrow and see what they say." He wasn't really much
interested in either. His mother couldn't swim and was terrified of the water,
and there was no point in giving her more to worry about. Then there was
the Air Corps, that was a possibility. Tom, his brother-in-law, was in the Air
Corps, and Buddy, too. He decided to let it ride. He wouldn't have long to
wait now anyway. He had spoken to the dean about withdrawing from
school, packed his trunk and shipped it home. "I figure I will get my call
around the last of the week," he wrote on February 17, "but I don't mind it
now that Tom and all my buddies are gone. . . ."

He took the L&N as far as Nashville, then changed to the Southern for
the final leg of the trip home. The trains were choked with people now,
soldiers and sailors wedged into the seats, standing in the cluttered aisles,
ducking to peer through the grimy windows as the train stopped at each
crowded station or lonely country depot. Home was a small manufacturing
town tucked into a fold of the East Tennessee hills just northeast of
Chattanooga. Cleveland, Tennessee, boasted some twenty thousand inhabi-
tants, a maple-shaded main street, a monument to the Confederate war
dead (although the town had been solidly pro-Union), and one six-story
hotel—the Cherokee—that rose up like a red brick silo from the dark
shadows of the hills. People worked in the woolen mill or the stove factory
or in the small stores clustered around the courthouse square, and on
Saturdays the streets were clogged with red-faced men from out in the
county, from the small family farms that stretched out north to the Tennessee River or south to the Georgia border only a few miles away.

The neat two-story house on Trunk Street where the Goodners had lived
since 1929 was an easy walk from the depot, and his father was standing on
the front porch waiting when he bounced up the steps. Ernest Goodner was
a thin, self-educated man with an ironic country wit and hands as strong as
pliers. As a young man he had worked for the railroad before becoming an
electrician with the TVA, and he had built the house and paid for it while
the market tumbled and times turned hard. Howard found his mother in the
kitchen. She had raised four children and seemed in Howard's mind never

to have left the stove. Standing in the familiar kitchen while she fried okra and his father read the paper, Howard recalled how all through the years of his childhood jobless men in seedy, colorless clothes had wandered down the street and smelled her food and stopped at the front door to ask for something to eat. His mother would send them around to the screened-in back porch, where she would place a plate of cornbread and beans on the long, white wooden table, and he and his kid brother, James, would stand shyly in the kitchen doorway and stare until she nudged them and frowned, and then they would slip back in the house until the stranger was gone.

His sister Mildred was there to greet him too. She was staying at home these days, waiting to hear from her husband, Tom. He was stationed at Keesler Field in Mississippi, completing his basic training, and Mildred was preparing to join him at his next post. Howard was anxious to hear the latest about Tom, about basic, about the Air Corps. Of all the recruiting pitches he had heard in the last month, the Air Corps's had been most impressive.

He spent the days at home with his folks and with Nancy, waiting, marking time. Despite the gas rationing, his brother James, a junior in high school, was learning to drive, and Howard took him in the big Chrysler out on Lee Highway, showing him the ropes. Tall and thin, James had never been much of an athlete, but he could sit for hours in the living room picking out show tunes on the old upright piano or listening to Benny Goodman on the radio. Even his older sister Sibyle drove across the mountains from Carthage, bringing her daughter, Elizabeth Ann. They would all be there to say good-bye.

When the county draft board released its March call for "white men," the name Goodner, Howard G. appeared as expected on the list, and on March 23, 1943, he packed a small bag, kissed the family and Nancy good-bye, and reported with the 120 other local boys to the small train station. There were all sorts—farm boys from out in the county, rough kids from the south side of town near the woolen mill, boys Howard recognized from high school and some he had never seen before. Sweethearts and parents and friends crowded around the platform as the boys, dressed in everything from coveralls to sport coats, carrying cardboard suitcases or duffel bags or nothing at all, stumbled into uneven ranks and listened intently as the roll was called. They waved good-bye as they climbed into the train, then sat with their faces pressed against the windows of the ancient Southern Railroad cars. Their destination was "an undisclosed induction center."

"Well, I am in the Air Corps," Howard wrote in the first week of April, "but don't know just what it is like so far. . . ." The stationery bore the inscription "Army Air Forces Technical Training Command, Miami Beach" and a logo depicting the silhouettes of palm trees, beach umbrellas, and couples playfully tossing a ball in the surf. He had spent ten days at Fort Oglethorpe, Georgia, not far from Chattanooga, being issued uniforms that didn't fit and taking psychological and aptitude tests that would determine his branch of service. At the end of the testing they stamped his papers "AAF"—army air forces—and he marched off with hundreds of other inductees to a railroad siding, awaiting shipment to basic training.

The trip to Miami in the crowded troop train took almost seventy-two hours. It was the first of many trips he would take in training, long days and restless nights squeezed into the packed coaches, reading day-old newspapers, munching yesterday's sandwiches, dozing between trains in crowded waiting rooms, watching at each stop the familiar tableau of farewells and homecomings. But for all the discomforts, that first trip carried an air of high adventure, the first step in an odyssey that would carry him into the world of momentous events he had only read about or seen in the newsreels. Like most of the boys he encountered in the crowded troop train or in the raucous mess halls or in the endless lines at the quartermaster annexes, Howard had never been far from home, had never seen the ocean or ridden in an airplane. Except for short trips to visit relations in middle Tennessee or North Carolina, the family had not taken vacations, and his only exposure to the world outside his hometown had been with the college sports teams, riding in the train to games in Youngstown or Memphis. His suitcase bore colorful stickers from those towns, and his mother still kept in her scrapbook the picture postcard he had sent of the train station in Dayton, Ohio. As the recruits disembarked from the troop train that first morning, the soft tropical sunrise playing off the pastel buildings and bungalows of Miami Beach bathed the world in a light so exotic, so magical, they might have landed in the kingdom of Oz.

On arrival they were herded through the usual battery of tests—the radio operator test, aircraft mechanic test, flexible gunnery test, and a bewildering array of general aptitude and psychiatric tests. They took physical exams and had their hair cut, their teeth checked, and inoculations for everything from tetanus to yellow fever. They wandered like sleepwalkers in long, meandering lines that wound into the medical annex, waiting as each man, dressed only in his shorts and dog tags, slogged through an interminable series of stations in the sweltering heat, waiting for their vaccinations. They stood passively while bored medical personnel, their starched khakis and white smocks stained with sweat, jabbed them with syringes and examined everything from their tonsils to their testicles. Side by side they peed in specimen jars, peered at eye charts, and bent over to touch their toes while dull-eyed medics strode down the line, probing them roughly for hemorrhoids. By the end of the day some were sick, some had fainted, and some could hardly lift their arms.

Set against a backdrop of palm trees and luxury hotels basic training was not at all what he had expected. "I'm crazy about Florida," Howard wrote after several days in his new quarters. "I am staying in the biggest hotel on the beach. They call it the New Yorker, [and] it would cost a civilian about $25 a day. . . . [We] march down the street going to the golf course to drill every day and . . . sing our flight songs. . . . There are 950 hotels here and all of them are larger than the Cherokee and are all white and blue and I mean they are full. We have a big rug on our floor about one inch thick and have a shower and bathtub to the room and a commode and sink. Five beds, one sofa, dresser, writing desk, five big easy chairs like in our living room and six windows on one side of the room with venetian blinds. . . . We have the ocean and in the backyard two swimming pools."

Not long after arriving at basic Howard began to think seriously about pilot training. "They tell me Buddy McLeod is a cadet," he wrote. "I sure wish I was." The cadet program led to an officer's commission, and even if you couldn't be a pilot there was navigator or bombardier school. His aptitude scores were strong, and after some prodding from his flight sergeant, he decided to look into it. In the meantime he thought he would be "going to gunnery school and radio operator-mechanic school and then to OCS [Officer Candidate School] if I don't get the cadet."

Letters from Nancy arrived almost every day, and Howard eagerly wrote back. They were not formally engaged, had not even really discussed marriage before he left for the service, but there was an understanding. They had dated throughout their senior year in high school and had written when Howard went off to college. They were in love. Calling on the telephone was out of the question. Howard rarely had access to one, and when he did the lines were impossibly long and the time short. So he looked forward to mail call, to the letters from his folks, from his older sisters, Mildred and Sibyle, and from his brother, James. But mostly he looked forward to Nancy's letters. She filled him in on events at home, on where their friends had been shipped, who was overseas, who was dating. He sent her a birthday gift just before Easter—it wasn't much considering he couldn't really leave the post—but he had a formal portrait made for her at a local studio. He was wearing his Air Corps hat, with its smart leather brim and propeller-with-wings insignia, and a trench coat, its collar turned up like Bogart's. The print was a bit fuzzy and the tint was dull, but he looked quite dashing. Everyone in the family knew they were serious, often adding little asides about Nancy in their letters and prodding him good-naturedly about their relationship. "I got a letter from Mildred and she said she heard I was married," Howard wrote in early May. "Well, don't believe it because it's not so. Old Howard isn't getting married or," he added in a meaningful clarification, "I'm not married yet."

By the end of May Howard and his group had completed basic and were awaiting their assignments. Some would go directly to gunnery, others to flight engineering, still others to radio school. Howard figured he would be heading for radio, but just where he didn't know. "I am on shipment now but won't be sent for at least a day or two yet," he wrote in early June. "They took up our khakis so I guess I am going north. Don't know just yet."

"Well, the old boy is in Scott Field, Illinois," Howard informed his folks on June 7. "We left Miami Friday at 4 P.M. and came through Atlanta, Chattanooga, and home (Saturday night at 12 A.M.), but we didn't stop. What I saw looked pretty good. Then Knoxville, Kentucky, Indiana, and Illinois. The first day here I caught KP in the world's second largest mess hall. I am now a private first class. I will be here until I finish school. Eighteen weeks . . . studying radio. . . . They say it is pretty hard."

An enormous, rambling base just across the Mississippi from St. Louis, Scott Field was the parent radio school of the AAF Technical Training Command. It was responsible for turning recruits into radio operators, the vast majority of whom would ultimately be assigned to a heavy bomber crew. Scott was also a port of embarkation (POE) for heavy bombers and their crews. He had heard them on that first morning, as he stepped down from the troop train onto the railroad siding and blinked into the harsh midwestern sun. A deep and distant rumbling rose from beyond the low-lying buildings as a squadron of giant, four-engine aircraft lumbered down an unseen runway. One after another they lifted off, roaring into the bright, cloudless glare. B-17s, he realized with a thrill, the Flying Fortresses he had read about and seen in the Movietone newsreels. Squinting, he strained to follow them as they rose above the rooftops, banked gently, and began to climb. The sight of the big silver planes was mesmerizing, but long after they had shrunk to sparkling shards of light high above the field, the relentless droning of their engines lingered, reverberating above the hissing steam of the train and the shuffling of the men as they fell in line on the platform. It was a sound that would be with them for months, would hover about them in the humid mornings and stifling afternoons of training, would so utterly envelop them that they would finally lose their awareness of it altogether. But in those first days the inescapable sound of the engines seemed as unnerving as the first rumbling tremors of an earthquake.

It didn't take long for the rigors of radio school to impress him. The demanding course included electronics, mechanics, code, and a comprehensive study of the radio set itself. Sitting in the labs during the long, hot afternoons or in the still, sultry hours of the night shift, Howard struggled to master the internal electronics of the radio, building generators, studying vacuum tubes and amplifiers, transformers and transmitters. He disassembled the sets, examined the intricate ganglia of tubes and wires, and reassembled them blindfolded. He learned theory and maintenance—how each part worked, how it could be repaired, how he might improvise in the air if the set were damaged or malfunctioned.

Electronics was a challenge, but the Morse code, bombarding his ears night and day with its relentless metallic chirping, was maddening. For weeks his head buzzed with electronic tapping—dot, dot, dash, dot, dot, dash—morning and night. Each day in code class Howard sat with his classmates at the long tables for hours at a time, trying to unscramble the clipped sequences of code beamed from tiny sets on the tables before them. "The sounds come through earphones," he wrote to his parents, "and they sound like a swarm of bees."

In late August Mildred wrote to tell him that Tom was on his way overseas. Like so many young wives she had followed him from training camp to training camp, from Keesler Field in Mississippi to Tishomingo,

Oklahoma, to Kellogg Field in Battle Creek, Michigan, living in hotels and boardinghouses until at last, in early August, she watched the troop train moving out for a POE somewhere on the east coast. New York, she thought. Mildred returned home to the house on Trunk Street, where she planned to stay while Tom was overseas. "I figure Tom was shipped to North Africa or to England," Howard wrote to her, "because he was shipped from New York. . . . Sure wish I was with Tom and I guess I will be after gunnery. I hope so."

Radio school was winding down, and Howard knew that he was doing well. He was ranked in the upper tier of his class. Still, he was a bit surprised when his squadron commander, after reviewing the class's personnel, sent for him. "I was called in . . . by the captain today," Howard wrote, "and he asked me if I would like to go to the communication cadet school. He said my grades were fine so far and if I wanted to go to come back tomorrow. . . ." The idea of the cadet program certainly appealed to him. "You stay here as an instructor from three to eight months, then in six weeks of cadet training at Yale you are a second lieutenant." It was tempting, even flattering, and he was confident that he could do it, but he wasn't sure if he really wanted to sit out the war as a communications instructor at Scott Field or one of the other radio schools around the country. For weeks Howard had watched the silver B-17s departing for Europe or the Pacific. If he refused the offer to become an instructor and finished up radio on schedule, he could be on one of those planes within a matter of weeks.

He agonized over the decision for days, turning over the pros and cons, talking to his CO, to his instructors, to the guys in the barracks. It would be a good job, a safe job, and although his folks didn't press the issue, he knew they wanted him to take it. Nancy, too. He wished he could talk to Buddy or Tom. Buddy, Nancy told him, had been home on leave recently, but there was no way to contact him now.

"Well, Mother," he wrote at last, "I didn't take the offer to become an instructor." He had almost completed radio school, he tried to explain, and after gunnery he would be assigned to a combat crew. If all went well he would be flying soon. "I would take [the instructor's job]," he added, "but you stay here too long." In the end it all came down to one central consideration. "I guess I just didn't want it. I couldn't take it and stay here while Tom is across and all the other fellows. I guess if you were a boy you would look at it the same as I." She didn't.

"We had commencement exercises Wednesday night," Howard wrote on October 29, "so now I am officially a ROM, radio operator-mechanic." He had completed his thirty hours of flying, operating the radio shoulder to shoulder with his classmates in planes specially modified for airborne radio instruction. They weren't B-17s or B-24s, but he *was* flying and he loved it. "I go up . . . and copy code and send a little and it sure . . . feels good to be flying around after going to school so long. I'll tell you what, they have some boys in the hospital who went code happy from taking code so much and that's no lie." He was in shipping and receiving now, waiting for his assignment to gunnery school. "I don't know where I'll go from here," he wrote, "but I hope it's Florida."

Howard got his wish. On Sunday, November 21, he wrote to tell his folks that he was in Panama City, Florida, at Tyndall Field Aerial Gunnery School. The barracks were only about one hundred yards from the ocean, and from his bunk he could hear the staccato rasping of machine-gun fire. "It sounds as if there is a war being fought here all the time and the obstacle course is one Superman cut his teeth on. After we start flying we get paid flying time." He was excited about flying. They would be going up not only in the usual two-engine trainers, but they would also get some air time in the "heavies," the B-17s and B-24s.

After the first week of orientation and classroom instruction flexible gunnery class 44-2 moved out through a desolate landscape of sandy hillocks and scrub pines to one of the many firing ranges. They began shooting skeet, then progressed to firing from moving platforms, from small arms to automatic weapons and finally to the heavy machine guns. They learned how to operate the power-driven turrets, how to sight and swing them and their twin fifties. Wedged into the tiny, cramped turret, they fired from the nose, the belly, and the tail, swiveling the Plexiglas and metal mechanism toward the moving targets downrange. They fired from fixed positions, and then from mounts on moving platforms on the ground, and finally prepared for air-to-air gunnery.

With the holidays approaching home was very much on his mind. It would be his first Thanksgiving away from the family, and it was clear that he would not be home for Christmas either. He wished he could see Nancy.

They spoke briefly on the phone from time to time, short, truncated conversations that left them both more lonely and frustrated than ever. Letters were better, but it was tough. "Say, how would you all like a new daughter-in-law?" he wrote just before Thanksgiving, and although he quickly added, "No, I was only kidding," he wasn't fooling anyone. He asked his mother "to tell Mildred to be looking for something for me to give Nancy. I can't get off the post, and it will be . . . impossible to send her anything. We can't get even one little pass. . . . I'll send her the money soon and tell her not to go by the price. . . ." It had to be a special gift. A few days later he had decided. "Tell Mildred to pick out a watch for Nancy. . . . Tell her to go ahead and get it but just pay a down payment on it and I will send her the money soon. . . . Tell her to get a good one, though." In the meantime his mail from home brought him a special Christmas gift. "I received a big box of eats," he wrote on December 13, and he added casually, "a beautiful ring from Nancy. . . ."

Howard completed gunnery on January 12, 1944, finishing in the top 2½ percent of his class. His instructors and squadron commander were still after him to consider the cadet program. It was not too late. A letter from Tom had just arrived, the first from his brother-in-law to reach Howard in almost two months. Tom was a sergeant in the Eighth Air Force now, assigned to the 390th Bomb Group "somewhere in England," and was, he told Howard, considering going for the cadets. Howard thought Tom would make a good pilot, but he was still not ready to apply for the program himself. "Don't worry," his squadron commander assured him, "you won't miss the war," but Howard was anxious to complete his training, anxious to move on to operational flying. "I was interviewed night before last again for communication cadet," he reported to his mother, "but I don't want it and I told Lt. Hay I didn't." She hoped he knew what he was doing.

With radio and gunnery now behind him Howard was ready for combat-crew training. That assignment, he assumed, would come at Kearns Field, near Salt Lake City, one of several bases where replacement crews for heavy bombardment groups were formed. He hoped the processing would not take long, and just a few days after the long train ride from Florida to Utah it seemed as if his wish had been granted. "I was assigned to a Flying Fortress and to a squadron," he wrote on February 7, "but it broke up or I would have been in England or the Pacific by now. England, I guess. We were ready to move, and they broke it up just like that. I can't figure it out. I thought for a while that I might get to see Tom, but no such luck." So he waited. Day after day he watched the clouds roll in over the jagged mountains beyond the runways, veiling the vast, empty landscape with rustling curtains of snow. He had never seen such snowflakes, giant gossamer crystals as large as robins' eggs that seemed to fill the thin mountain air with layers of delicate, fluttering lace.

He was playing basketball for the post team in early March when orders were cut transferring him to Buckley Field in Colorado. "We had a fine trip from Salt Lake to Denver," he wrote, "nice Pullmans, and it only took twenty-four hours to make the trip." He didn't expect to be at Buckley long. It was merely one more loop in the holding pattern, one more station in the seemingly endless conveyor belt of army processing. While he waited at Buckley for his crew assignment he trudged through the heaping mounds of snow to refreshers in communications, target identification, and first aid, but the courses, the drills and inspections and duties around the post were just something to keep them busy. He was treading water, waiting, and as he waited and watched his barracks mates ship out for combat-crew training, he was having second thoughts about passing up the cadet program. "James," he urged his brother, "you should try for the cadets when you come in, because it's the best deal [you] could get . . . I was crazy for not doing it when I came in, but gunnery and radio will do I guess."

When at last his orders arrived Howard discovered that he was to report to Westover Field, near Springfield, Massachusetts. It meant another tedious cross-country train trip, long, mind-numbing days in the stuffy coaches, sleeping upright in the threadbare seats, drinking coffee in the dusty stations between trains, but at last he would be assigned a crew. He would meet the nine men, four officers and five other enlisted men, who would fly with him. Friendships formed quickly in the army. On the different bases in the different phases of training he had met guys who seemed after only weeks like old friends, and whom he had forgotten almost as soon as that phase of training ended and they went their separate ways. But the crew would be different. He had watched other crews forming at Kearns and Scott, ten total strangers meeting awkwardly in squadron dayrooms or on the flight line under the wing of a plane, nervously sizing one another up. For the next twelve weeks his world would shrink down around them. He would live with them, eat with them, go through countless classes and training exercises with them, and finally, he knew, go to war with them. He hoped they would be good, hoped he would get along with them, hoped things would go well.

Westover, in the hills of western Massachusetts between Springfield and Chicopee Falls, was a major training facility for B-24 Liberators. After the bus deposited him at the gate he made his way to the barracks in the dark. Overhead he heard the droning of engines and could see behind the patchy clouds the red and green running lights of the four-engine bombers. "B-24s fly constantly here and one can't sleep well," he wrote the next morning, "but it didn't bother me last night." He was excited. Within days, he thought, he would be flying in one of those planes.

But weeks passed in processing and more refresher courses, and Howard was going stir-crazy. Then, in the second week of June, his orders at last arrived, assigning him to a training squadron for replacement combat crews. After months of close-order drills, chickenshit inspections, hours upon hours of straining at his radio headsets, he had at last arrived at the final phase of training.

Like an archaeologist examining the hieroglyphics on an ancient tomb, he eagerly deciphered the three pages of cryptic abbreviations and acronyms that made up his shipment orders. He was enormously relieved. There would be no torturous train trip, no new base. He would be staying at Westover, moving to another part of the field, and that, he realized with a jolt of anticipation, meant that he would indeed be flying the B-24s that thundered over the green Berkshire hills day after day, night after night, filling the spring air with their relentless droning rumble.

He met the pilot and copilot first, in the squadron dayroom on a hot, airless afternoon that announced the arrival of summer. Both were tall, lanky men, strong, soft-spoken, and easygoing. The pilot's name was Richard Farrington, from St. Louis. Well over six feet tall, Farrington was an athletic, powerful man, who exuded self-confidence. He had enlisted when he was nineteen and was not yet twenty-one when he finished flight school in March 1944. Jack Regan, the copilot, was also twenty years old, from the Elmhurst section of Queens in New York City, and like Farrington, he was a powerful man who carried himself with the easy gait of a natural athlete. His buddies growing up had nicknamed him Abe because of the slow, folksy cadence of his deep voice and his uncanny resemblance to the young beardless Lincoln. Howard liked them both right away.

One by one the others checked in, the officers arriving first. The bombardier was a squat, bearish man from Pittsburgh. Christ Manners was twenty-three and wore a thick, downward-arcing mustache that gave his round, swarthy face a misleadingly savage appearance. A full head shorter than Farrington and Regan, Manners was completely bald on top, and Farrington instantly christened him Curly. He had studied for two years at the University of Pittsburgh before enlisting shortly after Pearl Harbor. The eighteen-week bombardiers' school was behind him now, and he arrived at Westover with a high rating. Mel Rossman, the navigator, was also twenty-three. A thin, intense man with sharp, chiseled features, he had grown up in Denver. His mother, Howard would discover later, had died when he was twelve, and his father five years later, and during the hard times of the Depression he was raised in a household that included his grandparents, four uncles, and an aunt. After high school he came east and graduated from Yeshiva University in New York City. He had been planning a career in the law when the war broke out.

Later in the day Howard met the crew's five enlisted men. They were an eclectic bunch. They came from all over the country, from big cities and small towns, and ranged in age from eighteen to twenty-eight. Within the following weeks they would become his closest buddies, guys he would share a barracks with, go to chow with, go on pass with, guys he would depend on and come to trust like no others.

When Howard first saw him, Albert Seraydarian was playing cards and was down fifty dollars on his way to blowing a whole month's pay. With long, dark hair combed straight back from his broad, pleasant face, the man who would be the crew's tail gunner had a calm, unflappable air even as he drew one losing hand after another. When he spoke, casually swearing at the cards, the words sauntered out in a string of "dem's" and "dose's," a Brooklynese so thick and melodious it sounded to Howard's southern ear like something straight out of the Dead End Kids. Al was eighteen years old, the youngest of five children and barely out of New Utrecht High School in the Borough Park section of Brooklyn. He had enlisted shortly after graduation, hoping to become a pilot, but things did not work out and he was assigned to gunnery. They called him Brooklyn.

Sitting beside Seraydarian on the bunk that first afternoon, peering over his shoulder and offering a running commentary on each hand, was a big, broad-shouldered kid with a crew cut and an easy Irish smile. Jack Brennan said he was eighteen, but he didn't look that old. He had grown up in Cliffside Park, New Jersey, just across the Hudson from Manhattan, and had been a star football player for St. Cecilia High School in Englewood. When he graduated in June 1943 he was only seventeen, and he begged his parents to sign the release form for him to enlist. He wanted to join the Air Corps. They resisted at first, but in the end they relented, and Jack rushed off to join up. After basic training he completed gunnery school in Laredo, Texas, and was qualified as an armorer-gunner. He would man the fifties in the waist of the ship.

Harry Gregorian, the nose gunner, didn't talk much. He was quiet and intense, a nervous guy who radiated tension like high-voltage wires. At nineteen he had already begun a boxing career as a welterweight in Detroit. Short and wiry, Harry bristled with an air of quiet menace, a big-city tough with tense, pale eyes and a face that looked as if it had seen more than its share of trouble. Like Seraydarian's, Harry's family was Armenian, and he gravitated naturally toward Al, whose easygoing manner seemed to calm some of the tension that clung to him like static. Harry barely spoke when Howard introduced himself that afternoon, looking shyly down at his shoes or stealing a quick glance at the card game several bunks away. Howard couldn't get a read on him, not that day nor in the weeks that followed. Harry kept to himself.

The crew's flight engineer, Jerome Barrett, was small and compact, with dark, dancing eyes and a dashing mustache. The card game was over and the boys were sitting around getting acquainted when he pushed through the door, strolled down the aisle, and dropped his barracks bag on the bunk beside Howard. He was twenty, from New York City, and when Al and Jack heard his address—the posh Century Apartments on Central Park West in Manhattan—they whistled appreciatively. He had entered service just after high school, in October 1942, had completed the difficult flight engineering school, and because of his training would be, after Howard, the ranking NCO on the crew. His father, Howard later discovered, owned a very successful chemical company, occupying two entire floors of Rockefeller Center, and his older brother had begun a career in show business, encouraged by their next door neighbor, Broadway star Ethel Merman. Although Jerry rarely said much about the family and certainly didn't flaunt their well-heeled circumstances, he was from a world as far removed from the other boys as could be. Yet what struck Howard that first afternoon at Westover was that Jerry was bright and funny in a sophisticated sort of way, completely without pretensions, and right away the two boys, one from Central Park West, the other from Cleveland, Tennessee, hit it off.

When Howard first met Bob Peterson he was doing what he always did. Sitting cross-legged on his bunk, a group of photographs spread before him on the olive drab woolen blanket, he held his pen poised above a few scattered sheets of stationery. "Writing home to the wife," Jack Brennan whispered between hands of the card game, and it struck Howard as he glanced at the crew's ball-turret gunner that this was the first married man he had encountered in the service. Bob Peterson was trim and tan, having just arrived from gunnery school in Texas. He was from a small town in Illinois, near Peoria, and, as he explained to them on the way to chow that first evening, he was married and had two kids. His wife's name was Marie, and she and the two boys, one five and the other only four months old, were living with her folks in Chicago while he was away. Later, as they sat in the crowded mess hall, he proudly showed Howard the snapshots, one of Marie, one of Bobby, his older boy, and one of the four of them standing in the garden of his father-in-law's house in Chicago. It had been made only a few weeks ago, during his leave between gunnery school at Laredo and Westover—the first time he had seen the baby, Arthur. In the photograph, Marie wore a print dress and a broad smile and Bob, in his summer uniform, held the baby proudly in his arms.

He had been an electrician before the war, he told Howard later, and had been in the army for over two years. His first marriage had ended in divorce, and his son Bobby was living with his folks in rural Illinois when he met Marie at a factory picnic in Chicago. They both loved to dance, loved the beat of the big bands and the soft bubbling baritone of Bing Crosby, and they dated through the summer of 1941. In November, just on the eve of Pearl Harbor, they were married, and although he had a wife and small child at home, he enlisted in early 1942. He was convinced that he would be drafted soon and that by enlisting he would be able to enter the cadet program to become a pilot. But everything went wrong. He performed well in preflight and in the first phase of pilot training, handling the aircraft skillfully in the air, but he suffered recurrent bouts of airsickness, especially at takeoff and landing. He tried everything, but nothing seemed to work, and in the summer of 1943 he finally washed out of the program. Then, after passing the requirements for navigator's school, he was transferred out at the last, heartbreaking moment and assigned to gunnery school.

For a time in gunnery it looked as if he would spend the rest of the war as an instructor—he wrote excitedly to Marie with the news—but in late spring 1944 he was classified as an aircrew member ready for overseas duty.

It had been a hard two years, with long stretches away from Marie and Bobby, away from the baby, and now, as the crew assembled at Westover in June, he faced the prospect of going overseas. At twenty-eight Bob was the old man of the crew, and by the end of their first week together Brennan began calling him Pop.

After settling into their quarters the crew drew their flight gear—flying gloves, goggles, summer flying helmet, oxygen masks, the bright yellow inflatable life preservers, known to the crews as Mae Wests. They were issued an armload of technical manuals, instructional booklets—*Your Body in Flight, Army Air Forces Radio Facility Charts*—and other materials required for the classes and training exercises awaiting them. The first two weeks passed in a relentless grind of ground classes, familiarizing them with flight procedures, aircraft identification, first aid, and the operational doctrine of high-altitude strategic bombing. In addition, each man attended specialized classes: pilots in the Link trainer, a mechanical cockpit that simulated actual flight situations; the A-2 bomb trainer, for bombardiers and pilots; and communications reviews for radio operators. Almost daily the crew assembled at the flight line where the Liberators stood scattered around the runways. They clambered through the aircraft, going over the functions of the equipment at each station, familiarizing each man with the job of the others.

There was always a surge of adrenaline when the crew gathered on the flight line and confronted the mammoth plane they would fly. With a wingspan of 110 feet, a length of 64 feet, and a gross weight of forty-one thousand pounds, the B-24 seemed impossibly, monstrously big. The long, tapering wings were mounted high on the shoulders of the stubby fuselage, and the four 1,200-horsepower Pratt & Whitney engines sprouted propeller blades as large as a man. The Liberator was the most modern aircraft in the U.S. air arsenal in 1944. It flew faster, carried a heavier bomb load, and possessed greater range than its sister ship, the B-17, and more B-24s were in production than any other bomber. Yet, unlike the graceful Flying Fortress, which had become the glamour plane of the war, the Liberator was an ugly aircraft. Its squat fuselage, stubby nose, and enormous twin vertical stabilizers lent the ship an ungainly, pugnacious look. Dubbed the banana boat, the flying brick, the pregnant cow, and the old agony wagon, it was a plane that, as one of their instructors put it, "you just couldn't form an attachment to." None of the pilots coming out of flight school wanted to fly the Liberator.

The B-24 was a difficult plane to handle. The long, tapering Davis wing, which gave the aircraft its speed and power, also created problems. Although the Liberator could sustain considerable damage and still keep flying, hit that wing, one instructor delighted in warning them, and the plane would go down. Many veteran pilots also felt that the B-24 was less stable and more prone to high-speed stalls than the slower B-17, and at altitudes over twenty thousand feet the controls tended to go sluggish. These problems became particularly hazardous in high-altitude formation flying, which was the key to American air strategy in Europe. "You don't know what shit hittin' the fan means," one veteran told them, "till you've seen a Liberator flip over on its side in the middle of a forty-plane formation."

Pilots had to possess brute strength and extraordinary reflexes to handle the big ship, and from their very first trips up in the plane it was obvious to the crew that Farrington and Regan had both. Like so many men who flew combat in the war, neither Farrington nor Regan had set foot in a plane before entering service. They were both nineteen when they enlisted in 1943, determined to fly. By the time they met at Westover both had completed a grueling year of intensive flight training. After eight weeks of preflight—ground classes on navigation, aerodynamics, meteorology, and aircraft identification—both men proceeded through the three standard phases of pilot training. Including training casualties, which were stunningly high, almost forty percent of all who entered pilot training failed to complete it. In primary they learned to fly small, single-engine aircraft, tiny, skittish planes as unstable as canoes. After eight weeks they moved on to basic, where the planes were bigger and the classes more demanding, and advanced, where they learned military planes and tactics, until, at last, after thirty weeks of intensive training, they transitioned to multiengine aircraft, to the daunting B-24. When the crew assembled at Westover, Farrington had logged roughly one hundred hours in the big four-engine aircraft, and Regan was close behind.

The B-24 was not built for comfort. Even entering the aircraft was difficult. The bombardier, navigator, and nose-turret gunner were forced to squat down, almost on hands and knees, and sidle up to their stations through the nose wheel well of the ship. Once inside, the three men, fully dressed in their bulky flying gear, would be squeezed into a cramped compartment the size of a broom closet turned on its side. Harry Gregorian was the first to climb in, squirming up and inserting himself into the nose turret. The turret was so compact that he could not wear his parachute when he closed the metal hatch at his back. Following him in, Christ Manners, the bombardier, took up his position at the bombsight just behind and below the turret hatch. Squatting on a small seat, a bank of instruments rising on the aluminum wall to his left, he would be hunched over the bombsight or would simply sit on the sloping floor. Because of the turret Manners could not see directly ahead, but three slanting panels of Plexiglas in front and beneath him offered him a truncated view of the ground. Finally, Mel Rossman, the last to wiggle up into position, entered the navigator's torturous station. A tiny retractable stool, too small to sit on, was built into the right side of the fuselage, and the navigator's table, on which he had to arrange his charts and make his calculations, was little more than a thin shelf on the bulkhead that separated the nose from the flight deck. Just behind the shelf, at eye level, Rossman could see the feet of the pilot and copilot on the flight deck. In the air he would stand for hours at a time facing backward, leaning against the wall of the ship, while the bombardier squatted beneath him. The entire compartment was so unbelievably cramped it seemed impossible that three men dressed in cumbersome flying clothes could operate in such close quarters. Seeing it for the first time, Rossman understood why each crew member had been tested for claustrophobia.

The remaining members of the crew entered the plane by crawling up through the open bomb-bay doors, no more than three feet off the ground. Once in the bomb bay they would stand upright, step up onto the narrow catwalk, then scramble onto the flight deck or back into the waist. It was almost as difficult after a ten-hour flight to crawl back out. But compared to the cramped nose compartment, the flight deck, where the pilot and copilot were stationed, was spacious. Farrington and Regan could actually stand up and move around a bit after several hours at the controls. Just behind and below the copilot Howard sat at a small desk facing his radio sets. Through a small window no larger than a porthole he looked out over the right wing of the aircraft at the number three and four engines. A step down and just to his right was the bulkhead door that separated the flight deck from the bomb bay. Jerry Barrett, the engineer, stood between the pilot and copilot at takeoff, helping to monitor the engine and fuel gauges, but once in the air he slipped to his position behind the pilot and just across from the radioman. There, at the bomb-bay bulkhead, where the fuel transfer pumps and other gauges were located, he assumed his station. In combat he was also a gunner and had to operate the twin fifties in the top turret. When he was standing in the turret his feet swiveled on a metal bar inches above Howard's head.

A folding door just past the radio operator's table led into the bomb bay, where the narrow catwalk, less than a foot wide, passed between the racks of bombs toward the aft section of the ship. Pushing through the folding door at the rear of the bomb bay, Bob Peterson, Jack Brennan, and Al Seraydarian climbed to their positions. Al led the way, slipping past the retractable belly turret, past the open windows of the waist, where Jack Brennan would take his position, toward the tail turret. Standing on a small platform, he slipped his legs into the turret. Like Gregorian in the nose Al found that he could not wear his parachute while in the turret, and as a consequence refused to close the armored hatch to the turret behind him.

Jack Brennan stood in the waist. Earlier in the war the B-24s carried two waist gunners, but by mid-1944 fighter escorts in both the European and Pacific theaters had dramatically reduced the danger of enemy fighter attack, and on most crews one gunner manned both fifties in the waist. It was the position in the ship most exposed, both to weather and to enemy fire. There was no armor plating in the waist, and the walls of the plane were lightweight aluminum, so thin that a screwdriver could push a hole through the taut skin. Every position in the ship was cold, but at twenty thousand feet the wind howled through the open windows of the waist like a gale, covering the fifties and the ammo boxes and the gunners with a thin veil of frost.

Bob Peterson was assigned to the ball turret. A retractable Plexiglas bubble that hung beneath the belly of the plane, it was the most physically uncomfortable, isolated, and terrifying position on the ship. The gunner climbed into the ball, pulled the hatch closed, and was then lowered into position. Once the ball was lowered he rode suspended beneath the plane, staring down between his knees at the earth five miles below. If the plane was hit or started down the hatch could be opened, and the gunner was theoretically able to tumble out. Ball-turret gunners had to be small, but even so very few could actually fit into the turret with a chute on, so they relied on the waist gunner to engage the hydraulic system to raise the turret and then get them out of the ball. Bob Peterson had to have a great deal of faith in Jack Brennan, had to trust him to be there in an emergency, and he did. There were other positions on the ship that were more dangerous—the waist, for instance—but none was so unnatural or unnerving as the ball turret. It was ironic, Bob thought, that the oldest man on the crew, a man who had washed out of pilot school because of recurrent bouts of airsickness, should be assigned to ride in the ball.

Conditions inside the aircraft added to the hardships and anxieties of combat. Like the B-17, the B-24 was not pressurized, and the crews had to wear clammy, ill-fitting rubber oxygen masks for hours at a time. Malfunctions with the heating and oxygen systems were commonplace, particularly in the intense cold at operational altitudes. Whenever planes climbed above ten thousand feet it was necessary to go on oxygen, and each position had plug-in valves for the ship's oxygen system. Anoxia—oxygen deprivation—could sneak up on you, they were repeatedly warned in training, and while you might survive a minute or so, the loss of oxygen clouded your judgment and slowed down your reflexes. After only a short time, and with no warning, you would black out, and ultimately die. When temperatures inside the ship fell to thirty or forty or fifty below zero, sweat—and blood—froze, clogging oxygen hoses. Regular oxygen checks were therefore critical, and throughout a flight at operational altitude Regan used the plane's interphone to conduct a check on each crew member.

Then there was the cold. At twenty thousand feet frigid winds sliced through the turrets, through the open windows of the waist, and, on the bomb run, through the gaping bomb bay. To touch anything without gloves at operational altitude meant losing a finger or a hand. Frostbite was an ever present danger. The crew wore electrically heated flight suits, plugged into rheostats at each position, but if the electrical system shorted out or was damaged in combat, a crew member could freeze. So, in addition to parachute harnesses, inflatable life preservers, and heated suits, the men were forced to wear layers of bulky clothing for warmth, which made movement within the cramped, claustrophobic aircraft awkward and agonizingly slow. Each second counted when trying to escape from a burning B-24 before it exploded, and in the narrow confines of the plane many never made it to the escape hatches. The Germans, with good reason, referred to the American heavy bombers simply as "flying coffins."

The training schedule at Westover was intensive. They were either in class, studying weather, aircraft identification, or aircraft maintenance, or out at the flight line. On a typical day Farrington and Regan were up early, reporting for two hours in the Link, two more hours on the bomb trainer, and then flying in the afternoon. At first they went up with just a skeleton crew—pilot, copilot, bombardier, and navigator, and Farrington checked out his officers in their jobs. As radio operator Howard was required to make each of these flights. "Every time we fly or even if only the pilot and copilot go up alone," Howard wrote home, "the radioman has to go along, so every time the plane leaves the ground I have to go along also." Since the engineer also rode along on these flights, Howard and Jerry Barrett were getting to know one another well. Jerry always seemed in command of himself and the situation. Howard could see it in the airplane. Jerry knew the B-24 inside and out. It was his job to know the fuel and electrical systems, the engines, the hydraulics; he had to be able to handle any sort of technical problem that might arise in the air. During a mission he might roam around the aircraft, troubleshooting, checking for problems. Jerry knew his job, and Howard and the others quickly came to rely on his judgment.

They seemed to be on the flight line constantly. They flew every day, all sorts of flying. They flew formation with the other crews, practicing the tight combat formations that would be necessary for survival in Europe. They flew blind, relying on instruments to climb up through the clouds or land in foul weather; they practiced high- and low-altitude bombing and even air-to-ground gunnery. They flew long cross-country missions to Florida and Colorado and northern Canada, completing complicated navigational problems and simulated bomb runs. "We left here before dawn today," Howard wrote on June 21, "and flew to an island off the coast of Miami and back, and I'm plenty tired. We landed, checked our equipment, and were off like birds again. . . . Our bunch has new B-24s and are they honeys! I love them. I flew high altitude today, 28,000 feet, and it was 20 below zero and sometimes 30 and 35 [below]. It's hell and I'm not kidding." Just a few days later he added, "I'm sorry not to have written you sooner but my squadron has been to Canada and we couldn't write. P.S. We flew to Florida again yesterday."

They were learning a lot about each other, about their roles on the aircraft, learning to master their jobs and to trust in the skill and judgment of each man in the crew. They were also learning a lot about the Liberator and the hazards of flying the giant planes, even on training missions. "The B-24s are nice ships," Howard wrote, "[but] we lose a lot of them here. Since I got here we have lost seven ships. . . ." At briefing, their instructors grimly informed them about the costly mistakes of their classmates, about the Liberators that had vanished somewhere in the Atlantic when the navigator lost his bearings or the radioman missed a radio check. They saw the billowing black smoke at the end of the runway when a fully loaded Liberator failed to attain the proper airspeed, lifted tentatively off the tarmac, stalled, and slammed into the woods just beyond. They watched hair-raising near misses as eighteen planes, bucking erratically in the turbulence, flew nose to wingtip in tight combat formation, and the squadron commander, a veteran of thirty-five missions over Germany, bellowed at them to "close it up, close it up." Barely breathing, Howard watched the right wing of his ship slide steadily toward the waist of the flight commander's plane as Farrington edged them closer and closer. "Jesus," he heard Brennan muttering over the interphone, "I can shake hands with their tail gunner now."

They were kept to a demanding schedule. "I'm still going to classes and flying regularly," Howard wrote in late July. "It gets tiresome after the first five hours." Writing to his wife, Marie, Bob Peterson echoed that sentiment. "I'm so tired, I don't know whether I'm coming or going." The crew was "flying some time every day, at least four hours, seven days a week," he wrote. "We still have the schedule of 8 A.M. till 1 P.M. one day, and 3 P.M. to 8 A.M. the next, and 1 P.M. to 3 A.M. the next. Plus continual classes." He was hoping for a furlough about the fifteenth of September. "We may have only seven days or maybe as long as fifteen. . . ." It was a nice thought but, he added, "it's time to go upstairs for the night. . . . I'll be thinking of you as I fly over the homes below. I will be envious of the families together and their nice homes."

The long cross-country flights, especially the nighttime missions, were tedious exercises for gunners. On some nights Farrington demanded radio silence for hours at a time, practicing the interphone discipline that would be required in combat. But occasionally, while the engines throbbed hypnotically, bursts of conversation would erupt over their headsets, breaking the monotony.

"Howard," Farrington would snap, "can't you get the Cardinals' game on that radio?"

Farrington's father was a sportswriter for the *St. Louis Post Dispatch*, and night after night as they droned over the blacked-out towns and cities the pilot chided Regan about the sad-sack Dodgers and Giants.

"See how many games the world champion St. Louis Cardinals lead those New York teams by?" he would ask rhetorically to no one in particular. "Last time I checked, it was over twenty games each, and it's only July."

"Don't bother moving that dial," Regan would respond drily, "they don't have radio out in St. Louis yet."

Howard liked Regan. The copilot never talked much about himself, but the crew discovered from a buddy who visited from Elmhurst that Jack Regan was something of a local hero in the old neighborhood. He had grown up playing ball in front of the house on Ketcham Street and, Jack's old friend told them, they still talked about a home run he had hit on a Roosevelt Avenue field, a mammoth shot that had rattled off the top of the elevated train structure almost five hundred feet away. He had been been a terrific pitcher–first baseman—a southpaw—and Leo Durocher, the Dodgers' manager, had scouted the young left-hander himself. Offered him a minor league contract on the spot, the story went. But Jack had gone on to college, where he had played a season of basketball at Queens College and then another at NYU and then, of course, there was the war.

Sometimes, as they skirted the coast, high above the dark Atlantic, or saw the shadowy Rockies looming above the gray, featureless plains, the radio carried the soft strains of dance music to them from one of the blacked-out cities below, and they would hear Peterson humming or singing along. He would be riding in the waist, sitting just across from Brennan, and then the familiar argument would drift over the interphone. It would usually begin with Bob crooning one of Bing's western hits—"Don't Fence Me In" or "Pistol-Packin' Mama." He had spent much of his training in Texas, in flight school at San Antonio and gunnery at Laredo, and he loved those songs. Over and over again he sang them, his voice slowing into his version of a heavy Texas drawl, belting out verse after verse of "Deep in the Heart of Texas."

"I can't stand it any more, Pop," Brennan's voice would finally groan plaintively over their headsets. "Don't you know any Sinatra tunes?"

"Never heard of him," Bob would deadpan.

"You mean that scrawny TB case from Jersey?" Gregorian snorted.

"Hayseeds," Brennan grumbled, "I'm surrounded by hayseeds."

Then there was Manners, his voice crackling over the interphone from the nose, always asking Farrington to set the plane down in Pittsburgh so he could get a decent Greek meal.

"A little souvlaki, moussaka, taramasalata," he rattled on and on.

"Translate that for Howard back here, will you," Barrett would pipe up. "He thinks it's corn bread and beans."

"Manners doesn't sound like a Greek name to me," Al called out from the tail.

"The family name is Mugianis," Manners volunteered. "Changed it just before I enlisted. We came to the States from the Greek island of Icarus."

"Icarus! Not a good omen for a flyer," Barrett muttered. Manners didn't seem too worried.

By the end of August the crew had completed its combat training and was prepared for movement to a port of embarkation. The next stop would be overseas. They had no idea where that would be. Liberators were used in far greater number in the Pacific theater or, their instructors had told them, with the Fifteenth Air Force in Italy. The largest and best known of the army air forces, the Eighth, in England, where Tom was stationed, also had B-24s, so that was a possibility too. But uppermost in their minds was the furlough they had been hoping for since arriving at Westover, a last trip home before going to war. In early September it came through, and for the first time in weeks the crew dispersed, catching crowded trains from the small station in Springfield to Detroit, St. Louis, Pittsburgh, Denver, New York, Tennessee, and Illinois. They had ten days.

The time at home passed in a blur. The family gathered at the house on Trunk Street. Mildred had taken up residence there for the duration, and Howard's oldest sister, Sibyle, arrived from Carthage on the train with her daughter. James took the bus down from Knoxville when his classes were over for the week. He was in his first days at the university and was buzzing about his courses, his plans to pledge a fraternity, and playing in the band. Then, of course, day and night, there was Nancy. They spent as much time together as they could, driving out to Curly's Bar-B-Q and stopping in at the soda fountain at Central Drug Store. They visited all the old familiar places that seemed to Howard to have changed in some intangible yet undeniable way in the months since he went away. They did not talk much about his leaving, about the war. They talked about friends, about her job. They talked about the time when he would be coming back, when their life would begin anew.

Some of Howard's buddies were home on furlough, too—C. L. Bivens,

Ralph Chancey, and Medal of Honor winner Paul Huff. They got together at
the old football field and horsed around, trading stories about the service.
Howard told them all about his crew, about the pilot, the airplane, the
places he'd been. The crew had come out of training with a very high rating,
Howard related, and it was obvious that he was proud of them. He was not
sure where they were going, but just before the furlough home came through
they had turned in their summer khakis and were issued wool olive drabs.
Sounded like England, everybody agreed. Howard had hoped that Buddy
McLeod might be home, but he had just begun crew training. He had
graduated from cadets in July and was assigned as a bombardier to a B-17.
Maybe they would meet on the other side.

On his last day home they ate lunch on the back porch, as they had done
so often in the years before the war. The lush watermelon-red blossoms of
the giant crape myrtle pressed tightly against the screen, and late-season
cicadas whined in the small backyard. Next door Mr. Ryden was mowing
the narrow swath of lawn between the houses, and the metallic grinding of
the blades cut the humid stillness as they passed the food and sipped the
iced tea. It was as hot as a day in August. Everybody was there, squeezed in
at the long white table, and the meal passed with the usual light banter and
a resolute determination not to speak of parting. Howard's duffel bag was
packed, waiting on the front porch.

When the time came to leave he wanted no wrenching, teary farewells,
and they all did their best. He asked his brother to drive him down to the
station, and while James backed the car out they gathered on the sidewalk
in the deep shade of the maples. Howard kissed his mother and sisters and
Nancy good-bye and hugged his father. Almost exactly a year before,
Mildred could not help thinking, on a day not unlike this one, she stood in
the steamy station at Battle Creek, Michigan, straining to catch a glimpse of
Tom as the train passed through, bound that day for overseas. She waited for
hours as troop trains slid through the dusty sidings, their open windows a
blur of olive drab and khaki. Men waving, blowing kisses, clowning. She
never did see him, and in the late afternoon she took the bus back to the
boardinghouse, packed her bag, and came home. Now her brother Howard
was saying good-bye, tossing his duffel bag into the car, sliding in beside
James, and it seemed to her that the war had been one long, shuddering
succession of partings, of farewell kisses and tears on train platforms and
bus depots and front porches. James released the brake and the car moved
slowly away from the curb, and despite the sweltering heat she shivered. At

the corner Howard shifted in his seat and waved one last time, then James
turned left onto 8th Street, and he was gone.

"Parting this time was very hard," Bob wrote to Marie when the crew
assembled back at Westover. "Not that I fear war or anything in the world of
that nature. I am not much of a coward in most things, but I dread being
apart so long. I do hope the war ends . . . [soon]. Every time that I have sat
down to write since arriving I found tears blotting out clear vision. . . .
Guess I am a baby at times. Anyway, I hated to leave my loved ones. . . . I
was glad to be home, even if for only a few days. Precious days in my
memory! I hope this is our last good-bye."

On September 21 the crew departed Westover for Mitchel Field to begin
final processing for assignment overseas. "It took six hours to get here,"
Howard wrote after settling into their new barracks. "It is located on Long
Island . . . and tomorrow night I will be off and get to see New York. . . . I have
no idea how long I will be here at Mitchel Field, but I don't guess it will
be long."

The boys spent their days filling out insurance forms, drawing equipment, just waiting for shipment, but their nights were free. They watched
movies on the base, went to the USO, and wrote letters, their last before
being subject to army censorship. "Last night I saw Pat O'Brien and Jinx
Falkenburg and their camp show," Howard reported. "Tonight they are
having someone else." But he was not very interested. The boys from the
New York area could actually make it home, and shortly after arriving
Howard spent a day in Cliffside Park with Jack Brennan. He ate dinner with
the family, said a quick hello to Jack's girl, Fern, who was a junior in high
school, and dropped by Jack's school to meet his football coach, a young
chemistry teacher named Vince Lombardi.

"I like it here at Mitchel Field," Howard wrote several days later. "I
actually believe there are more civilians working here than . . . soldiers."
One civilian in particular had caught his attention. Her name was Alice,
and they met at the PX where she was working. She was gorgeous and
energetic—a knockout, in Jerry Barrett's words—and he could tell from
their very first conversation over the sundries counter that she liked him.
She didn't wait for him to take the initiative but asked him out right away.

"Would you look at that," Brennan muttered in admiration, as the boys
watched Howard and the slender, well-dressed woman leave the base that

first night. "How does he do it?" Over and over again at the dances at Westover or at the USO mixers in Springfield they had watched in awed astonishment as girls gravitated directly to Howard, asking him to dance, to get a Coke, to take them home. They gave him addresses and phone numbers and photographs. "Hey," Al would say, "why don't you send a few of 'em over this way?" Howard would smile and wave his hand dismissively, as if embarrassed. He never seemed to care about the attention, to take much interest. Alice was different.

He didn't really know much about her. She had worked as a model in a fashionable store in Manhattan, she told him, and her father worked as an artist for one of the big movie studios. She was twenty-one and had studied art in school and found him, with his soft southern speech and courtly manners, as exotic and mysterious as he found her. For two weeks they saw each other almost every night. They met at the front gate and drove in Alice's stunning yellow convertible to Jones Beach, walked along the nearly deserted shore, went swimming in the cold surf. They took the train into Manhattan and she showed him around Times Square, Rockefeller Center, Radio City Music Hall, Broadway. They strolled arm in arm up Fifth Avenue and, at his insistence, took a carriage ride around Central Park. They rode the subway to Chinatown and sauntered through the fish and vegetable markets on Mott Street. They danced in nightclubs he had read about in *Collier's* and heard Walter Winchell talk about on the radio but had never dreamed of seeing. She took him to the Stage Door Canteen, where they saw the Andrews Sisters from so close Maxine reached over and kissed him on the cheek. Howard called her Gypsy, like in the Ink Spots' song, and for days they spent every spare moment together.

They were playful, never serious. She was funny and he laughed easily and each night was an adventure. He never really knew what she might do or say or what to expect from himself. He never allowed himself to think much about what they were doing, never analyzed what it meant, how it related to Nancy, to home, to the future. Whenever he tried to focus, to get a grip on things, his thoughts, like a handful of marbles dropped from a table, scattered in all directions. He was not going to worry about it now. He had a week, maybe two, before they shipped out, and he was making no long-term plans. Things would sort themselves out later.

"Since I came to Mitchel Field I haven't done a thing but sleep and go to New York nights," he wrote rather vaguely to his folks, but to James, who had moved into the dorm at the university, he sent a photograph of Alice in her bathing suit. It was a snapshot taken of the two of them at a pool on Long Island, but he did not reveal much. He didn't know what to say or how to explain what had happened or what he wanted. And there was so little time. They were already packing their gear, preparing to leave any day now. "I liked Mitchel Field very much, and the pilot seemed to do okay for himself," he joked. "My copilot, Regan, took my pilot, Farrington, to his home in Queens and fixed him up with some of the Queens chorus girls and I think he took a few dancing lessons. . . . He hated to leave." Thinking of the last ten days and Alice he added, "It was nice at that."

"Here I am in Hempstead at the USO," Bob wrote to Marie on September 27, "waiting for some of the fellows to come in so we can see a show." He had heard a "rumor that we will get off the post tomorrow night but not again," and he was expecting to leave for the port of embarkation by the weekend. "We have a permit to buy cartons of cigarettes, candy bars, and chewing gum. I am stocking up . . . to have things to trade for souvenirs abroad or maybe for food . . . to get a change of diet from K rations. . . ." Some of the guys were adding nylons and perfume for emergency situations. After all, you never knew when they might come in handy.

"Today is the last day to write mail without the APO (Army Post Office) censor," Bob wrote two days later. "We are all packed [and] ready to leave. . . . We may be at embarkation from one to five days. They issued us pistols today . . . [and] took all our sun tans, so we must be going to a winter climate." That probably meant England, he thought, but his letters from overseas would be censored and he would not be allowed to divulge his location or to say much about their activities. "I think I have a plan worked out so you will know how I am overseas and how many missions [we have] completed. After every mission . . . I will write a sentence thusly if all is well: 'This is letter number one (or whatever number it is). How do you like it? I like it.' If anybody is hurt I will write: 'This is letter number one. How do you like it? I don't think much of it.' " It was hard to believe, Bob thought, that after two years in the army he was at last on his way overseas, on his way to war.

"Everything here is just fine and I feel good today," Howard wrote on September 30, "because I may see Tom soon. . . ." He was sitting in the squadron dayroom, waiting to be paid. He had filled out forms for war bonds and insurance, making his mother the beneficiary, and he explained how it worked. He made the usual inquiries about the family, about his sisters, his father, about James and his studies. "I guess it is funny not having that crazy James around, hanging on the piano, etc. He sure wants to be a doctor and . . . he will make a good [one]. . . . I'm hoping he doesn't have to leave school but I just don't see how he can miss, do you? . . . Sure wish I could go on to school but. . . ." That just wasn't in the cards. "Just wish this [war] would end. I don't know if I want to study engineering, law, or dentistry. I would settle for [any of them]," he wrote in closing, "if only this would end."

CHAPTER II

SOMEWHERE IN ENGLAND

Before sunrise on October 4, 1944, the Richard Farrington crew climbed into the truck that would take them to Pier 40 on the West Side of New York. The convoy left Mitchel Field in the predawn darkness, moving slowly through the sandy flats of Long Island and into the sparse early morning traffic of the city. When at last the line of trucks halted and the men clambered stiffly out onto the pavement, they saw among the cables and cranes the great white bow of the ship that would carry them to war.

The *New Amsterdam* was a Dutch passenger vessel designed for transAtlantic luxury travel in happier days, and in the early morning light it seemed to hover above the gloomy pier, suspended in the black waters of the Hudson. Thousands of GIs, sweating in their brown wool uniforms and lugging their bulging barracks bags, already stood in ragged lines, waiting in the cavernous shed along the pier.

Inside, a thick cloud of cigarette smoke coiled around the beams, mingling with a powerful stench of oil, water, and sweat. A bewildering cacophony of instructions and orders, frantic questions, and shouts of recognition boomed through the dismal shed above the metallic clamor of unseen machinery and the mysterious bustling of the stevedores.

"355 Squadron form on me."

"Hey, buddy, is this A Company?"

"Anderson, John C., anybody seen Anderson?"

"D Company, saddle up, move forward. Let's go, move it!"

A group of matronly Red Cross women bobbed cheerfully about in the sea of brown wool, dispensing coffee and doughnuts, smiling at the wise-cracks, asking the usual questions.

"Where you from, soldier?

"Tennessee? Really! You ride the Chattanooga Choo Choo?"

"You're from Detroit? My brother-in-law lives in Detroit."

"No, no, sorry Corporal, I'm afraid I can't go along in the cabin with you."

"Then how about you taking my place, honey bun?"

The men jostled and swore, stood and waited, edged forward, stopped, and waited again. The aircrews had formed up together, waiting their turn to process. Howard recognized many of them. They had been together at Westover and Mitchel. They were all replacement crews and would be assigned to bomb groups in either England or Italy. No one was sure just where.

The processing and loading dragged on for most of a day, until each individual soldier and airman filed up the gangplank and onto the converted liner. When their time came the ten men of the Farrington crew stepped on board, called off their names, waited for the checker to mark them present, and then trudged off to find their assigned bunks somewhere down below. The crew had been excited when the day began at Mitchel Field as they prepared to embark for the war, but the endless army processing, the hurry up and wait, had gradually worn them down. How many times in the past year, Howard wondered, had they stood in lines at PXs and medical exams, had they been pressed shoulder to shoulder, belly to belly in troop trains and trucks all across the North American continent? The excitement, the edgy sense of adventure—even the the dull presentiment of dread, like the first faint hint of a toothache—with which the day began, was utterly stifled, deadened by drab army routine.

Still, when at last the tugs began to ease the great ship out of its moorings, swinging it gracefully into the river, the excitement returned. Those who could crowded along the railings to watch the skyline of Manhattan glide past. On the starboard side the Statue of Liberty, the stuff of postcards they had religiously sent home to Alabama and Arkansas, to Des Moines and Minneapolis, slid by. For almost an hour the ship maneuvered gingerly through the congested harbor, past the Brooklyn shipyard with its giant cranes and pulleys, past the swarming wharves of Jersey City and Newark, until at last, moving under its own steam, it turned for the open sea.

Standing on deck in the brisk salt spray, Howard took one last look at the already distant shores of Long Island, of the United States of America, of home. Amid the laughing and horseplay he stood quietly watching, lost in thought. Somewhere out there Alice would be making her way to work at the PX, expecting him to drop by in the late afternoon. He had thought he would see her one last time to say a proper good-bye, but maybe it was better this way. He had her address. Maybe he would see her again. The war in Europe would be over soon. Everybody seemed to think so. The new Allied offensive in the Low Countries was moving ahead, the Germans were reeling. Maybe they'd be home by Christmas, maybe early next year. Maybe the war would end next week, next month.

But now, room assignments in hand, the crew had to find their bunks. Down they went, through brightly lit corridors that had once resounded with the tinkle of champagne glasses and whispered sighs of shipboard romances. On A deck, above the waterline, the officers peeled off in search of their quarters, while the enlisted men continued to move down the steel stairwell, to C then to D then to E deck. As they descended the air grew stale and warm, the corridors narrowed, and the light faded. Deep in the bowels of the ship they could distinctly feel the pulsing of the engines and the growing swells of the Atlantic. Checking their papers against the room numbers, they plunged into the cabin that was to be home for the voyage. At first sight it didn't seem that the room could possibly accommodate the six of them with their equipment. The walls of the tiny cabin were festooned with bunks that seemed to climb, like stairs, from just off the floor to the very ceiling. Consisting of a metal pipe frame hinged onto iron stanchions along the wall and held in place on the front by chains at the head and foot, the canvas bunks were arranged in tiers of four, so that twelve men could be sardined into a tiny space intended to hold a vacationing couple. Two men, boys from another crew they recognized from Westover and Mitchel, were already lying in their bunks. One dozed peacefully, the other lay with his head over the end of the bunk, his face ashen. As they entered, he raised his dull eyes to greet them, gagged, and emptied what was left in his stomach into his steel helmet.

The men claimed their bunks, stowing their gear as best they could. Could twelve men actually stand in the room at the same time? There was no place to sit except on the floor, already littered with barracks bags and stray bits of equipment, and once in the bunk it was almost impossible to turn over. Lying on his back, each man stared at the torso etched into the sagging canvas twelve inches above him.

Just miles from the shores of North America they entered a combat zone. Although the crossing was not as hazardous as in the early years of the war, German U-boats still prowled the North Atlantic, sinking tons of Allied shipping each month. As the sun rose after their first night at sea, burning away the early morning mist, the men standing on deck were in for a shock. The rolling swells of the vast ocean stretched from horizon to horizon, unbroken by the presence of a single ship. They were alone. Surely there would be a convoy, escort ships? Would other vessels be joining them at a rendezvous point? Would they intercept a convoy already forming from other ports? At briefing that day they were told that the *New Amsterdam* could do almost thirty knots. It would try the hazardous Atlantic crossing without an escort, zigzagging so that U-boats could not track their garbage trail. The men were issued life jackets and briefed on evacuation procedures, and they conducted periodic lifeboat drills. These exercises in pandemonium broke the tedium, but it was perfectly obvious to those who chose to think about it that if the *New Amsterdam* were torpedoed, most of the men jammed into the ship would never make it to the lifeboats.

As the days passed and the novelty of thinking about a possible U-boat attack faded, the men confronted more pedestrian problems. In New York Harbor they had joked about seasickness, but after days of swaying and bouncing, of watching the clouds dip and surge above the relentless waves, the laughing stopped. Puddles of vomit stood on the slick floors of the latrines and collected in helmets in the rooms. Its ubiquitous smell hung in the motionless, sweltering air of the lower decks, mixing with the thick, greasy steam of the dining hall. Conditions all over the ship were terribly crowded, and ventilation was nonexistent. Any movement through the corridors, in the latrines, or in the rooms was extremely difficult. In this cramped environment, even changing clothes required considerable acrobatic skill, and with each passing day fewer and fewer men felt it was worth the effort. Washing also quickly became a source of frustration. Fresh water on the ship was strictly rationed and not available for "ablutions." The men were to wash in seawater and were issued a soap specially developed for the purpose. With great determination and more enthusiasm than most could muster, they might work up a lather using it, just as the navy boys advertised, but the combination of soap and seawater also produced a prodigious rash that sent them into a frenzy. As the days dragged by, fewer and fewer bothered to wash or to change their clothes, and belowdecks the air turned dank and fetid, laced with the pungent aroma of sweat and vomit.

Each day the crew assembled to talk, to exchange rumors, to speculate on their destination and their assignment. They groused about the crowded conditions, complained about the boredom and the food. Those who were not sick were almost constantly hungry. In the giant galley the cooks ladled out sardines and hot dogs, hot dogs and sardines, lunch and dinner, day after day. Everybody grumbled. They grumbled about the food and then grumbled because there was never enough of it. The enlisted men in one crew bitched to their officers so much about the lack of food that their pilot "volunteered" the lot of them for KP. "That son of a bitch," one of their cabin mates commiserated. "Hell, no," Hudson Coombs, a ball-turret gunner from Nashville, replied, "Best thing that could have happened to us. At least we get enough to eat."

For those who were not seasick time hung heavy on their hands. There were movies at night, Betty Grable and Hopalong Cassidy and Woody Woodpecker, and during the day there were boxing matches, which both Harry and Howard entered. Howard had not boxed since Camp Kearns and, though in excellent shape, he was very much an amateur. Harry, on the other hand, had fought professionally in Detroit before the war. He had talked about it some at Westover and Mitchel—not bragging, just matter-of-fact—and Howard had watched him working out with the heavy bag in the gym, but the boys had never seen him in the ring. As soon as he set foot between the ropes it was frighteningly clear that he knew what he was doing with the gloves. "Look at that little sonofabitch punch," a GI at ringside yelled as Harry cornered his first opponent, and the crew cheered him on. He pounded away at the burly private, slamming him with blow after blow, first to the body then to the head. The infantry boys from the man's unit hooted and howled as Harry's gloves thudded savagely into their buddy's suddenly shapeless, blood-flecked face. The punches continued in an awesome flurry, delivered with such brutal efficiency that the crowd fell into an awed, uneasy silence. The PFC was finished, helpless to defend himself, but Harry would not stop. Even the referee couldn't get him off until the infantryman was slumped on the canvas mat, his eyes rolling glassily toward the wire-covered lights above them. Harry had hardly broken a sweat. The guys were stunned.

Aside from walking the deck, which could only be done in the daytime, exercise for most of the men was a virtual impossibility, and despite efforts at classes, and rumormongering, boredom was rampant. Belowdecks the *New Amsterdam* became a poor man's floating casino, and Al Seraydarian loved it. Card games of all sorts, poker, blackjack, red dog, and some Howard had never heard of were going night and day. Men sprawled on blankets on the cabin floors and huddled in stairwells and even in the latrines, dealing, rolling the dice. Whole cabins were given over to a game, sometimes with a dozen cramped participants straining to focus under the dim blackout lights. Al sampled them all. Almost every night, it seemed to Howard, Brennan would press breathlessly into their cabin, summoning them to rescue their tail gunner. Al was down two hundred dollars in a crap game on C deck or four hundred dollars at blackjack. Howard and Jerry would roll out of their hammocks and edge their way down the corridor, peering into one crowded game after another. Inevitably they would find him, his T-shirt plastered to his chest in the sweltering cabin, surrounded by cards and piles of bills. Perspiring heavily, Al would look up and smile sheepishly as his crewmates appeared above the circle. The conversation was always the same.

"Just one more roll, fellas," Al pleaded. "I'm due."

"You're overdue," Howard groaned, "way overdue. How much you in for?"

"I'm down $320."

"Unluckiest guy I ever saw," Howard sighed, patting Brooklyn on the shoulder. "Come on, let's go."

On the thirteen-day voyage Al Seraydarian's luck didn't change. When the ship at last docked he had lost thirteen hundred dollars.

It was night when the *New Amsterdam* eased its way up the Firth of Clyde, docking at last at the port of Greenock. After being confined in the cramped quarters of the ship for almost two weeks the men were excited and eager. They gathered their equipment and formed up for disembarking, a process that miraculously went much faster than the loading in New York. It was pitch black when they filed off the ship. Along the pier where they assembled only narrow wedges of dim light slashed the gloom at irregular intervals. The blackout lights from the lanterns overhead or the trucks that ground slowly around the dock were so faint, so illusive, the men had to blink to be sure they had seen them at all. Above them, etched against the murky gray clouds, ominous black ovals hovered like giant gnats. "Barrage balloons," someone whispered.

It began to rain.

From the quayside the troops boarded a ferry to another pier, then marched through a maze of cobblestone streets in utter darkness. Someone said that this was Glasgow, but it might have been Morocco or Sicily for all they could see. The men of the Farrington crew followed in their places, scarcely talking, until the column at last turned into a quiet, darkened building. Passing through the thick blackout curtains into the light, they found themselves in a dim, cavernous shed. Along one wall women of the Scottish Red Cross stood on hand to serve tea and some warm food. Speaking with a thick Scottish brogue, a vigorous British officer welcomed them cheerfully to the war, and a U.S. Army captain gave the men a brief orientation about life in wartime Britain, distributing a pamphlet prepared for all U.S. troops stationed there. "Read it, remember it, follow its suggestions, and your interaction with your British hosts will be enjoyable." Quoting liberally from the *Guide* he reminded them, "All Britain is a war zone and has been since September 1939. . . . The British have been bombed, night after night . . . thousands of them have lost their houses, their possessions, and their families. . . . The British will welcome you as friends and allies. But remember that crossing the ocean doesn't automatically make you a hero. . . . There are housewives in aprons and youngsters in knee pants who have lived through more high explosives in air raids than many soldiers saw in first-class barrages in the last war.

"The British are friendly, and they're glad to have us here. But they are often more reserved in conduct than we. On a small, crowded island where forty-five million people live, each man learns to guard his privacy carefully—and is equally careful not to invade another man's privacy. So if Britons sit in trains or buses without striking up a conversation with you, it doesn't mean they are being haughty and unfriendly. Probably they are paying more attention to you than you think. But they don't speak to you because they don't want to appear intrusive or rude.

"The British have seen a good many Americans and they like

Americans. They will like your frankness as long as it is friendly. They will
expect you to be generous. They are not given to backslapping and they are
shy about showing their affections. But once they get to like you they make
the best friends in the world. The British are like the Americans in many
ways—but not in all ways. The language, for one thing. Someone once said
that the British and Americans are two people separated by a common
language. You'll find out what that means soon enough. Trucks are 'lorries,'
flashlights are 'torches,' the movies are the 'cinema.' There are things you
shouldn't say in polite company, such as 'I'm stuffed'—has an entirely
different meaning over here; a 'bum' isn't a panhandler, it's what you sit on.
They'll say some pretty odd-sounding things to you, too. If they send
someone to knock on your door, they're 'knocking you up.' Don't get
excited. And don't be surprised when somebody tells you to 'keep your
pecker up.' It's not what you think."

The men laughed, and despite the chill in the room they began to relax.
"You will quickly discover differences that seem confusing and even wrong.
Like driving on the left side of the road and having money based on an
'impossible' accounting system and drinking warm beer. But once you get
used to things like that you will realize that they belong to England just as
baseball and jazz and Coca-Cola belong to us.

"Look, listen, and learn before you start telling the British how much
better we do things. They will be interested to hear about life in America,
and you have a great chance to overcome the picture many of them have
gotten from the movies of an America made up of wild Indians and
gangsters. . . . It is always impolite to criticize your hosts. It is militarily
stupid to insult your allies. So stop and think before you sound off about
lukewarm beer, or cold boiled potatoes, or the way English cigarettes
taste.

"There's a war on, and the contrast with the States is going to be stark.
You are coming to Britain from a country where your home is still safe, food
is still plentiful, and the lights are still burning. So it is doubly important for
you to remember that British soldiers and civilians have been under
tremendous strain. Sixty thousand British civilians—men, women, and
children—have died under bombs, and yet the morale of the British is
unbreakable and high. Our British allies are plenty tough," he added. "A
nation doesn't come through if it doesn't have plain common guts—you
won't be able to tell the British much about 'taking it.' They're not particularly interested in taking it anymore. They are far more interested in

getting together a solid friendship with us so we can all start dishing it out to Hitler.

"You haven't had a chance to see much out there in that blackout tonight. Tomorrow when you look around Britain might look a little shabby, the shops barren, the clothing and the people a bit washed out. Don't be fooled. The British people are anxious to have you know that you are not seeing their country at its best. There's been a war on since 1939. The houses haven't been painted because factories are not making paint— they're making planes. The famous British gardens and parks are either unkempt, because there are no men to take care of them, or they are being used to grow needed vegetables. Britain's taxis look antique because Britain makes tanks for herself and Russia and hasn't the time to make cars. If British civilians look dowdy or badly dressed it is not because they do not like good clothes or know how to wear them. All clothes are rationed, and the British know that they help war production by wearing an old suit or dress until it cannot be patched any longer. Old clothes are 'good form.'

"It's a small country," he reminded them. "England is smaller than North Carolina or Iowa. The whole of Great Britain—that is England and Scotland and Wales together—is hardly bigger than Minnesota. England's longest river, the Thames (pronounced 'Tams') is not even as big as the Mississippi when it leaves Minnesota. You don't need to comment on it. Don't brag. The British dislike bragging and showing off," the officer emphasized. "American pay is the highest in the world, and," he suggested, "when payday comes it would be sound practice to learn to spend your money in accordance with British standards. They consider you highly paid. They won't think any better of you for throwing your money around; they're more likely to feel that you haven't learned the commonsense virtues of thrift."

Finally, he stressed that English women were to be treated with the same respect the boys would show the girls back home. "You'll have a lot of money to spend, and the female population of these islands have done without a lot of things." Howard and Jerry instantly thought of the perfume, handkerchiefs, and nylons waiting in their A-2 bags. "Be sensible. Use your head, stay away from the Piccadilly Commandos. There's been a lot of talk about the only problem with the Yanks being that we're oversexed, overpaid, and over here. Let's not contribute to that."

After some warm food and a mercifully short processing period, the crew received orders to proceed to a transportation depot for assignment to their permanent base. At daybreak the Farrington crew climbed aboard a personnel truck and began a long overland trek southward. Sitting under the dark canvas awning of the truck, the men had no idea where they were headed. Throughout the long day, as the vehicle lurched and swerved, the crew dozed, speculated on their destination, and strained to catch a glimpse of the countryside as it bounced past them. The truck rumbled through a landscape soft with moisture, through sleepy pastoral villages and market towns. The fields were ochre with grain, and although it was early October, patches of startling green lay shimmering between the dense hedges and scrubs. Occasionally they caught sight of a horse-drawn cart or an ancient plow or thresher. In the larger towns they saw on the railroad sidings flatcars lined with tanks, artillery pieces, and the wings of fighters en route to the Channel ports and the war.

By afternoon the rolling hills of the north had given way to the flats and marshlands of Norfolk, and toward evening the 6 × 6 slowed and the driver consulted his map. "Almost there, Lieutenant," he yelled above the grinding gears as the truck passed into the village of Weston-Longville. There a small cemetery, its tombstones worn smooth by centuries of wind and rain, embraced an ancient Norman church, and a single public house, the Ringers, catered to a small band of farmers. A narrow country lane twisted among a handful of cottages, past the rectory and a small grove of trees to a flat expanse of earth stripped of its trees and shrubs. At its center lay an elongated triangle of tarmac, and scattered along its periphery, half obscured by the few remaining trees, clusters of tin half-moon huts, giant hangars, and tar-paper shacks hugged the ground like mushrooms. Air Station 120 had been carved out of this piece of pastoral tranquillity, this vision of English arcadia.

The truck deposited the crew at group headquarters, a long Nissen hut bustling with activity. An assortment of 6 × 6s, jeeps, and staff cars stood outside the entrance. While the boys waited in a faint drizzle, an orderly escorted Farrington to the duty officer. Typewriters clattered, a Teletype stuttered metallically, and the insistent ringing of a telephone could be heard through the thin walls.

"Welcome to the 466th Bomb Group, Lieutenant," said a surprisingly boyish-looking major, glancing up from behind a desk strewn with papers. "We've been expecting you." He rose to shake Farrington's hand.

"Glad to be here, sir."

"We'll get you squared away here, get your squadron assignment, quarters, and let you and your boys get over to the mess hall. You could probably use some chow."

"We've been in that truck for about twelve hours. My backside could use a rest."

"Right," the major chuckled. "I understand. You're being assigned to the 787th Squadron. They're desperately short of crews. In fact, they've been stood down now for almost two weeks."

Farrington said nothing but looked inquisitively at the major.

"Few weeks ago on a routine training flight near the field," the major said after a pause, "we had two planes collide in midair. Ten officers were killed, four enlisted men. The squadron commander was up with them, testing several new pilots, fresh from the States. Damn good officer, damn good pilot." He sighed. "You'll be doing several practice missions, Lieutenant. New pilots, we've found, need more formation flying if they're going to survive in the ETO. One of the new pilots was nervous in formation— you've got to really tuck it in over here—he slid in too close to his wingman, lost it. The two planes collided. Fourteen men died. Six others managed to bail out. The 787th is still reeling. Your crew is one of three we're assigning to the squadron this month."

Farrington said nothing. The major handed him a sheaf of papers for the crew and went on for a few more minutes about the 466th, Air Station 120, and the 787th. Farrington's mind wandered. You always heard about these collisions in every phase of training in the States. Carelessness, bad weather, mechanical trouble. It was one more thing to think about. One more pressure point.

"Do you have any questions, Lieutenant?" he heard the major ask at last.

"Yes, sir. Where exactly are we?"

"Norfolk, East Anglia. Almost the whole Eighth Air Force, over 40 heavy bomb groups, 20 fighter outfits, and approximately 130 airfields are jammed into an area about the size of Delaware. It's the largest aircraft carrier in the world. You are now approximately ninety miles northeast of London. The closest city of any size is Norwich, about nine miles away. Trucks run daily into town. When you get a pass, they'll take you in and carry you back out here. Liberty Run, we call it."

The reporting over, Farrington saluted smartly and trudged back to the truck.

The drizzle seemed to have stopped, though it was hard to be certain, and the men stood about smoking. "Let's go, boys," Farrington said, "this looks like home for a while." The men grabbed their gear and climbed back in the truck. The driver deposited the officers in front of a hut just inside the main gate. The barracks was not a typical Nissen but a larger dwelling, a light frame structure of tar paper, stuccoed or plastered on the outside. It held twenty-four cots, and most were full when Farrington, Regan, Rossman, and Manners jumped down and disappeared inside. The 6 × 6 swung around and, passing along a network of small roads, proceeded to the enlisted men's quarters. Howard peered out from under the canvas at the air station passing on both sides, the revetments with the silver planes, half-moon Nissens of every size, hangars, jeeps, trucks, and, everywhere, men on bicycles, pedaling through the gloom to the mess hall, to the movies, to their huts.

Then the buildings vanished and the truck rumbled down a narrow lane, bordered by potato fields, into a cluster of Nissens and other structures. It slammed to a halt in front of a hut. "End of the line, boys," the driver called out. "Everybody out."

Exhausted, the crew tossed their bags down, jumped down onto the pavement, and surveyed the gloomy little half-moon hut before them. In the failing light the pale green concrete front shaded into gray. It was one of several huts of different sizes clustered among the trees. In the distance they could hear the rumble of engines, but the runways, the hardstands, the mess hall, the main sites of the base were out of view. A faint mist was falling, enveloping them in a fine coat of moisture.

The men gathered their duffels and entered the hut. Twelve frail bed frames lined the arching walls, six on each side. The ceiling was only about eight feet at its center. In the middle of the hut a tiny stove, almost comical in its lilliputian proportions, squatted on the concrete floor. It was cold; a faint scent of burnt coke hung in the damp air, the only hint that a fire had once burned there. Arcing above the beds along one wall, calendars, photos from home, a stray aircraft identification chart, maps, pinups, Rita Hayworth, Betty Grable, the usual Vargas and Petty girls, rose in clustered profusion. Light was provided by three dim, naked bulbs dangling from the ceiling.

"Jeeze," Brooklyn wailed, "what are these things?" Al stood above a bunk and raised a large heavy slab from the frame.

"Biscuits, buddy, biscuits," a muffled, disembodied voice called from the rear of the hut. From under a bundle of blankets the shape of a man slowly unfurled. The figure swung his legs over the edge of the bunk, yawned, and faced them. Pale and unshaven, he was fully clothed.

"You boys just get here? Well, you've slept on your last mattress for the duration. The cots here don't have mattresses. These are 'English biscuits,' instruments of torture, as you'll soon discover. Three hard cushions stuffed with cotton. About like sleeping on the floor. But worse yet, if you don't make up your bed real tight your ass end'll slip down between the biscuits to the slats. You boys fresh off the boat?"

"Just got here today," Barrett answered, testing the biscuits on his bunk with his fingers.

"Where are we, anyway?" Howard asked.

"You're at the WAAF site—honored home of combat enlisted personnel. Latrine's in the shed just behind us. You can grab some chow at the enlisted men's mess hall just across the way here. You'll get the hang of it."

"Sunday evening in a metal hut in England is a new experience for me," Bob Peterson wrote to Marie. Twelve men, the enlisted men from two crews, he explained, lived together in the small hut. "We are not at the Ritz by any means, but we are a million times better off than the infantry boys," Bob believed. The little buildings "with half-moon shape and concrete floor . . . seem to be very cozy. There is a very small stove in [the] center of the room [and] a washroom . . . a few steps away. Looks like a farming community on all sides. There are trees in front of the barracks and a field of grass. Makes me dream of where I long to be. In the countryside . . . and in our own home."

Shortly after daybreak the men reported to the headquarters of the 787th Squadron. The headquarters building was an unimposing brick and stucco shack, its entry marked by a dummy bomb and propeller. Like the other structures they had seen along the way, it perched forlornly on a slab of concrete in a sea of mud flanked by a pair of dismal, scraggly shrubs. A light rain was falling, as it had off and on for hours, when the Farrington crew pressed into the orderly room.

After a brisk welcome a captain introduced them to the group and to Air Station 120. "Gentlemen," he said, "you're now members of the 787th Squadron, 466th Bomb Group, 96th Combat Wing, Second Air Division, of the Eighth Air Force. Like every other group, the 466th consists of four squadrons, the 784th, 785th, 786th, and us. At full combat strength each has eighteen crews. We're a little short just now—the group lost ten planes last month—but we expect to be at full operational strength shortly."

The men shuffled their feet, shifting their weight, but they were listening intently. "Ten planes," more than one of them thought.

"The Eighth is made up of three bomb divisions," the captain continued, taking a long drag from his Lucky Strike. "The First and Third fly
exclusively B-17s, the Second, 24s. There are four combat wings in each air
division. A lot of airplanes, gentlemen, a lot of airplanes. The 466th is one
of three groups in the 96th Combat Wing, meaning we fly our missions
usually with the 458th and 467th."

He paused. "By the way, the base is officially Attlebridge Aerodrome,
because Attlebridge is the closest rail station, about five miles away, but for
security purposes it's Air Station 120. It was a former RAF base—the
WAAF site is the former quarters of the RAF's Women's Auxiliary Air
Force. The village just at the edge of the base is Weston-Longville. Good
pub. I'm sure you'll discover it soon enough.

"The group was activated at Alamogordo, New Mexico, in August '43.
We began combat training at Kearns Field in Utah and moved to the ETO in
February 1944. The 466th flew its first mission in March—it was a beaut—
to Big B—Berlin, the longest inaugural raid by any group in the Eighth's
history. At this point the group's logged approximately 130 missions. Had
our hundredth mission party in August. Glenn Miller and his orchestra
played here in the north hangar. Terrific.

"You won't be flying combat for a while. For the next few days you will
be in school—aircraft identification, combat procedures for pilots, navigators, bombardiers, radio, and gunners. And you'll get some flying time, as
much as we can give you. You'll get some practice at night flying, but your
missions will be in daylight. Daylight precision bombing is the name of the
game in the ETO, and that means high-altitude formation flying." None of
this came as a surprise to the crew. For months in training they had heard
about the American policy of daylight strategic bombing. They had read
about it in the newspapers and magazines, and their instructors in crew
training had emphasized it. During the 1920s and 30s the U.S. Army Air
Corps had developed the strategic doctrine of daylight precision bombing,
the doctrine that would guide its operations during the war in Europe. Air
Corps strategists were convinced that American bombers equipped with
high-tech aiming devices and flying at altitudes above effective enemy
antiaircraft fire could identify and destroy carefully selected strategic
military and industrial targets.

The British and Germans had tried daylight strategic bombing early in the war, but both had suffered disastrous losses and had almost entirely abandoned daylight operations well before the Americans entered the conflict. Both had adopted a policy of nighttime area raids, the military value of which remained highly controversial, but which certainly resulted in heavy civilian casualties and would in time, the argument went, break the will of the enemy to continue the war. But U.S. Army Air Force planners remained undeterred by the British and German experiences. They were confident that the United States possessed the necessary technology to make daylight strategic bombing work.

The prime instrument of that policy was to be the four-engine heavy bomber—the B-17 and B-24, equipped with the top secret Norden bombsight. The doctrine called for a mammoth armada of these machines, flying in tight defensive formations, to deliver knockout blows to the enemy's ability to conduct the war. The organization chosen to implement this doctrine was the Eighth Air Force. Activated in January 1942, the first combat elements of the Eighth began arriving in Britain in the early summer and launched their initial raid in August. In the course of the next eighteen months the Eighth would become the largest, most powerful air force in the world. When it reached full operational strength in the summer of 1944 it was able to mount missions of gigantic proportion, dispatching over one thousand bombers and eight hundred fighters to targets in German-occupied Europe.

Yet for the first year of operations the effectiveness of the Eighth was tenuous at best. Throughout 1942 and into the new year the Eighth battled against horrendous weather in northern Europe, a chronic shortage of planes and crews, and the competing demands of Operation Torch—the invasion of North Africa—which stripped the Eighth of its most experienced flying units and ground personnel. It was only in the early summer of 1943 that Ira Eaker, commanding general of the Eighth, felt confident that the men and machines were in place to mount the kind of massive raids envisioned by air force doctrine.

Between July and November the Eighth launched a series of daring raids deep into the heart of the Third Reich, inflicting severe damage on a number of strategic targets but suffering shocking casualties in the process. The Regensburg–Schweinfurt raid of August 17, in which 60 heavy bombers—600 men—were lost, was a preview of what awaited the Americans if they attempted a deep penetration into Germany without fighter escorts. In one grisly week in the autumn the Eighth Air Force lost 148 bombers (1480 men), and in the aftermath of these losses the British urged their American allies to abandon the entire project and join the RAF in its nighttime area bombing. The losses were reported in *Time* and *Newsweek*, setting off a firestorm of debate in the United States. Farrington had read all about it in phase training. He had heard the veterans, survivors of a combat tour in the ETO, talking about the casualty rates. Until mid-1944 the life expectancy of a bomber and crew was fifteen missions, and a flyer had only one chance in three of surviving a tour of duty. Still, the American leadership believed that improvements in formation flying, an increase in the number of aircraft and trained crews available, and the development of long-range fighter escorts would ultimately prove the feasibility of daylight strategic bombing. And so, despite appalling losses, the Americans continued their strategic experiment into 1944.

It was the introduction of the P-51 Mustang, the long-range fighter, early in that year that ultimately turned the tide, making the successful daylight bombing of targets in Germany possible. By the autumn swarms of Mustangs filled the sky, escorting the colossal bomber formations deeper and deeper into Germany and routing the increasingly beleaguered Luftwaffe. "The German Air Force has taken a terrific beating," the captain continued, "and Göring can't put up the planes the way he did just a few months ago. But Jerry is still out there. You never know when you'll encounter fighters, especially the new jets. We've seen a few of the Me 262s. So stay alert. Learn to fly tight formation. It'll save your life. Biggest problem you're going to run into right now is not fighters, though, but flak—ground-based antiaircraft fire. With the war going the way it is now, most of your targets will be in Germany, and Jerry has concentrated his flak batteries around the major targets. You'll see plenty of it.

"A tour of duty in the Eighth Air Force today is thirty-five missions. Used to be twenty-five, then thirty, and now it's thirty-five. Do your job, stay on the ball, and it'll all work out. Finish up, we give you a "Lucky Bastard's Certificate," and send you home to a grateful nation. Odds of earning that certificate have gotten better and better. In the Eighth's first year of combat only about one man in three finished a tour. About half never made it through the first five missions."

"Jeez," Al whispered, half audibly. During training nobody had ever really talked about casualties.

"Fighter escorts have made all the difference," the captain continued. "Broke Jerry's back. You'll fall in love with our 'little friends,' the Mustangs and Lightnings and Thunderbolts. They'll be with you all the way to the target and back. Any questions?"

No one said a word.

"Good. Now, squadron procedures. Each of you is responsible for checking the alert list every day here at squadron headquarters. That list will tell you who is alerted to fly the next day's mission. It doesn't mean you'll actually go, but if you're on the list, you're restricted to the base and should be prepared for a mission the next day. The CQ will wake you next morning with all the poop on chow, briefing, et cetera. If you're not alerted, you can, with permission, go off the base, take the Liberty Run into Norwich. Schedules are posted in the *Daily Bulletin* here at headquarters. You're responsible for the info in that, too. Some of the men have been known to visit local pubs in the area around here as well." He smiled. The boys smiled too, a bit uneasily.

"Now," the captain continued, "you'll need to check in with the quartermaster to pick up flying equipment. Class schedules will be posted this afternoon. Check the *Bulletin*. If there are no questions . . ."

"Our aircraft, sir," Farrington began, gesturing to a map of the station on the wall.

"You will not be assigned a permanent plane. You'll fly different ships from the squadron. The 787th's area is across the field, Lieutenant, revetments 15 to 28," indicating an area north of the main runway. "Anything else?"

From squadron headquarters they walked out to the hardstands, eager to get a view of the planes they would be flying into combat. Following the perimeter track that wound around the triangular runways, they passed through the 784th's revetments. The 784th, they had learned at breakfast, was the pathfinder squadron, made up entirely of lead crews. They were responsible for leading the formation to the target and putting the bombs "in the pickle barrel," as they had heard so often during training. They continued on past the squat control tower, past the combat-crew equipment sheds, past the tech sites, where oil-spattered mechanics bustled and the high-pitched whine of drills and the thunderous clamor of sheet metal and machinery echoed from the aluminum huts. They skirted the western terminus of the main runway, reaching at last the dozen or so revetments of the 787th.

In the bleak overcast the great silver planes stood gray and lusterless on their hardstands. Around them a small shantytown of ragged tents and huts had sprung up. Made of ammunition crates, irregular bits of metal siding, and boxes of all sorts, topped in some cases with a shaft of stovepipe, the huts were the prized possessions of the ground crews who often had to work through the night to get the planes ready for a mission. Cramped and cold, but at least offering some protection from the wind, some were equipped with crude bunks, a chair, the inevitable pinups, odd tools, a washtub, even a radio. "All the comforts of home," Manners said, as they peeked into one.

Everywhere there was noise and motion. Mechanics from the ground crews crawled into nose wheel wells or emerged from bomb bays, stood on mobile platforms or on a wing over an open cowling, their coveralls slick with rain and grease. Occasionally an engine coughed, a prop swung into a halo of motion, and a plume of black smoke shot into the gray mist. A tail turret whirred, swiveling left, whined, and stopped. "The son of a bitch is still jammed," a voice behind the Plexiglas shouted above the din.

The boys sauntered from hardstand to hardstand, examining the aircraft. Many of the planes carried colorful, ribald names, outrageous scatological puns, or the titles of songs. Just back of the nose turret and below the navigator's tiny window, they sported vividly painted renditions of cartoon characters from the funny papers or generously endowed, scantily clad women sprawling in a variety of lusty poses.

"Hey, there's a plane for you, Brooklyn," Regan called out, pointing to revetment 18, where the *Hard Luck* rested.

"Yeah, and there's one for you, Lieutenant," Al responded, pointing to *The Joker*, just beside it on number 16.

"Tennessee's got one over here," Farrington shouted, pointing to *Earthquake McGoon*, the *Li'l Abner* hillbilly on revetment 25.

"That one's for you, Jerry," Howard laughed, gesturing toward *The Madame*.

"Or this one," Brennan added, *Oh Mona*.

"Harry's got one, too," Barrett suggested, nodding significantly at *The Troublemaker*. Gregorian did not laugh.

Walking to the edge of the hardstand, Howard stopped, gazing out across the fields to the west. Beyond the great lump of earth that served as backdrop for the base's firing range, a vista of peaceful undulating fields, each framed by low-lying hedges and stunted shrubs, stretched out to a distant tree line. Neatly cultivated wedges of barley, sugar beets, and potatoes glistened in the lingering mist, a blur of muted yellows and greens as far as the eye could see. But it was the sky that struck him. A vast expanse of lowering leaden gray loomed above, a sky so immense it dwarfed the tiny sliver of verdant earth on which he, the planes, and the aerodrome stood. Even in Utah or Colorado or Florida he had seen nothing like it. Spellbound, he watched as a billowing mountain of cloud rose above the vast horizon. Roiling as if caught in a surging, turbulent current, the clouds tumbled across the landscape, fluid vapors that dissipated and regrouped, transforming themselves from second to second in endless mutations. Ghostly, diaphanous streamers trailed across the terrain, leaving wispy tufts to settle eerily in the treetops. A soft, driving rain spread quickly across the field, and a blanket of cold mist enveloped the landscape. As he watched, transfixed, the flowing canopy of gray opened for an instant, revealing through a tiny rift a patch of brilliant, boundless blue, as if a sapphire had been rubbed suddenly clean on the dusty hilt of an ancient sword. The clouds closed quickly again, and bursts of pelletlike drops began to fall. Pulling up his collar, Howard rushed to catch up with the crew. They were on their way to chow.

"Well, I guess you are wondering just what has happened to your son," Howard wrote that evening to the family, sitting cross-legged on his bunk, the rain drumming relentlessly against the metal roof. "I am in England and arrived here safe and sound. The country here is somewhat different from what I just left in the States. My mail hasn't caught up with me but it will in about two weeks, I guess. Hope everyone at home is fine and well." He paused momentarily to watch as Barrett, armed with a poker and several crumpled sheets of *Stars and Stripes* tried without success to coax some heat from the tiny stove.

"Let me try," Brennan said, crouching beside him. He had just come in from the mess hall, and a hint of steam was rising from his damp sweater. Everything in the hut was damp.

"Boy, it is awfully cold here and I'm not kidding," Howard wrote. "I'm not any too crazy about it, either." A tiny, feeble flame flared for a moment in the stove's belly, spent itself, and died. "The son of a bitch is just impossible," Barrett said in disgust.

Seeing a map of the Eighth's air stations at squadron headquarters in the afternoon, Howard had been quick to locate Tom's outfit, the 390th, in Framlingham. "I am quite a ways from Tom," he wrote, "but am hoping to get in touch with him soon. I am about ninety miles out of London and as yet

I haven't had a chance to arrange a date with him, but I will in not long though." The censors, he would later learn, had cut the mileage reference from the letter. "Has James heard from the draft board? Will he get to continue school or not? I sure hope so, but I doubt if he will." There was little of substance to report, little that he could say without the censors blocking it. "So far I haven't done anything exciting," he concluded, "but expect to in not too long."

As usual, Bob's thoughts were with Marie and the boys. "Sunday afternoon and pretty quiet," he wrote on the fifteenth. "No mail since leaving the States. I sure will hug one tight when I do get a letter from the good old USA. One doesn't really appreciate the United States till you leave them. Then you count every hour till you return." He had hoped the crew would get a pass to go into the nearby village, but it didn't materialize. Instead, he learned that he would draw detail. "Tomorrow morning I have KP at 5 A.M. That will be midnight in Chicago. I would rather be in bed in Chicago at midnight than getting up in England for KP. I guess one is never in the army too long to draw KP." In the hut, his small book of snapshots open on the olive drab blanket, Bob struggled against a mounting swell of loneliness. "[Whenever] I see the time I subtract five hours, which gives me Chicago time. I imagine what you are doing and dream of you. Sure helps pass the time." He flipped again through the small collection of photographs. "They offer some consolation," he wrote. "Hoping to see Bobby with new clothes soon. I do have a wonderful family and am indeed proud of them. I . . . miss you, sweetheart, and am looking forward to a lot of loving when I become yours again and not Uncle Sam's. . . . My prayers are for peace and a better world to live in."

During its first few days at Attlebridge the Farrington crew settled into life in the squadron, learned the layout of the air station, and began combat orientation. From the quartermaster they drew their personal flight gear—parachutes, harnesses, Mae Wests, electric suits, pile-lined jackets, pants, boots, flight helmets, and oxygen masks—to be stored in the combat-crew locker room. Their hut was over a mile from the mess hall and other major communal sites on the base, and although trucks made regular rounds most of the men preferred to use a bicycle for day-to-day transportation around the post. Black and spare, with numbers painted on the rear fender for identification, bikes whipped along Broadway, the tiny paved road that led from the WAAF site to the flight line, or slogged through the ubiquitous gravel and mud. They clustered by the dozen in racks in front of every building, stood propped against the walls of huts, or simply lay strewn about on the ground outside buildings as if they had been shot. English models with handlebar brakes rarely seen in the States, they tested the uninitiated with sudden stops and dramatic spills, especially after a night in one of the nearby pubs. The boys bought bikes.

Combat orientation began with ground school. The men attended classes on medicine and first aid, intelligence, personal equipment, and aircraft identification. They practiced emergency procedures for ditching and listened to lectures on the Articles of War and evasion. Each man in the crew also attended specialized classes—Rossman studied navigational problems, Manners worked in the simulated bomb run, Farrington and Regan spent more time in the Link trainer and autopilot. Howard learned combat radio procedure, the call signs and letters of the squadrons and groups, as well as the bomber code used by both the Americans and the RAF. The gunners had additional practice in the mock-up turrets and on the firing range.

After a week of ground classes the crew was scheduled for high-altitude formation flying. Despite their training in the States and their confidence that they were a good crew, the men were uneasy, especially after hearing the horror stories about the mid-air collisions that seemed to plague the 466th. The veterans in the barracks and in the mess hall delighted in offering all green crews particularly vivid macabre details of the catastrophes they had witnessed in the air. It was not surprising, then, that everybody seemed jittery when the whole crew assembled on the hardstand for their first full-fledged practice mission in the ETO. The weather was terrible, with clouds stacked up to almost five thousand feet and a driving rain lashing across the field. The end of the runway was shrouded in fog, and as the men assumed their positions for takeoff nobody, least of all Farrington, thought they would be going up that day. It was only practice, after all. But the mission was not scrubbed. The control tower gave the start signal, and Farrington watched as the ships before them hurtled down the runway, vanishing behind a veil of low-lying clouds. And then they were on their way, roaring down the rain-blackened tarmac into the void. When after what seemed an eternity they broke through the clouds, emerging suddenly into the bright, cold, clear air, they could not locate the other ships in their formation. After circling for several minutes, all eyes scanning the horizon and the thick carpet of sunlit clouds beneath them, Farrington followed his flight plan, heading for The Wash and the practice bomb run.

Suddenly Gregorian's voice rang out over the interphone from the nose turret.

"What is that stuff down there?" he yelled.

Brooklyn saw it too. "Puffs of black smoke, sir, a thousand feet below us and off to our left. Jeez, I think it's flak."

"Flak! In England?" Farrington barked incredulously.

"They're shooting at us, sir," Peterson called out from the ball. "No doubt about it."

"Let's get the hell outta here," Regan said calmly.

Farrington swung the plane away to the right and began a steady climb, leaving the sooty black smudges behind them in a matter of seconds.

Back at Attlebridge in the afternoon an embarrassed Farrington discovered to his chagrin that they had strayed over a restricted zone, well off the flight plan, and the British antiaircraft batteries had fired several warning salvos. "Lieutenant," the debriefing officer deadpanned, "we in the 787th hate to lose a crew to enemy flak. Losing one to the British is a bit hard to take."

Despite this screwup it quickly became apparent to the squadron commander and to the veteran pilots who evaluated the rookies that Farrington and Regan were both calm, competent men. In their subsequent practice missions they handled the Liberator with skill and confidence, especially in high-altitude formation flying, when so many pilots fresh from the States were shaky and timid. Farrington in particular seemed to have a knack for sliding the giant bomber neatly into his assigned position in formation. Flying wing tip to wing tip didn't faze him. It was in these days that the boys in the crew began calling him Fearless Fosdick.

Air Station 120 was now definitely home, and the crew was making adjustments. For one thing, their mail had at last caught up with them and everyone was jubilant. "Glad to get your letter today," Howard wrote to his brother on the twenty-fifth. "It was the first mail I received since I left the States. I got sixteen letters, including nine from Nancy." Among the letters was also one from Alice, a long airmail written the day he left. It contained a snapshot of them together in New York, posed against a tree at the Central Park Zoo. Jerry Barrett had taken it. He had invited them to dinner at his parents' apartment just across the park, but they had declined, preferring to spend the evening alone together. The letter surprised him. It was jaunty and upbeat, as she always was, but she begged him to write, not to drop matters. She was expecting to see him again soon in New York, she wrote, and to hear from him in the meantime.

As they quickly discovered the base was a surprisingly self-contained town of more than three thousand men, much larger than the villages and rural hamlets scattered about the surrounding countryside. In addition to the combat crews, they met ground personnel assigned to engineering, maintenance, ordnance, intelligence, operations, weather, training, base defense, personnel, and even public relations. Each day the group's *Bulletin*, posted at squadron headquarters, announced an astonishing array of activities that sought to preserve a semblance of civilian normality. During their first week at the field the base movie theater, dubbed ironically the Opera House, showed *Girl Crazy* with Mickey Rooney and Judy Garland and *Heavenly Body* with William Powell and Heddy Lamar. Shows were at 6:30 and 8:30, with matinees every Monday, Wednesday, Friday, and Sunday. If they didn't take in a show, the officers had their club and the enlisted men could head over to the Aero Club. Run by the Red Cross, the club was open daily at 11:00 A.M. and offered, as the *Bulletin* advertised, "excellent recordings, hometown newspapers, warm fires, and Marge, Mary, and Nell on deck." The three women were American Red Cross volunteers who staffed the club and tried to impart a touch of home to the base. The Aero Club also sponsored other special activities, offering in the crew's first week dancing lessons, instruction in conversational French, a classical music hour, a quiz show, news talk, and "the gala weekly dance" with the group's orchestra on Thursday night. To their astonishment dozens of local girls from nearby villages and Norwich arrived at the base in "liberty trucks" for the festivities. For the more sedate, Big Bingo was the event on Fridays at 7:00. The Shamrock Tavern, "featuring that famous piano stylist Paul Bowers," was open every night except Sunday at 7:00 in the WAAF site across from the Special Services office. Unlike the Aero Club, the Shamrock served beer.

The group also offered correspondence courses and other educational activities. "Study, Brother, Study," Special Services urged. "Why not get ready for those years AFTER the war? Correspondence courses now available with top U.K. universities offering four hundred courses on everything from livestock management to the history of philosophy. Uncle Sam pays one-half of the bills. And if you wish to go to Oxford or Cambridge for a week, see Special Services." In addition, the men could sign up for courses

on how to handle the personal finances of war. "Have some jack when you
get back," it advised. Howard was particularly taken by the base's athletic
activities. Ping-Pong tournaments, boxing, basketball, and even a football
team was fielded. The group's baseball team, he learned, had won the
Eighth Air Force championship in August.

"Finally I have a permanent base for a while," Howard wrote on
October 22, "so now I can find a few minutes of my own." He was finding his
way around the base, adjusting to the new routines, and staying "busy at all
times." He had met about a dozen guys he had known during the phases in
the States—men he had met at radio school, Tyndall, or Westover—so it
wasn't totally alien terrain. He still hadn't been able to contact his brother-
in-law, but he hoped to soon. "I know where Tom is located but he doesn't
know I'm here yet and it will be quite some time before I can get a pass. If
only he knew where I was, he could see me without any trouble at all."

The casual atmosphere of air stations in the ETO was well-known, but
the boys were pleasantly surprised at just how relaxed the military routine
was. "We have no reveille," Bob explained to Marie. "They wake us for a
mission or ground school. Otherwise we sleep. No formation for retreat. We
just stand wherever we happen to be when the national anthem is played
and the flag is lowered. Eat whenever we get up and before 8 A.M. Meals at
noon from 11:30 to 1:00 and evening chow from 5:30 to 6:30." There would
also be no KP for them when they went on combat status and that, Bob
concluded, was certainly a plus. "Don't have to put up with much chickenshit around here," one of the guys in the hut told them, though occasionally
local commanders would try to crack down. Not long after the Farrington
crew arrived, the 466th's CO complained that "personnel on this station
have been apprehended by the London Military Police for minor offenses,
such as unbuttoned clothing, lack of insignia, improper identification,
mixed uniform, lack of dog tags, et cetera. These offenses have been a
reflection on the station as a whole and must cease. Future violators will be
subject to severe disciplinary action." Just two days later he cautioned his
personnel, "an intensified check is being made during the next ten days in
Norwich, Lowescroft, and King's Lynn for military courtesy and discipline.
Unit commanders will insure that all personnel are instructed as to proper
behavior." He also warned, "all personnel are reminded that a pass is a
privilege and *not* a matter of right." These injunctions apparently had little
effect, since shortly thereafter he felt moved to comment, "Military courtesy
on this base has reached such a point of indifference that it is necessary to

take drastic steps to remove this condition. Unit commanders have been directed to bring this matter to the attention of the personnel of their command, and action will be taken to insure compliance. Any officer or enlisted man of this command who fails to render the prescribed salute will be subject to disciplinary action." It was a warning repeated for weeks on end.

The food on the base was plentiful and suprisingly good. To one another, and certainly to the cooks, they might bitch about the grisly powdered eggs, which sometimes appeared in a startlingly bilious green or a suspicious rusty gray, and virtually everybody grumbled about the mutton and omnipresent brussels sprouts, but to the folks at home the men, as Bing Crosby's hit song urged them to do, accentuated the positive. "Meals are not bad over here," Bob reported, "except we have no fresh milk."

The weather was another matter. "It is raining here as usual," Howard wrote in what became a standard refrain even in their early days in England, "and probably will for a week or so." "It rains nine out of ten days on the average," he added glumly. Rain became the dominant element of their lives. It pelted against the windows, it rattled on the tin roof. It dripped from every ledge and stood everywhere in puddles, turning the world into a morass of mud. Sometimes it cascaded down in fluttering sheets, driven by gusts of howling wind. It poured in torrents from clouds so low they could reach out and touch them. It turned to sleet, to hail, and back to ponderous drops. It lingered as fog, as haze, as mist. And, most mystifying and maddening of all, it came in a form so fine they could never feel anything as distinct as a drop, so invisible it failed to stir even the placid surface of a puddle, and yet after walking ten yards their faces, their jackets, their caps would be drenched as if they had somehow generated the moisture from some elusive internal source.

Everything was damp. Even inside the hut, its cold concrete floors caked with mud, the condensation from the stove added its contribution to the inescapable dampness. "Chills you through to the bone," Bob wrote. "Most of us are wearing long woolen drawers and shirts. . . . This is the first time I ever wore long woolens and just keep wearing them." The little stove could put out just "enough heat to keep you warm if you lie on the bed and keep your feet off the floor. . . . The climate is the worst I have ever experienced," he complained. "It is not too cold as for the thermometer readings, but chilly because of the moisture in the mists. . . . [I] never realized there was such a damp spot on earth or such a changeable atmosphere," he ruminated. "After being here I even appreciate Illinois."

On October 23 the promotions for the enlisted men on the crew finally came through, but in those early days at AS 120 they had little opportunity to spend any of their money. "We still haven't had a pass to see the civilians of England," Bob wrote on the twenty-seventh. The guys had talked about walking over to the village, but it was over two miles away and the blackout made navigation difficult for newcomers. Some of the old hands at the WAAF site had already briefed them about the nearby pubs. "You just slip out the back gate down Broadway here. It's about a mile over to The Dog. Great place," a gunner in their hut explained. "On the main road from King's Lynn to Yarmouth. Ales, stout, the works. You need a bike, though. If you get tired, you can always stop off for a visit with one of the farm girls along the way. Couple of houses there where they're real friendly with the GIs. There's The Swan and The Union Jack over in Ringland or The Bush in Costessy. Great fish and chips shop there, too, if you make it before closing time. Brennan even showed up at chow with a pub map, drawn up by a fellow in the 786th, detailing routes, distances, and destinations of note.

Still, the crew stayed put. "We could have gone several times lately," Bob wrote, "but the gang goes to the free movies or to the Aero Club on the post for extra activities." After a day of ground school and practice missions the men congregated around the small stove, "writing letters home and warming our feet." They hoped to get into Norwich soon. "From the air the towns look much different from the U.S. towns." The sight reminded him of a picture folder of England he and Marie had seen on his last leave home. "Sure some quaint old brick houses here. Also they have those country lanes you read of." But the United States was "far advanced ahead of anything I have seen over here. Automobiles are small with steering wheels on the right side. They drive on the left side of the road. . . . Trains are smaller and look like toys beside our giants. Roads are narrow and are more like country lanes."

Although his contact with English life was limited to what he had observed enroute to AS 120 and, of course, from hearsay around the station, Bob had already formed what was a typical impression. "England has a class system and a lot of poor people. I feel sorry for [them]." Everything seemed grimy, encased in soot, and the people appeared as gray as their surroundings. The poor housing, the lack of fuel, clothing, sanitary facilities, and even soap, "except for the privileged few," shocked him. By contrast, the base, with its abundance of food and entertainment, was an island of prosperity, of home.

It was a curious, anomalous existence, difficult, if they chose to think about it, to fathom. On this sheltered base in England, with its movies and Ping-Pong, its dances and Liberty Run girls and drinks at the Aero Club, war lurked all around them, and with each passing day it edged inexorably closer. "Doesn't seem possible to be overseas," Bob mused, struggling to grasp the reality of their strange new life. "This is the real thing. Over in the States you just read of robot bombs etc. . . . They really land in England." In early October a giant V-2 had slammed into a farm about four miles away. The concussion could be felt as far away as Norwich, and the crater, according to the rumors that circulated around the base, measured twenty-two feet deep and sixty-five feet wide. Every Wednesday was gas-mask day, and everyone carried a mask from 0800 to 1200. From 10:00 to 10:30 they wore them as they went about their duties.

During their first week at Attlebridge the 466th flew almost daily missions to targets in Germany—Mannheim, Cologne, Mainz, the Ruhr. Each morning in the pale light of dawn the Farrington crew stood mesmerized as the mammoth planes lumbered from their hardstands, taxied along the perimeter track, lined up for takeoff, and roared into the mist above. Stopping on their way to ground school, their necks craning upward, their eyes followed the group as it formed above the field, joined with others, and disappeared at last beyond the horizon. For over an hour on a stunningly clear morning the bright blue sky would be tesselated with contrails as hundreds of heavies passed on their way to targets on the continent. It was an awesome sight. In the afternoon they stopped to watch as the group came back. Like everyone else, they counted the planes.

Later, at the mess hall, the boys observed the crews as they straggled in from interrogation. Some were tired and listless, others buoyant and loud. Some wanted to talk, recounting what they had seen in the sky that day, others sat quietly, expressionless, preoccupied. Farrington and his crew watched them. They listened. As the days passed and combat drew nearer, they found themselves almost viscerally alert to every recounted experience, to every fragment of advice, to every breath of instruction about equipment, about first aid, about weather, which two months before would have left them straining to stay awake. They reviewed their jobs and procedures, checked out their equipment, inspected the returning aircraft, peering into burnt-out engines, splintered Plexiglas, and ragged shrapnel holes, some as large as footballs. They watched the veteran crews as they went about their business on the base, as they ate at the mess hall or drank at the Aero Club. What were they looking for? What did they hope to find? Some hint, some clue, some discernible quality that might guarantee survival?

They had been on the base for more than two weeks, and although they could use more practice missions they knew that they would be flying combat soon. Each day they checked the alert list with mounting anticipation, searching the neat, typewritten rows of names for their own. Then, at breakfast on November 4 they learned that one of the new crews, assigned to the squadron on the same day as they were, had gone on the mission that morning, bound for a target in Germany. They were all jumpy when they reported to the 787th orderly room at 0900, anxious for the alert list for tomorrow's mission to be read. The ops officer opened the door, stepped into the limpid sunlight, and called for attention. "The following crews are alerted for tomorrow," he coughed, "and are restricted to this base." Howard listened intently as the officer, squinting at his clipboard, slowly read off the pilots' names, followed by the individual members of their crews. Then he heard it.

"Farrington, Richard!"

"Here," his pilot's voice rang out, and then one by one the members of the crew sounded off as they heard their names called. He had been expecting this for days, and yet as he stood silently outside the shabby operations hut on the small, muddy knoll, Howard was stunned, almost breathless.

They flew a practice mission that morning, twenty-seven ships taking off for an exercise in high-altitude formation flying. They had flown practices for days, logging air time, making cross-country navigational flights, dropping dummy bombs on target barges in The Wash, but today was different. They had attended a full briefing, and spent just over three hours in the air, bobbing in the prop wash of the ships in front of them, hugging their wingman as tightly as Farrington dared. Everyone on the crew was sharp, excited.

Back in the hut after evening chow, no one was tired. For some time they talked, joked, put their equipment in order for the next day. They wrote letters, they stoked the fire. They rechecked their clothing. They went to the latrine. Then one by one they climbed into the sack, and the lights were extinguished, and the chatter dwindled, and the hut fell silent, leaving each man alone with his thoughts.

Howard lay on his back, eyes wide open, staring at the slope of the metal ceiling. A jeep pushed slowly along the road outside the hut, and above the grinding of its gears he could hear the rumble of the Lancasters and Halifaxes, the RAF on its way to the continent and death. In the darkness he could see the form of Jerry Barrett, sitting upright on his bunk, a dim figure punctuated by the red glare of a pipe. Howard turned on his side, pulling the blankets tautly over his shoulder, straining to hold the mattress together beneath him. At the other end of the hut Al, too, was smoking. Someone—was it Brennan?—muttered drowsily in his sleep. It sounded like a prayer.

Howard tried to relax. Stray thoughts, forgotten moments from school, from training flashed through his mind. He thought about the house on Trunk Street, about the back porch where they ate in the summer, the blood red blossoms of the crape myrtle just outside the screen. He saw the ornate lobby of the Tivoli Theater in Chattanooga, where he had gone with his sister Mildred and Tom just after they were married. What did they see that day, before the war? He thought about swimming at Fillauer Lake on sweltering, cloudless days with Buddy McLeod and C. L. Bivens. He thought about Central Drug Store, with its bright rows of greeting cards, the rich powdery scent of the cosmetics and candies, the soda fountain. He thought about Nancy. Then these images dissolved, routed by a jumbled sequence of radio frequencies, call numbers, codes. He did not want to think about tomorrow, but with an unshakable, primitive clarity he wondered, for perhaps the hundredth time that day, what he, Howard Goodner from Cleveland, Tennessee, was doing in a cold, dimly lit hut on the flatlands of East Anglia. Someone—Al, he thought—got wearily up, slipped on his jacket over his long johns, and quietly stepped outside, heading for the latrine.

Howard had written home earlier in the evening, just before lights out. He would mail it on the way to chow in the morning. "I haven't seen much as yet," he wrote, "but, Mother, don't worry about me at all because I am going to be okay and if I didn't feel like I was, I wouldn't say anything." He warned her that he might not be able to write as much in the coming days, but she was not to worry. "I promise you," he concluded, "nothing will happen."

CHAPTER III

THE WINGS OF MORNING

While thousands of men tossed in a fitful, restless slumber in huts across East Anglia, senior operations officers gathered for the day's final weather briefing at VIII Bomber Command. Smartly dressed despite the hour, the officers stood at a small wooden table in a large, windowless room. In front of them a gigantic map of Europe, its topographical signatures and political boundaries punctuated with diagrams and symbols, extended across a brightly lit wall. A young officer stood at the base of the map. A pointer, fashioned from bamboo and over six feet long, rested at his side. Consulting the papers clutched in his left hand, he traced with the pointer a broad parabola across the map. As he spoke, the men glanced from the open folders on the table in front of them to the map and back again. They asked questions. The pointer moved again to points east and stopped. Another officer, fresh faced and confident, no more than twenty-five years old, rose from the table and joined him, took the pointer, and followed a line that doglegged from the south coast of England eastward toward France until it vanished in a clot of red along the German border.

Throughout the day, while monitoring the progress of the mission already under way, the senior operations staff of VIII Bomber Command had been anxiously following the course of an unstable high pressure system that was easing its way eastward across the continent. Weather was always a problem, always a critical factor in planning, not only over the target but over the bases, where hundreds of aircraft would have to form up and then, the mission completed, land in the dangerously congested air space over East Anglia. The staff had convened as they did every day in the large, square room buried under thirty feet of reinforced concrete on the grounds of a former girls' school at Wycombe Abbey. Located northwest of London and code-named Pinetree, High Wycombe had served as the headquarters of VIII Bomber Command since the Americans began arriving in England in 1942. It was the nerve center of the vast and complex machinery of war that the U.S. Army's Eighth Air Force had assembled for the assault on Hitler's Europe. At the daily 1015 and 1600 weather briefings updated reports had indicated that the high would probably hold for the next day's mission, though weather over eastern France and northern Germany might be spotty. By late afternoon status reports from the groups involved in the current mission had also begun arriving, allowing the staff to determine aircraft and crew availability for the coming day. On the basis of these projections the staff, following standard operating procedure, had selected a number of targets from the priority list drawn up by the Combined Bomber Offensive. In the late afternoon the chief of operations had evaluated his staff's recommendations and made his preliminary decision. He had selected the targets, the number of planes necessary for the mission, the type of bombs required to destroy the targets, and the order of battle for the Eighth's three air divisions. A warning order giving this information had been dispatched down the chain of command following the 1600 weather briefing, alerting all the Eighth's formations for a mission the following day. Now, hours later, with the latest meteorological data available, the final decision had to be made. Seated at the small table, a bank of telephones to his left, the commander closed his folders and looked one last time over the map. They would go.

At just past 2200 the Teletype began to clatter in the operations block at a country estate just southwest of Norwich. Ketteringham Hall served as headquarters of the Second Air Division. It commanded all the Eighth's B-24s—fifteen bomb groups divided into five combat wings scattered across the marshy Norfolk flatlands. The officers assembled in the operations building that night had been anticipating the field order from Pinetree all evening. They knew that a weather conference had indicated favorable conditions for a mission tomorrow, and a warning order had arrived in the late afternoon over the scrambler—a specially designed telephone that electronically garbled the words spoken into it, rendering it unintelligible to anyone seeking to tap the line, before restoring the words at the receiving end. That message identified the target by coded number and specified the ordnance requirements. Operations and intelligence staffs had already begun planning the mission, studying target maps, calculating bomb loads, plotting routes and times, arranging for fighter support, and determining the number of aircraft needed, the order of the division's combat wings, and the number of squadrons in each.

With these preparations under way, Second Air Division headquarters alerted its five wing commanders. The combat wing was a purely operational organization with no administrative responsibilities. Wing officers were charged with calculating takeoff times and assembly points for the three groups under their command. They also determined the position of the groups in the wing formation—which group would fly lead, which would be high, which low. Takeoff and assembly were nerve-racking, dangerous phases of any mission, and the planning had to be meticulous. At the headquarters of the 96th Combat Wing at Rackheath, operations officers scanned the advance order. All the information wasn't in, but already they knew that they would be sending up approximately one hundred aircraft at almost the same time in an area the size of greater Philadelphia. Maybe the weather would be good, with ceiling and visibility unlimited—CAVU, the weather boys called it. Usually it wasn't. Maybe the high pressure system would hold. But they couldn't count on it. The weather changed with a rapidity and unpredictability that defied description. They got to work.

The three groups constituting the 96th Combat Wing, the 466th at Attlebridge, the 458th at Horsham St. Faith, and the 467th at Rackheath, received their first warning of a mission for the following day in the form of a telephone message on the scrambler in the group's operations' message center. The call from wing HQ had come into Air Station 120 in the late afternoon, while the the the last of the crews returning from that day's mission to Gelsenkirchen were still wearily answering questions in interrogation. The watch officer in the group operations building immediately notified all services on the base to expect a field order for a mission tomorrow. A quick call alerted the group commander, group operations officer (S-3), the intelligence section (S-2), the group navigator and bombardier, the weather office, flying control, the ordnance and armaments sections, the engineering office, the signals and photographic units, the mess hall, the motor pool, and finally the charge of quarters (CQ) on each squadron living site.

The combat crews were still in the mess hall or, exhausted, wandering back to their huts to catch some sleep, when key personnel began filtering into the operations building. They would be there all night. Waiting for the field order to arrive, they were already poring over the advance information from wing HQ for clues about tomorrow. Where would they be going? How many planes would they be expected to put up? What was the bomb load? What about fuel? A full fuel load meant a deep penetration, a tough mission, and the number of aircraft indicated whether this was to be a big show—a maximum effort that would send all four of the group's squadrons into combat. But the advance field order was rarely complete, and those in the ops building often had to wait, sometimes for hours, for the Teletype to spew out the relevant data from wing or division. Late weather updates, new intelligence on flak or the Luftwaffe, or other factors might provoke changes in the orders. Annexes and amendments would continue deep into the night. Nobody in this building would sleep.

The target arrived in coded form, a cryptic set of numbers, which sent the group's S-2 duty officer scurrying to the locked code office. There he checked the top secret codebook to decipher the target reference and withdrew the appropriate target folder from the hundreds on file. Each target folder contained a map and a clear vertical photograph of the target to a standard size. Taking a transparency with numbered grid lines, the intelligence officer carefully placed it over the photograph and, referring to a number code in the Teletype order, determined the center of the desired bomb pattern on the target, the so-called MPI, or mean point of impact— the bull's eye for the mission's bombs. Having established the target, intelligence transmitted this information to the S-3 and to the group bombardier and navigator offices. The intelligence staff also began to assemble the maps, photographs, and other relevant material for navigators and bombardiers, while the photographic laboratory copied flak charts and mission flimsies, which would be used for briefing the crews.

On a large wall map the ops staff began to chart the route to the target and the group navigator's office plotted courses, distances, and times for assembly. They checked and rechecked the weather reports, especially the temperatures and wind data expected at altitude en route. They calculated the airspeeds and drift on various legs to be flown and checked them against times received from division. Precision was essential. If the group failed to take off on time, if its assembly was too slow, if it missed a checkpoint by as much as a minute, disaster could result. With a thousand bombers forming up in the crowded clouds above East Anglia, each one had to find its assigned spot at the assigned altitude and at the assigned time.

Meanwhile, officers from the group bombardier's office hovered over a large table, its surface a clutter of maps, aerial photographs, and the latest information from the weather officer. Reading from the glossy high-altitude vertical photographs, they studied the crucial landmarks—road junctions, railroad lines, bridges, a bend in the river to be checked on the bomb run. They had to anticipate conditions at the target, calculating speeds, drift, and heading data that would be computed into bombsight settings for the attack altitude.

Late in the evening squadron operations officers began arriving, anxious to see what they would need for tomorrow. By midnight the air in the windowless rooms of the ops block was heavy with stale cigarette smoke. Coffee mugs and ashtrays littered the desks and tables. The room was chilly, and the men, even those who had been there for hours, wore their jackets. The squadron operations officers drifted in, fresh from assessing the impact of the day's mission on their men and planes. Their immediate task was to make any last-minute amendments to the crew and aircraft status boards on the walls of the operations room. From these a tentative availability list was drawn up. Working with the information from the advance field order, the operations officers selected the aircraft and crews for the mission. They examined their squadron alert lists. Not everyone alerted would fly. They made their choices and wrote the names on a large chalkboard, using a schematic formation plan. As the squadron officers checked their rosters, duty clerks from equipment, engineering, armaments, and other sections involved arrived at operations to obtain pertinent information.

As soon as the bomb load was known the ordnance section swung into action. Ordnance was responsible for fusing and loading the required bombs into each of the group's planes. Working in the pitch black, men from ordnance loaded the massive bombs—thousand-pound general-purpose bombs, five-hundred-pound fragmentation bombs, incendiary bombs— onto the special trailers at the bomb dump for their trip to the hardstands. It was a dangerous job. Struggling in the slippery wet and numbing cold, they gingerly wheeled the bombs to a position under the open bomb bay and, using winches and tractors, hoisted the unwieldy, blunt-nosed bombs into their racks. The bombs had to fit precisely and securely. A mistake could mean a hung-up bomb load over the target or a sudden, blinding explosion on the ground. It happened occasionally.

As ordnance crews crawled about in and under the bomb bays and armaments personnel placed ammunition for the machine guns in the aircraft, ground crews were already at the hardstands, checking and re-checking the planes. They, too, would work through the night, snatching only a moment of rest in the tents or shacks they had erected beside their hardstands. They tested the oxygen and fuel systems. They checked the controls. They ran up the engines. They would remain with their planes throughout the night, as trucks rumbled ceaselessly along the base's small roads, and jeeps darted from headquarters to hangars, and the giant Pratt & Whitney engines, first one, then another, then another, bellowed at intervals from their hardstands, their roars reverberating like the rumble of distant thunder across the dark, silent countryside.

By 0200 the planning was complete. The last weather update had been issued. The final intelligence annex to Field Order 510 had been dispatched by VIII Bomber Command and had been received and passed on through the Eighth's elaborate apparatus of command. And in the dead of a cold English night at more than forty airfields in East Anglia, men tossed restlessly in their bunks, struggling for sleep. In only a few hours a thousand planes and ten thousand men would be sent into the deadly skies over Germany.

At 0300 in the predawn darkness of November 5, 1944, the door of the hut snapped open and the CQ of the 787th Squadron stepped in, flashlight in hand.

"Barrett, Brennan, Goodner, Gregorian, Peterson, Seraydarian," he said, in a voice somewhere between a bark and a whisper, "mission today. You're flying. Breakfast at 0330, briefing at 0400."

The men stumbled out of their bunks, frozen, scared, and, despite the hour, wide awake. Whatever heat had huddled in the half-moon shack before lights out had slunk timidly away in the night, and the stove stood forlorn and cold in the center of the room. No one had slept much. As they shaved awkwardly in the clammy water and fumbled with their clothes, hung in varying degrees of disorder on the rack behind their beds, the usual complaints and ribbing filled the hut, but the laughter was thin and the banter hurried, distracted.

Howard rose quickly, scrambling into his clothes. He had slept in his cotton shorts and T-shirt, topped with the woolen long johns. He could not remember when he had them off last. Over his white cotton socks he pulled on a heavy woolen pair and then, bouncing nervously to dispel the dank chill, slipped on his ordinary uniform pants, shirt, and the heavy fleece-lined flying jacket. He looked down at the New Testament—the pocket-sized Heart Shield Bible, with its front cover of gold-finished steel, that Nancy had given him—and decided to leave it behind on the bed.

Outside the hut the weather was miserable, pitch black, wet, and raw. All along the road between the huts the silent shapes of men passed in the gloom, some on foot, some, despite the mud and the darkness, on bicycle. A light truck with a makeshift ramp on its tailgate stopped in front of the shack to carry them the mile or so to the combat mess, and in the truck, with its smell of metal, gasoline, and wet canvas, there was little talk.

Jumping down from the truck's platform, they shuffled through the blackout curtains into the yellow glare of the mess hall. The air in the large Nissen hut was heavy with smoke and the aroma of burnt grease, cigarettes, and coffee. Amid the clatter of mess kits and the scraping of wooden chairs on the muddy concrete floor, they filed through the line for chow. There were no officers present. They had their own mess. All around combat crewmen sat at long wooden tables, some in their light leather jackets, others in their heavy sheepskin jackets and fatigues. Most wore their hats. Occasionally a laugh, a taunt, a shout of recognition would rise above the murmurous hum, but the atmosphere was subdued, somber, as if each man in the crowded room had deserted the present and crawled into a small, secret space just behind his eyes. A treat—French toast—was being served that morning, and the cloying smell was ghastly.

The crew found seats at the end of a table and settled in facing one another over the steaming food. Howard could not eat. He glanced at his buddies. Across from him Barrett sipped fruit juice, his cap pushed back jauntily on his head, his arm draped carelessly around Al's chair. An irresistible air of self-confidence, of control always seemed to radiate from Jerry. Is he worried about where we're going today? Howard thought. Did Jerry wonder, as he did, if they were ready? Beside him Al, a great shock of dark hair falling across his brow, pawed indifferently at the French toast.

Just looking at Brooklyn's broad, pleasant face was somehow reassuring. At the corner of the table Harry appeared drawn and tense. He sat motionless on his chair, gripping the thick, white coffee mug tightly in both hands, his eyes fixed on a spot in the ceiling. Brennan and Peterson were at Howard's side. Alone among them Jack seemed relaxed, as if they were back at Westover, headed out on a cross-country flight to Florida. He was chattering amiably to Bob, who sat quietly, apparently absorbed in his coffee. Howard distinctly heard the word *Hoboken*, but he could not concentrate. Bob never turned toward Jack, never acknowledged his rough nudges or easy, flowing banter. Did he even hear? He is somewhere in Chicago, Howard thought, with his wife and kids.

Howard looked carefully at each of them, scrutinizing the faces he had not known a year ago, faces that were now as familiar to him as his brother's. He had known them all for only a little more than six months, guys from Brooklyn and Detroit and Chicago, from places he had never been, from lives he would never know, could not even imagine. And yet he knew them. Knew them well. Knew that at this moment they were all thinking the same thing: When the weary crews straggle back to this mess hall this afternoon, another mission behind them, will I be among them?

Only Jack ate.

From the mess hall the men climbed into the trucks that shuttled along the base's winding roads to the long Nissen hut that served as the main briefing site. It was still dark, and a light mist was falling. The wind had picked up, rippling the black surface of the puddles. At the crowded entrance the crew separated for the first time that morning. Jerry, Jack, Bob, Al, and Harry joined the crowd pressing into the special briefing for gunners, while Howard, after drawing his headsets and mikes, hurried into the meeting for radio operators. At another entrance the pilots, navigators, and bombardiers were filing into the main briefing room, a cluttered, brightly lit space with folding chairs arranged in ragged rows on a concrete floor. In the front a low platform, illuminated by a bank of overhanging spotlights, waited empty in the harsh glare. On that platform stood a chalkboard bearing a diagram of the day's formation, and across the wall stretched a large map covered with a black cloth that concealed the target for today.

MPs stood guard at the entryways, and just inside the door Farrington, Regan, Rossman, and Manners signed in, their names checked against those on the master loading list by an officer seated at a small table. The

tension was thick as the men, sleepy, anxious, ill-tempered, found their
seats and waited. Some smoked—cigarettes, cigars, pipes. Some chewed
gum. Some did both. Some—perhaps the new men—were already jotting
notes on small pocket notepads. Some wore garrison caps, some their soft
flying helmets, the earflaps pushed up, some the jaunty "fifty-mission
crush" hats. No two men seemed to be dressed alike. Only one item of dress
was identical. As officers, they were expected to wear ties, as if headed for a
day at the office.

At promptly 0400 a voice behind them boomed "Ten-hut," chairs
scraped on the concrete as the men rose to attention, and the group
commander strode briskly into the room and up to the platform. With the
men again seated the colonel spoke. His words were crisp, businesslike. He
praised them for their work of the day before. He wished them good luck for
the day's mission. He wished them good hunting. The target for the day was
Crécy. The name meant nothing to them. But as he spoke the black curtain
over the map was removed, and their eyes were drawn to a thin red ribbon
that moved in sharp angular tangents from the bulge of East Anglia due
south to Folkestone near Dover, then doglegged across the English Channel
to a point near Boulogne on the French coast. From there it veered
southeastward, past Paris and Reims, dodging the flak concentrations at
Nancy and Metz, before turning abruptly at the German frontier.

The intelligence officer who would conduct the briefing stepped forward. He nodded at the men before him and began to speak. His voice was
matter-of-fact, succinct, his manner knowledgeable and confident. The
men fell silent. The target, he told them, was a large fortress constructed of
reinforced concrete just southeast of Metz. Erected during the First World
War, the fort housed a battery of heavy guns and was holding up the advance
of Patton's Third Army. The Ninety-sixth Combat Wing would be leading
the entire Second Air Division to the target, and each of the roughly three
hundred B-24s in the mammoth bomber stream would be carrying four
2,000-pound high-explosive bombs.

The crews usually liked these tactical targets in France, far away from
the dense belt of flak that ringed targets in Germany, but today's mission,
the S-2 warned, would be a tricky operation. "Friendly troops will be four
miles west of the target. No bombs," he paused for emphasis, "will be
dropped early. If *any* doubt exists as to the identity of the target, bombardiers will hold their bombs. Bombing of the primary target will be by visual
methods only. Friendly forces will put up a line of red flak to seventeen

thousand feet two miles inside their front lines. Be alert. Bombing altitude will be twenty-three thousand feet."

His pointer moving along the ominous red ribbon, the intelligence officer traced the routes in and out. He covered expected enemy air activity and flak near the target and along the route, including its anticipated intensity and range. Although division intelligence predicted only minimal enemy fighter action on this mission, he discussed possible fighter attacks, current Luftwaffe tactics, and the location of enemy airfields along the way. Friendly fighter cover would be provided by three groups of P-51s. Flak at the primary was expected to be light, but since the weather was questionable for visual bombing the briefing officer devoted great attention to the secondary target, the railroad yards at Karlsruhe just across the German border. Because the Eighth's two other bomb divisions would be operating in the area and air space would be tight, it was necessary to approach the secondary target through its most heavily fortified section. If the primary was socked in and the group was forced to attack Karlsruhe, the crews could expect intense and accurate flak.

As the men made notes the intelligence officer signaled to an aide, who lowered a screen on the platform behind him. On this same cue in the ritual choreography of the briefing, another aide maneuvered the belloptican, a large, awkward, overhead projector, forward into position in the narrow center aisle. The lights dimmed and the machine whirred, sending a shaft of stark white light toward the platform. "This is your target," the briefing officer said from the black fringes of the screen. The men strained forward in their seats. In the darkened room a crisp aerial photograph of a congested urban landscape materialized. At first it appeared as a giant geometric puzzle, a bewildering maze of tangents, ovals, interconnected rectangles and squares. But as they watched and the pointer moved and the officer's voice resumed, the shapes resolved themselves into the unmistakable vertical topography of a city. Buildings, factories, rail lines materialized. And clearly marked on the photograph and on the maps that followed was the target for the day. The briefing officer explained each map, each photograph, each diagram in painstaking detail, pointing out key terrain features, enemy camouflage, dummy targets, or crucial landmarks along the bomb run.

When he concluded and the lights were turned back on, another briefing officer stepped forward to go over escape and evasion procedures. He spoke quickly, covering what for most of the crews in front of him was grim but familiar terrain—what to do if shot down over enemy territory. He discussed escape routes in Holland, Belgium, and occupied France. He pinpointed the location of rescue ships in the North Sea. For days, Farrington thought fleetingly, the crew had practiced ditching procedures, climbing laboriously out of the plane, inflating the rubber rafts, grappling with paddles and flares. If they were forced to ditch, would everybody know his job? Only a third of the crews who ditched in the frigid waters of the North Sea or Channel ever came back.

The briefing officer was talking now about what to expect if captured by the Germans. "Wear your dog tags, gentlemen; carry your GI shoes and no other private items," he concluded. "If captured, give only name, rank, and serial number."

These warnings given, the weather officer took the stage. He reported on the anticipated meteorological conditions on each leg of the planned route, first from AS 120 to the English coast, then over the Channel, then from the enemy coast to the target, and finally along the route back. The weather was not good this morning, he acknowledged. Visibility and ceiling were currently poor, both over England and over the target, but projections were for improving conditions as the morning wore on. Dick Farrington looked over at his copilot. If things stayed like this, they both realized, it would mean an instrument takeoff and maybe an instrument landing on return. There would be no easing into combat flying in the ETO.

His report concluded, the weather officer stepped aside, yielding first to the radio officer, who spoke briefly about radio procedures, and finally to the group navigator, who provided additional details on the schedule and order of takeoff, assembly, and the position of each plane and squadron in the group's formation. Farrington and his crew listened anxiously as the pilots' names, their aircraft, and their positions in the formation were ticked off one by one. The names and numbers droned on until they heard it. "Farrington, flying spare, position 2-10." All four men scribbled it down. They glanced at one another. Was this good news or bad? Being a spare meant that they would fly into combat only if one of the other planes dropped out. "Takeoff—H-hour—is 0710, gentleman," the briefing officer continued. "Taxi, 0635, engines at 0630, and stations, 0530." The group navigator now called for a "time hack," the synchronization of all watches. Farrington, Regan, Manners, and Rossman, sitting shoulder to shoulder in the crowded room, readied their watches as the group navigator counted down: "five, four, three, two, one—hack!"

The main briefing was now over. All the information from the field order and its myriad annexes had been synthesized and dispensed. The planning was almost at an end. The men rose stiffly from their chairs, shuffling in their thick flying boots toward their different destinations. Farrington and Regan moved quickly to the front of the briefing room to check the flight diagram once again. They noted which plane they would follow out onto the perimeter track and then into the air. They would go now to the combat crew's locker room to draw their flying equipment and then head out to the hardstand to preflight the plane.

From the main briefing the navigators and bombardiers adjourned to their special meetings. Rossman joined the other navigators as they filed into a neighboring room in the ops block to study the flight plan in detail. The group navigator went over it carefully, examining airspeeds, routes, times, and altitudes, until each man was certain that it was correct, that he understood it fully. They rechecked the latest weather report for any changes that would affect winds or times. The briefing lasted almost an hour, ending with each navigator placing his maps, flight plan, and log into a small satchel before leaving to draw his flying gear.

Surrounded by the other bombardiers, Manners had taken a seat at a long table covered with maps and target photographs. A bombardier from the 785th had asked to see the briefing photo of the target area again on the screen, and the projector once more whirred into action. Manners stared from the photo in front of him to the picture on the screen and back, locking it into his memory. He made notes as the group bombardier reviewed the latest weather data, determining ground, air, and mean temperatures at the target. He made notations on his maps, gathered his notes together, and, the briefing at an end, he, too, departed for the combat-crew lockers.

The radio operators' meeting had already concluded, and Howard stood in line in the combat locker room across the road, waiting to turn in his personal effects. When he reached the front of the line he placed them on the counter—a handful of British coins he still hadn't mastered, his wallet, with his social security card, a five-pound note, and a picture of Nancy. The quartermaster officer sitting behind the wire-mesh screen looked up and smiled warmly as he accepted the articles. He was heavyset, wore glasses, and appeared to be in his thirties. He collected Howard's things, slipped them neatly into a small bag, recorded the name and number, and handed them to a corporal behind him. "See you this afternoon, sir," Howard said confidently as he turned away. The officer nodded. "Good luck, Sergeant," he answered. The corporal stored the small bag alongside the dozens of others on the neatly arranged shelves and returned, without expression, ready for the next man.

Howard claimed his flight gear. He stowed his goggles, oxygen mask, throat mike, heavy gloves, GI shoes, canteen, rayon gloves, heated gloves, and a steel helmet into his flight bag. These he would put on at the hardstand, under the wing of the plane. In the crowded locker room he struggled into his flying clothes. He proceeded carefully, methodically. At twenty thousand feet today the frigid crystalline air would howl through the unpressurized aircraft like a gale and the temperatures would plunge to minus thirty or forty degrees Fahrenheit. All around him the men prepared themselves as best they could for the ordeal. Over the cotton underwear, woolen long johns, and ordinary wool uniform of shirt and trousers he wore to briefing, Howard pulled the electrically heated F-3 flying suit. Small, well-insulated wires, which would be plugged into the electrical system at his station in the aircraft, ran like veins throughout the dark brown jacket and overall pants. By adjusting the rheostat just beside the radio operator's table he could control the temperature. Over his two layers of socks he slipped the heated shoe inserts, and plugged them into the tab connections along the ankles of his F-3 pants. Finally, he pushed his legs into a baggy pair of wind- and moisture-proof pants, tucking them into the fleece-lined, rubber-coated flying boots, and slipped on his green, pile-lined flying jacket. Over his head he pulled the inflatable yellow life preserver, the Mae West, and securely fastened the straps of his parachute harness, adjusting them around his chest and legs. On his head he wore his leather flying helmet.

Standing in the cluttered chaos of the locker room, he wondered if he had forgotten anything. He ran down a mental checklist, but it was hard to concentrate. The sweat coursed down his back and sides. It ran down his neck, matted his hair, and burned his eyes. Waddling ponderously toward the exit, Howard claimed his parachute, a small bundle that he would attach to the harness on his chest, and pushed out into the darkness.

Jostling along the narrow perimeter road in the truck headed for the 787th's dispersal area, Howard tried to recall details of the communications briefing. He carried with him a sheaf of communications maps, a logbook, and mission flimsies giving the numerous call signs and various frequencies he would need. The flimsies were made of rice paper, wafers that were to be eaten in the event of ditching or bailing out. He had scribbled notes throughout the briefing and had felt confident when he left for the locker room. Now his mind was a complete blank. In the chill of the darkened truck the sweat along his back and sides had turned clammy. At altitude it would freeze. A shudder rippled through his limbs, cramping his shoulders. "I'll be all right," he found himself muttering, "I'll be all right."

When Howard jumped down from the truck, swinging his flight bag onto the tarmac, the rain had stopped, and to the east, beyond the water tower and the low trees of the WAAF site, a light fringe of luminous gray had risen along the horizon. Through the gloom he could see the ground crew at work around the silver plane. A man in colorless overalls, a heavy sheepskin jacket, and a baseball hat, bill upturned, squatted on the left wing, topping off the fuel tanks. A powerful odor of aviation fuel, so pervasive it seemed to coat the lungs, filled the wet air. Farrington was talking with the crew chief beneath the number two engine on the concrete hardstand. He and Regan had already finished their preflight checks inside the aircraft, and now the pilot inspected the exterior, listened to a bit of the plane's recent repair history, and prepared to sign off the A-6 form. Drawing near the open bomb bay, Howard could hear the plane's auxiliary generator chugging as Barrett ran through his checks of the plane's various internal systems. At the plane's extremities, cramped in their swiveling Plexiglas bubbles, Al and Harry were working with the turrets. They would be testing their operation, their hydraulic and electrical systems, inspecting the solenoids, examining the metallic belts of gleaming fifty-caliber shells for oil or rust.

Shoving his bag in ahead of him and squeezing up through the bomb bay, Howard climbed to his station just behind the copilot's seat on the flight deck. He would go through the preflight checks on the radio equipment. Using a portable generator, he checked the interphone for noise, turned on the receiver, the liaison transmitter, and radio compass to see if they were working properly. He called the tower on the command set for frequency and modulation and turned on the VHF, which would be used on the command set to communicate with other aircraft and with the ground. He sent Bob to inspect the headsets and mikes and to make a visual check of the antennae. Finally he opened his folder, took out his log, and placed it on the small black desk in front of him. He was no longer nervous.

Glancing up through the small porthole window that faced him, Howard caught a glimpse of Manners as he strode up to the dispersal tent just beside the hardstand where the crew chief and Farrington were still absorbed in conversation. Curly was the last of the crew to arrive, and

Rossman was helping him adjust his parachute harness. Looking down at his watch, Howard realized that it was only fifteen minutes until stations. A surge of adrenaline shot through him. Regan, sitting above and in front of him on the flight deck, uncoiled suddenly from the copilot's seat and turned toward the bomb bay. "Got to take a leak," he muttered as he crawled past. Howard was suddenly seized by a violent desire to follow him. There was no safe or comfortable way to urinate at twenty thousand feet with the temperature at forty below zero. The little tubes provided in the plane were useless, and besides, it meant pulling off or opening layers of clothing and equipment. Howard climbed out of his seat and struggled out through the bomb bay.

The rain had started again, and the clouds hung low and heavy over the field. From their position just north of the main runway they could hardly see the tower. The raw breeze that had buffeted them throughout the morning had picked up again. The plane swayed gently on the hardstand, the heavy canvas flaps of the ground crew's tent fluttered wildly, and bits of gravel scudded across the concrete. Straggling back from the weedy fringes of the revetment where they had lined up, side by side, to urinate, the men gathered beneath the wing. Al was helping Jack adjust his parachute harness. Howard glanced at his watch. Five minutes to stations, when all the crews would climb into their planes and assume their positions for takeoff. All across the squadron's area he could see other crews clustered under the wings of their aircraft, having a few last words about the mission.

"I think I'm supposed to give you a little pep talk," Farrington began. "But I'll be damned if I can think of anything to say." His voice was hoarse and edgy. He hadn't slept much either, Howard realized, but his lean, angular features betrayed no sense of nerves. "This is what we've been waiting for, boys. Let's do our jobs, stay on the ball, and we'll get this one behind us." He paused, glancing from face to face at the men huddled around him. They fidgeted, looked blankly at the menacing sky or stared down at their boots.

"Any questions?"

No one spoke.

"Good," he said. "Just one last thing." He paused dramatically. "Remember to take a piss before we leave, Brennan. I'm not going to stop to let anybody out once we're on the way." Everybody laughed.

"All right then, let's get this show on the road," the pilot said, slapping Regan on the back.

Bundled in their layered flying clothes, their oxygen masks dangling from their flying helmets, the men trundled toward their stations in the aircraft. One after the other Farrington, Regan, Howard, and Jerry squatted awkwardly, squeezed up through the gaping bomb bay, and climbed onto the flight deck. Manners, Gregorian, and Rossman squirmed into the cramped Plexiglas nose compartment through the front wheel well. In the rear of the plane Al peered into the turret, checked the ammo belts and feeder, then turned back to the waist to join Brennan and Peterson at their stations for takeoff.

The plane rocked as the men clattered through the metal ganglia of the crowded fuselage and settled into their positions. Each man attended to his final preflight jobs, losing himself in his own routine. They tested their heated suits, checked their oxygen, adjusted their throat mikes. In the cramped quarters inside the plane most could not wear their small chest parachutes, and so they stowed them close at hand, within easy reach. At their feet flak vests, thick leaden aprons weighing about twenty pounds, lay on the floor at each position, waiting to be donned like medieval armor when they entered enemy air space.

In the cockpit Farrington and Regan went through their final checklist, systematically examining again the maze of gauges, valves, switches, and controls that surrounded them. Barrett stood between them, monitoring his own set of instruments, following the methodical preflight ritual. From his station just behind the copilot Howard caught snatches of the familiar incantation above the crackle of his headset.

"Fuel shutoff switches."

"Okay."

"Gear switch."

"Neutral."

"Cowl flaps—open right."

"Open left and locked."

"Idle cutoff."

"Check."

"Throttle."

"Check."

And on and on, as the moment to start engines drew inexorably near. Howard looked again at his watch. 0625. Five minutes until the signal to start engines. He took a deep breath. And another. He flexed his fingers, spreading them wide and closing them, an exercise he had practiced to relax before basketball games. It didn't work. He opened his log in front of him on the small black desk. He would sign on watch and make his first entry as soon as the engines were started and then at five-minute intervals throughout the mission. He was ready to go, to get under way. With all the preflight checks completed and equipment squared away, these final few minutes before takeoff crawled by, caught in an undertow of time. He glanced at his watch. Still four more minutes.

At precisely 0630 a bright green flare rent the gray mist above the field, rising eerily from the railed balcony of the control tower where the group's operations officers stood clustered in the cold. From the small porthole in front of him Howard caught a glimpse of its glimmering arc as it sputtered across the field and almost instantly heard the first reluctant cranking of the number three engine, the yellow tips of its giant propeller only six feet from him. First one of the Pratt & Whitney engines, then another coughed, sputtered, and fired, belching flame and bursts of black smoke, until the whine of the giant propellers filled the air. A member of the ground crew, crouching low, sidled under the plane, removed the chock blocks from the wheels, and retreated cautiously. Slowly the planes, ghostly silhouettes in the dingy mist, nosed ponderously out of their hardstands and began their lumbering procession along the perimeter track that wound around the triangular runway. Regan consulted the formation diagram again. His finger found the place that told him which plane they were to follow. They watched the squadron's planes—*Hard Luck*, *Delores Jean*, *Peggy Anne*, *Moonlight Marge*, and the others—taxi past them, each groping awkwardly toward the main runway.

"That's it," Regan said at last, and Farrington eased the ship gently out of the hardstand into the moving line. The planes inched forward, nose to tail like elephants in a circus parade, their pilots advancing, then throttling back, braking, then pushing forward again. Inside the aircraft the noise was deafening, and the plane vibrated in jolting anticipation. The smell of exhaust and aviation fuel filled the plane like a physical presence. Waiting for takeoff was the worst moment of the entire ritual of combat missions. With a full bomb load and a full tank of one-hundred-octane aviation fuel, Farrington had little margin for error at takeoff. Standard procedure called for aircraft to take off at thirty-second intervals in good weather, one-minute intervals in bad, and in either case a mechanical failure, a pilot error, or a sudden shift in the wind could spell disaster. It had happened in almost every group, in every training command.

Everyone knew that this would be an instrument takeoff. They would be flying blind. In the waist Bob struggled with a rising tide of nausea. It was always bad on takeoff and landing, this old affliction that had washed him out of pilot training. Today, as he crouched against the walls of the ship, it was worse than ever. Closing his eyes, he could taste the bile rising in his throat. Brooklyn, his face utterly blank, sat slumped shoulder to shoulder with Brennan near the right waist-gunner's post. As Bob watched them, Brennan muttered something. Who was he talking to? He crossed himself. So did Bob.

The ungainly serpentine procession shuddered to a halt at the end of the main runway. Like pearls bunched on a string, the thirty-six silver planes stood poised, their engines idling. They waited. At exactly 0700 a green flare hissed into the sky, and far in front of Farrington the first plane rushed down the runway into the murk. The mission had begun.

The Liberators moved forward, braked, moved again, until at last they pivoted onto the tarmac and at precise thirty-second intervals sped down the long, fog-shrouded runway. Farrington was at almost the very rear of the formation. The turbulence from the preceding aircraft would be terrific, he realized, and he would be on instruments in the bargain. He watched the plane in front of him swing onto the runway and speed away.

Farrington edged the mammoth plane into position. Locking the brakes, he revved up the engines to a shrill, deafening pitch. The plane shuddered violently, straining as Farrington opened the throttles to 1000 rpm. Every nut and bolt, every rivet and tube rattled and shook. Then he released the brakes, and the plane pitched forward, lunging down the runway. As the aircraft accelerated, Farrington and Regan, and Barrett crouching between them, stared intently from the runway to the airspeed meter. The field whipped by as the needle nudged upward, 70, 80, 90 miles per hour. They were committed now. Even if they lost an engine, Farrington would have to try to lift off. Only one-third of the runway left, and beyond, now clearly visible through the mist, a grove of black, leafless trees the size of skyscrapers rushed toward them. Straining forward, lifting upward ever so slightly in their seats as if to help, the ten men held their breath, waiting, waiting. If Farrington delayed too long, they would never clear the trees. If he pulled up too soon, their airspeed would drop and the plane would stall. In either case there wouldn't be enough left of them to send home. At 120 miles per hour Dick Farrington eased back firmly on the stick and thirty tons of B-24 rose gently, improbably, off the earth. In that moment of liftoff, with the whirring hum of the landing gear retracting into their sockets, the great machine, like the men coiled inside it, seemed to sigh in audible relief.

As they cleared the trees and began their ascent into the clouds, every eye on the plane peered into the enveloping soup, watching intently for disaster. Farrington was flying the artificial horizon, flying blind, ignoring his instincts, his senses, and relying instead on his instruments. He would follow the briefed heading for a set number of minutes and seconds, while climbing at a specified rate and speed. Somewhere in this impenetrable murk thirty-five other planes from AS 120 were also flying blind, following, Farrington prayed, the same briefed route. Dead silence on the interphone. Hardly anyone breathed. Up, up, up, groping through the clouds for what seemed like an eternity, Farrington followed his heading. He was drenched in sweat. Past the briefed altitude for assembly he continued through the clouds. "Where the hell is the ceiling?" Regan muttered. Still they climbed. At last they sensed a brightness above them, and then suddenly, as if they had entered another dimension, the plane broke into the clear, into a world bathed in brilliant sunlight.

No amount of practice could have prepared them for what they encountered. B-24s, glittering like mica, were popping up out of the clouds all over the sky. Corkscrewing upward, they seemed to be everywhere, at different altitudes, going in every direction, searching for their squadrons, their groups. Farrington and Regan scanned the crowded sky for the group's rally ship. An old, battle-weary crate painted in outrageous bright colors and with a distinctive design, it was always the first to take off, and the elements of the group's formation aligned themselves on it. After the group had assembled the rally ship would slide out of formation and drift back down to the base, its job done for the day.

Despite the apparent chaos Farrington could see the distinctive silver and red lightning bolts of the 466th's rally ship above and ahead of him. The "strip-ed ass ape," the other pilots called the old bucket, and Farrington heaved an inward sigh of relief to find it climbing steadily to the north, its lights blinking. As he watched intently, the swarm of circling silver planes resolved gradually into distinguishable elements of three, of six, of nine. The group's squadrons were forming up. Squinting into the glare, Farrington found his assigned niche and slid the giant bomber, already bucking in the turbulence, into position. Now they would climb and circle, climb and circle, following a racetrack route around the group's two radio beacons, until all the 466th's aircraft were assembled. The process would take perhaps an hour.

Off to the east, across the placid surface of sunlit clouds, they could see other groups forming up. Probably the 458th and 467th, Regan thought. He stole a glance at his watch. In exactly forty-three minutes the 466th's thirty-odd planes would move to rendezvous with them to form the 96th Combat Wing. They would continue to circle and climb, more than a hundred B-24s, until they had assembled into a tight combat box formation. If all went well, this phase of the mission would take just over an hour, then the 96th Combat Wing would move to the briefed rendezvous point and join the long bomber column, a stream of one thousand heavy bombers bound for the continent.

It was a time-consuming and harrowing phase of the mission. Planes from as many as forty airfields would be surging through the thick clouds into the packed air space over East Anglia at approximately the same time. If they were late or slightly off course or at the wrong altitude disaster could strike. They had heard the horror stories about forming up, stories about planes, sometimes whole squadrons, lost or late, blundering through a formation, scattering planes in every direction until, in a split second, a spectacular chain reaction of brilliant, blinding explosions would shudder through the sky and a shower of burning men and metal would spin sickeningly toward the earth.

"We're at ten thousand feet," Regan spoke into the interphone. "Going on oxygen." Throughout the plane the men fastened on the clammy rubber masks they would wear for at least five hours. The formation continued to circle and climb for what seemed an eternity, until at last, still climbing, it began to move toward the south and the coast. In the nose, Mel Rossman checked his watch and his maps. The 96th Combat Wing had formed up without incident, he realized, and now was climbing to operational altitude where they would link up with the other wings from the Second Air Division. In ten minutes he calculated they would leave the English coast at a point between the radio beacons at Dover and Folkestone. They were on schedule. In front of him Curly Manners was staring intently through the Plexiglas. Far below he could see nothing but a blanket of cloud and swirls of B-24s. He had never seen so many airplanes.

Thirty-six planes had lifted off from Attlebridge, and as the formation crossed the coast, now at operational altitude and in its assigned position in the gigantic bomber stream, Farrington and Regan scanned the sky around them. Things had gone off without a hitch so far. But would they be going on to the continent? They were a flying spare and would only go if another aircraft dropped out. They had come this far, gone through the gut-wrenching ordeal of takeoff and assembly. Nobody wanted to turn back now.

In the waist Jack Brennan adjusted his oxygen mask. What the hell is going on? he thought. He was having trouble breathing. He looked down. Across his chest a thin sheet of ice cascaded down from his oxygen mask like a beard. With his gloved hand he swept the ice away, clearing the discharge vent in his mask. The frigid wind howled through the open windows of the waist, and all around him a fine layer of frost was forming on the guns, the ammo boxes, the yellow oxygen bottles. He could feel numbness creeping into his fingers. Fumbling with his rheostat, he turned up the heat in his electric suit. He was still cold. In the thin, bone-numbing air of northern Europe at twenty-three thousand feet the temperature inside the plane plunged to thirty below zero. If the rheostat failed now, if the electric suit shorted out, he would freeze. There had been a lot of talk about frostbite in training and practice. The Eighth, their instructor warned them, lost more men to frostbite than to enemy action. Stamping his feet to keep warm, Jack could believe it.

Farrington's flight plan told him that they were over the Channel, though he could still see nothing below except a vast veil of cloud. "Gunners, test fire your guns," he ordered. Peterson had already climbed down into the cramped ball turret. Brennan had helped him in and lowered it. Glancing back toward the tail, Jack could see Brooklyn's back swiveling in the turret. His chute lay on the small platform just outside the turret. Al never closed the bowed hatch door behind him, and when he swung far to the left or right his back actually hung outside the plane. "You're gonna slice your whole backside off one of these days," Jack had warned him repeatedly. "And if I close that door," Al always answered, "I'd never get out of this crate." Suddenly the fifty calibers erupted, the roar of their short, crisp bursts rumbling through the ship. The plane shuddered with a quick violent spasm and the smell of cordite hung for a moment in the frigid air.

They had been in the air for almost three hours now, and the sun had risen high above them. Great white vaporous ribbons, contrails from the lead formations, expanded across the cold blue sky. Just ahead, one aircraft was clearly having trouble, losing power in two engines. For several minutes it struggled on but could not keep up. As Farrington and Regan looked on, the plane, with one engine feathered, began to slide out of formation.

They watched as it dropped down and began a wide banking turn to the left. It was turning back. Without hesitation Farrington pulled up and tucked his plane tightly into the vacant slot. He swung the ship in so close that Regan, glancing over the number three and four engines, could see the left waist gunner of the adjacent plane adjusting his oxygen mask. The gunner waved. They rode in utter silence for several minutes. Then the men heard their pilot's voice crackle over the interphone. "This is it, boys," he said. "We're on our way to the war."

As Farrington struggled with the prop wash Manners gave the order to arm the bombs. From his position in the tail Seraydarian tumbled out of the turret, climbed through the waist past Peterson in the ball, opened the bulkhead doors, and stepped gingerly into the bomb bay. Squeezing out onto the narrow catwalk, a steel girder only ten inches wide, he took a deep breath from the portable oxygen bottle he carried and tried to relax. The four 2,000-pounders, huge, blunt-nosed monsters, hung ominously in their racks on both sides of him. It was his job to arm them. Standing on the slippery frozen catwalk, he stretched to pull the cardboard tags from the nose fuses, then reached inside the fins at the other end to pull the wire arming pin from each of the mammoth bombs. The catwalk was too narrow for him to wear his parachute, so as he leaned out in the frigid bomb bay, holding with one gloved hand to the vertical stanchions, his movements were slow, deliberate. A false step, he realized, would send him plunging through the doors to his death five miles below. Stuffing the pins into the knee pocket of his flying suit, he edged his way back again out of the bomb bay.

As the formation crossed into enemy air space over France, the first flak appeared. Riding in the nose turret, Harry stammered out on the interphone: "Flak, one o'clock low!" His voice sounded high and brittle, as if it would snap off in the cold like an icicle. A few small black puffs off to the side and below the formation, that was all. Distant, silent, harmless looking. Out his window Howard could see nothing, but something in Harry's voice sent a ripple of fear down his spine. His stomach turned to stone.

At the French coast Jerry climbed into the top turret. As he moved the turret, scanning the skies for enemy fighters, his boots swung just behind Howard's head. At briefing they had been told that enemy fighters might appear. What if they encountered the new Me 262s, the jets that occasionally rose to screech through the bomber stream? Although significant Luftwaffe action was not anticipated, you could never tell. What did they mean by "significant," anyway?

In the cramped nose Mel Rossman scanned his charts. According to his calculations they were only minutes from the initial point, the beginning of the bomb run. At the IP, usually a prominent geographic feature easily identifiable from the air, the formation would swing onto the path that would lead directly to the target. During the fifteen minutes of the bomb run, from the IP to the rally point just past the target, the planes and their crews were at their most vulnerable. If the bombs were to find their targets, the formation had to fly at a constant speed at a set altitude. They could not dodge the flak or take evasive action from enemy fighters.

As the formation turned onto the IP, a small village just south of Verdun, a 10/10 cloud cover extended as far as the eye could see. Manners squatted in the nose, peering through the Plexiglas. Staring between his knees, he could see nothing but a mountain of cloud below him. There would be no visual bombing today, no easy target in France. The coded message had already passed through the formation. Howard heard it on the command frequency. They were diverting to the secondary, to Karlsruhe and the flak.

Flak. They had heard plenty about it in their combat orientation and from the veterans around Attlebridge. In training in the States they had always thought about fighters, had seen combat footage of the sleek, cigar-shaped Me 109s or the chunky Focke-Wulf 190s, the sinister black cross emblazoned on their sides, roaring out of the sun to swarm the formation. Now the Germans were introducing a wonder weapon, a jet fighter that Hitler maintained would revolutionize the air war. But the most dangerous enemy the Farrington crew would confront in October 1944, the orientation officers had made clear, was not the single-engine fighter, but flak.

The intelligence briefers had explained to the new crews that, as the Luftwaffe lost strength in 1944, German air defenses concentrated more and more on antiaircraft fire. By October 1944 German antiaircraft units employed almost a million personnel, operated over fifty thousand guns, and could collectively fire five thousand tons of shells per minute. Over the heavily defended cities of the Reich, dense clouds of flak formed on virtually every mission. The Germans placed their flak batteries in concentric circles around all likely targets and in a belt along their western frontier. Some batteries consisted of a dozen light or medium weapons, but by the autumn of 1944 most held four to eight heavy guns, the dreaded eighty-eights. The eighty-eights' shells were time fused, traveling at a speed of one thousand feet per second, and were effective up to approximately twenty thousand feet. When they exploded, each bursting shell sent shards of white-hot metal in all directions, and, the Americans calculated, each had a killing zone radius of about thirty feet. When an approaching formation came into range, all weapons in the battery fired at the same target, at the same time. Some batteries still relied on visual aiming, but others employed a sophisticated radar system. If the guns were radar-aimed, the big eighty-eights were trained on the center of each bomber formation. If visually aimed, the target was the lead aircraft in each formation. Now, Farrington thought, as the group swung away from the primary and set a course for Karlsruhe, they were going to get a chance to see it firsthand.

The giant formation droned on, maneuvering to the secondary IP, and began a gentle turn. The lead bombardier would use radar to identify the target, bombing through the clouds. Manners would toggle his bombs when the lead ship in the squadron did, and so he watched intently, his hand moving nervously to the lever, ready to open the giant bomb-bay doors. Off to the left, several miles away, a dark storm cloud the color of a gun barrel rose above the gloomy gray cloud bank below. As he watched, it widened, its color deepened. It did not seem to move or dissipate, but spread like a pool of oil across the azure sky. Then he saw the first flight of B-24s, the lead elements of the entire formation, disappear into it. Rossman tapped him on the shoulder and pointed. "The target," he said, nodding at the tower of flak. "Je-sus," Manners whispered.

In an instant Farrington, holding his place in formation, wheeled the plane into a gentle left turn. They were on the bomb run. In the nose Harry watched the billowing black shroud draw nearer, watched the first elements of the group disappear into it. The dense cloud had now dissolved into a multitude—hundreds, thousands—of dull sooty bursts, each hurling hundreds of shards of razor-sharp steel through the air. It was everywhere, flak so thick, he had heard the veterans say, you could get out and walk on it. Nobody could get through this. It was impossible. "Mary, Mother of God," he heard himself muttering, "Mary, Mother of God, get me out of this."

Then they were in its midst. The sky turned dark around them as the flak engulfed the ship. Gritty puffs of black smoke appeared off both wings, in front of the nose, but below them. Jarring detonations erupted in clusters, roiling the sky into a turbulent fury. The plane bumped and shuddered, staggered by shock waves that slammed into it from every direction. This was what they meant by a barrage-type fire, Farrington thought almost abstractly, when, instead of tracking the formation, the Germans sent up a

dense box barrage over a point through which the formation would have to
fly. Funny, he marveled, it made hardly any sound at all. There was only the
concussion followed, if the burst was really close, by a clattering metallic
sound as slivers of steel slashed into the aluminum skin of the plane. Even
that sounded oddly harmless, like rocks thrown by a kid against an empty
garbage can. The only sound was the droning of the engines and the
whistling of the wind through the ship. It lent the scene an eery, unearthly
quality, as if they were merely spectators, distant, detached observers,
insulated from danger by a curtain of silence. Farrington watched his
instruments and struggled to hold the plane steady. They were, he thought,
still three minutes—an eternity—from the target. Hunkered down in their
flak vests and helmets they would sit helplessly, waiting for the lead ship to
drop its bombs, praying that miraculously the fire in the sky all around them
would not consume them. Gripping the wheel tightly, Farrington made a
discovery that countless others had made before him—that it was possible
to sweat at thirty below zero.

As the bomb-bay doors of the squadron's lead ship rolled open, Manners pulled the lever beside him, and a howling blast of wind roared
through the gaping bomb bay. His hand was poised on the toggle switch. He
strained to keep the lead plane in view. Wallowing sluggishly in the
turbulent air, the whole formation seemed to hang suspended over the
invisible target. Time slowed, then stopped, frozen in the menacing darkness. A bone-jarring tremor rattled through the ship, then another, and
another. Fragments of flak clattered along the fuselage. They bounced and
trembled and waited. The interphone was as silent as the grave.

"Bombs away," Manners barked at last, and the plane heaved suddenly
upward as its deadly cargo tumbled out, vanishing into the clouds below. In
the tail Al looked down, following the flight of the bombs, but there was
nothing to see, nothing to hear. How odd. Tons of bombs raining down, gone
without a trace.

At last able to take some evasive action, Farrington quickly banked
the aircraft and headed for the rally point. Climbing, they cleared the
cloud of flak, emerging once again into the bright sunlight. Regan called
for the crew to check in, and one by one they sounded off. Their voices
were tense. There was no chatter, no wisecracking, but everyone was okay.
Farrington swung the plane into formation as the group reformed. In the
top turret Jerry surveyed the formation. He was counting planes. "Amazing," he muttered to himself, breathing heavily into his oxygen mask. As

best he could tell, they were all there. All thirty-five planes in the group had made it.

They began the long trip out, following the briefed route that would take them along a narrow corridor between the known flak installations back to the coast. The gunners remained alert, searching the sky for enemy fighters, but there were no Me 109s or FWs lurking in the clouds today. They passed again the coast of France, following a northwesterly course. There was no flak. Gradually the formation loosened and began to let down. The men were able to come off oxygen. To the west, over the North Sea, the skies had cleared, and far below them they could see pale sunlight glinting off the cold, wind-driven waves. The engines droned, and the plane continued to descend, down through faint, wispy clouds.

Howard reached into his jacket pocket. Removing his gloves, he fumbled with the wrapper of the candy bar he had been given at briefing. It was a Tootsie Roll, frozen solid.

"There she is, boys," Farrington said.

Beyond the gray expanse of sea and sky, a dull gray green form rose steadily from the haze to meet them. Slowly the blunt snout of East Anglia materialized below them.

"Hot damn!" Jack cried, pounding exuberantly on the cold fifty caliber. His voice over the interphone was loud, jubilant.

"I can taste that beer already!" Al shouted.

"Even that warm Limey stuff will taste good tonight," Jack laughed.

They all spoke at once, laughing, kidding. Their giddy voices gurgled over the interphone like bubbles, buoyant with relief, rising from the depths of dread.

Bob stood in the waist. He had not spoken since climbing out of the ball turret over the North Sea. As the plane dropped and Farrington maneuvered it into the landing pattern, Bob watched the houses and fields and villages slide silently by beneath the wing. Then, as if they had passed magically into another dimension, the visibility suddenly dropped to zero and the world outside the aircraft went dark. A local rainstorm engulfed the ship. The plane bucked in the churning crosswind, and Bob felt the left wing rise as the ship seemed to slide sideways through the cloud. They were going in. He prayed to God that Farrington could see more than he could, that the instruments were correct, that the landing gear held. The nausea that usually gripped him at takeoffs and landings surged and fell away. His ears popped. He slumped down beside the ammo boxes, exhausted, his mind an utter blank. He closed his eyes. When he opened them, Jack and Al had scrambled into their landing positions across from him. He listened as the pitch of the engines dropped and the flaps began to drag through the air. Fighting a surge of queasiness, he felt the plane easing down, down, until at last the wheels bounced with a screech on the main runway of AS 120. Bob leaned back, ran his hand wearily across his face, and sighed. When he looked up, Al was smiling and Jack winked at him.

CHAPTER IV

I'LL GET BY

H oward had been awake for almost twenty hours, but he was not tired. Sighing, he glanced around the dimly lit hut. The floor was cluttered with equipment and clothes. In the next bunk Brennan was sound asleep. He still wore his jacket, the dark, pile-lined collar pulled up around his ears. His mouth was wide open, a picture of pure exhaustion. Just past the cold stove Harry was doing sit-ups on his bunk, his feet hooked under the metal frame. He had been at it for what seemed forever, and with each repetition the bed creaked piteously, scraping the rough furrows of the concrete floor like fingernails on a chalkboard. Nobody seemed to notice.

They had flown their first mission and survived, Howard thought. He was scared, scared at takeoff, scared in the flak over the target, scared in the fog at landing. He was scared all the way through. And yet all the months of training, the intricate routines, the painstaking preparation had paid off. It was a rough mission, bad weather and flak, but everyone performed. The ground crew rushed out to the plane when the giant props were at last still, with congratulations for the rookies and rough praise for Farrington. The fog and rain at the field were as bad as he had seen, the crew chief grunted, and Fearless Fosdick had brought the ship back without a scratch. Nice job. They horsed around a bit at the hardstand, waiting for the truck to carry them to debriefing. Jack fell theatrically onto the ground, patted it lovingly, kissed it. Everyone was relieved, everyone was happy.

Howard slumped at interrogation, barely able to stay awake for the questions about flak and friendly fighter coverage. Sitting around the table, surrounded by other crews at other tables in the crowded debriefing room, he munched a sandwich handed him by the Red Cross girl and sipped the bitter black coffee. Some of the guys took a shot of the scotch they were offered. "Rotgut," Jack snorted in disgust, but he downed his and Howard's. The room was buzzing about the weather. Planes from the group had been diverted to fields all over East Anglia, feeling their way down in the soup. One of the new crews, somebody said, had gone down in the fog not far from the base. Crash-landed. The Nelson crew, somebody thought, but nobody seemed to know for sure.

After interrogation and chow the fatigue, like the fog, had suddenly lifted, and riding a wave of adrenaline, Howard stopped off at the squadron dayroom to place a call to his brother-in-law at the 390th. Making a personal phone call from the base was difficult to manage, but over the past two weeks he had tried several times to get through. They had never connected, and he did not expect to reach Tom now. But tonight in particular he felt like talking, like hearing a familiar voice, a voice from home. He had not seen his brother-in-law for over a year. Tom had shipped overseas in August '43, and for almost a year before that they had written as each shuttled around Air Corps training bases in the States. Tom's letters would arrive weeks old and in bunches, forwarded from post to post, and they had not spoken, even on the phone, for what seemed an eternity. So the sound of Tom's soft southern voice echoing suddenly over the wire came as a shock. Howard could hardly believe his ears. They talked quickly, stumbling over each other's sentences, blurting out snatches of news, formulating plans. They talked about London, about home, about his mission. Tom knew just where AS 120 was located. He had found it on the map after Howard's first letter and thought he could swing a jeep, maybe even a staff car. He had been in the ETO for over a year and knew a guy in the motor pool. Maybe he could get away on the seventh, day after tomorrow, and could come to visit. Get there in the afternoon. Howard was buoyant as he made his way along the small road to his hut, following the pale beam from his flashlight as it danced on the puddles like a firefly.

Harry had finished his exercises and Howard was listening to Jerry talk about his brother, an aspiring actor in New York, when Farrington came in. They were surprised to see him. The weather outside was dismal, even by British standards—fog, rain turning to hard crystals of sleet that beat on the metal roof of the hut. A mission in the morning didn't seem likely. Still, they were alerted.

"Anything more on the crash?" Jerry asked. "Was it Nelson?"

"Yes," Farrington said wearily, "it was Nelson." The pilot stood hovering over the pitiful stove, shaking off the damp. "It doesn't look good." They all knew guys on the Nelson crew. They had come into the group at the same time, and for the past three weeks they had gone through combat orientation and practice flights together. Today they had flown their first mission together.

"What happened?" Jerry asked.

"They were pretty badly shot up over the target," Farrington said. "They limped back home, and in that fog the pilot apparently mistook a stretch of road for the runway. They were about a mile from the base. He dropped down just over the treetops with his landing gear extended, caught his mistake at the last second and pulled back on the stick. The ship reared up like a spooked horse. All four motors died." They could all visualize it, the Liberator, nose up, hanging motionless in the mist, its engines suddenly, sickeningly silent, then dipping, dropping like a stone into the field. "Three crew members—bombardier, navigator, and radio operator were killed on impact, the others are all in real bad shape." Howard thought of the radioman, tried to remember his name. They had sat in procedures class together, taken the code tests, compared notes. He had seen him in the communications briefing this morning, nervous, full of anticipation, eagerness etched in his earnest face—a mirror image of himself.

Farrington ambled out into the rain, and Howard felt suddenly very tired. Fully clothed, he crawled under the blankets. He should write a letter to Mildred. Tell her about Tom. He would get up in a few minutes and do that, he told himself, when Jerry got the stove going. Howard turned on his side. He drifted, wavering at the edge of sleep. "Jungers," he mumbled to no one in particular. "What's that," Jerry asked. "The name was Jungers," Howard muttered. "Eugene."

At 0600 the briefing officer pulled back the black curtain and, as he cleared his throat with a dramatic cough, the men followed the course of the bright red ribbon as it veered across the map. It departed England between Cromer and Great Yarmouth, angling gently to the southeast toward the Belgian coast just north of Bruges. From there it passed Antwerp, then turned sharply north to the IP in Holland. The ribbon did not extend far into Germany, but a low groan rose from the men when they saw it disappear into an ugly ball of red. It was the Ruhr.

The men hooted and jeered. Someone let out a long, low oh-shit-we'll-be-sorry whistle, and the S-2, pointer in hand, waited patiently for the hubbub to subside. The 466th, he told them calmly, would dispatch twenty-seven aircraft as part of the 96th Combat Wing to attack a synthetic oil installation at Sterkrade. The oil refinery had a monthly capacity of ten and a half metric tons. Repairs had been in progress since the last Allied attack on October 6. The target was on the number 1 priority list. That was bad news. The Ruhr, as they all knew, was the industrial heartland of the Third Reich and one of the most heavily defended areas in Europe. Although division intelligence predicted only minimal enemy fighter action on this mission, over three hundred heavy guns, eighty-eights, guarded the area.

Sterkrade, a grim smudge of a city a few miles north of Duisburg, lay on the northwestern fringe of a sprawling industrial megalopolis, and the routes to and from the target, the S-2 assured them, had been drawn to minimize exposure to known flak concentrations. Still, they could expect flak over the target to be intense and accurate. The formation would be in range of known defenses for approximately two and three-quarters minutes before bombs away and approximately three minutes after. The 466th would make up the last elements of the Second Air Division formation. Three other combat wings—roughly three hundred aircraft—would be in front of them on the bomb run, so the prop wash would be awesome and the flak gunners would have plenty of time to find their range before the group passed over the target.

As if that weren't enough bad news, the group's formation diagram revealed that Farrington was slated to fly the tail-end Charlie slot in the low-left squadron. It was the most difficult and dangerous position in the whole formation. If there were fighters out there, hiding in the clouds, they would pick this last squadron to jump, and if the fighters didn't get them, at that lower altitude they would be more vulnerable to flak. They were riding in the coffin corner.

At the hardstand everybody was tight as a drum. Farrington was all business, barely spitting out a few last reminders before they climbed into the ship. Even Jack could think of nothing to say. As they taxied out onto the perimeter track, Bob's stomach rebelled, erupting in a violent spasm of dry heaves. Leaning out the left waist window, he choked convulsively, but there was nothing in his stomach to vomit, and as he slumped down into his station for takeoff, viscous beads of green bile trailed across the bright yellow Mae West like a necklace. At altitude it would freeze.

There were no delays at takeoff, no problems in forming up, and they departed over Clacton on schedule. The intelligence briefing was right. No enemy aircraft showed up along the route, and flak over the target was subsequently described as "moderate and inaccurate," a big improvement over the day before. But it was bad enough. As they turned onto the bomb run they watched it sprout below them, dark blossoms of soot against the platinum sky. Just over the target the bursts of a box barrage, coming in dingy groups of four, walked closer and closer to them. The plane pitched and shuddered, buffeted by the powerful prop wash of three hundred B-24s and jolted by the muffled detonations of the flak. The next battery might get their calculations right, and the next box, they all knew, might close on them like a coffin. But today the flak gunners, five miles below and buried beneath a blanket of cloud, had their altitude wrong and did not make the necessary corrections. There were no close calls. The low-left squadron passed without incident over the target, released its bombs on cue, and turned for the rally point.

On the way out, as the formation neared the Dutch coast and the relative safety of the Channel beyond, the tension eased. The weather to the west appeared to be clearing, and maybe today they would not have to sweat out the landing. Jack began to hum a Sinatra tune, and in the nose Manners stretched his legs into the wheel well. Suddenly Harry's voice, taut as a piano wire, pinged over the interphone. "B-24 out of control," he screeched. "Ten o'clock high." In stunned silence they watched as a Liberator in the formation in front of them, two engines spitting smoke, spiraled down toward the patchy clouds below. "Anybody see any flak?" Regan called out. "Any fighters?" The turrets whirred, scanning the sky. Nothing. Burning like a sparkler, the silver plane plunged into the clouds and was gone. "Anybody see any chutes?" Farrington asked at last. Only static crackled over their headsets. For all the accidents in training and all the horror stories they had heard from the vets, none of them had ever witnessed such a scene, a giant bomber careening out of the sky like a kite, ten men pinned inside by the centrifugal force. Howard noted the time and coordinates in his log. There was no banter as the formation let down over the Channel, no joking as Farrington settled them into the flight pattern for landing. They were home in time for lunch, but nobody was hungry, especially when they discovered that they were alerted again for the following day.

"Another Monday night and I am tired," Bob wrote. A copy of *Stars and Stripes* lay on Jerry's bunk. Its headlines trumpeted the massive American air offensive against German oil. A grainy photograph of B-17s stacked like cordwood in the skies over Germany, bombs cascading from their open bomb bays, accompanied the story. "I imagine you are reading the papers and listening to the radio," Bob wrote. "Please, don't worry. I am okay and doing the best I can, for God is near me on all my missions. I really do pray through those long moments over the targets. Go to mass after every raid." He thought fleetingly of the base chapel, just up the road from the WAAF site, and of Father Collins, the Catholic chaplain. He attended every briefing and held a short service afterward, saying a few words of comfort to anyone who chose to listen. He had plenty of takers. "I'm doing my best and sure hope this will make it so our children will never have to go to war." Bob sighed. "Do I get scared????? Who wouldn't!"

Howard was disappointed. Tom was due to come up to AS 120 the next day. He had begun a letter home to the folks at Trunk Street, excited that at last he had something to report. "Well," he wrote, "I talked to Tom last night and, boy, I was really glad to hear his voice." He paused, looking up. Harry was sleeping fitfully, and beside him Al was folding a letter. Al's mother was sick, and he wrote regularly in Armenian—drove the guy who censored their mail crazy. Rain had begun to drum on the roof of the hut. Maybe the weather would be bad tomorrow. No point even thinking about that, Howard concluded. The weather seemed to change every hour. He turned back to the letter. "We are close together and he is coming over tomorrow to see me." The distance, Howard calculated, was about fifty miles as the crow flies, but Tom would have to navigate the narrow Norfolk roads. Smiling, he recalled the times he had borrowed Tom's car, the old mustard-colored Packard, in Chattanooga when he had gone to visit for the weekend after

Tom and Mildred were married. They lived in a small apartment on Cameron Hill, just up from the L&N station and not far from the river. "It will take about as long as it took him to see Mildred before they were married and, boy, I am really looking forward to seeing him." He thought about tomorrow and the mission. "I'm afraid he won't get to see me," Howard added obliquely, "because I won't be on the base for quite a while." He hoped they wouldn't go to the Ruhr again. If all went well, maybe they would be back by early afternoon. You could never tell. "I'm hoping he will wait on me to get back. Tell Mil that I'll take care of Tom for her," he concluded jauntily. "He and I are going on a 48-hour pass from the third to the fifth of next month." A nice idea, Howard thought, something to look forward to. Next month.

He folded the letter and stashed it with the address book and stationery on the shelf above his bunk. The wind was picking up, and a chill draft slipped beneath the blackout curtain on the window behind him, its clammy breath brushing the back of his neck. He crawled under the blanket. Maybe they wouldn't fly tomorrow after all. He slept.

On November 7 the dawn came and went and the door of the hut remained closed. Outside in the dim morning twilight the wind moaned through the WAAF site. Rain lashed at the windows, and a loose piece of metal roofing clattered somewhere close by. One by one the men awoke, stretching, groaning, luxuriating in the slowly dawning realization that they were still in the sack, that today, it appeared, they would not be flying.

Barrett was the first to get up. Dressed in his long johns and jacket, he rummaged noisily under his bunk. Emerging with a soiled burlap sack, he opened the stove and began neatly arranging the contents of the sack in the tiny heating chamber. He painstakingly arranged the kindling, strips of splintered bomb crates and assorted sticks he had gathered from the nearby woods. Crumpling the pages of an old *Stars and Stripes*, he laid the tightly packed wads of paper inside. He paused, looking around. "And now," he said with a dramatic flourish, "for the pièce de résistance." Reaching into the sack, he produced three jet-black clods, each the size of a grapefruit, and placed them gingerly onto the pyre he had fashioned in the stove.

"That looks an awful lot like an illegal substance," Howard smiled, sitting up in his bunk at the foot of the stove.

"Coal," Al exclaimed, "You got real coal?"

"The very commodity," said Jerry proudly. They crowded around to examine such an exotic, valuable item. The soft coke issued weekly to each barracks stubbornly refused to burn, and staying warm in the cramped, poorly insulated Nissen huts was a never-ending effort. No matter how much coke they burned, it was never enough, and the miniature English stoves, with their tiny heating chambers, never seemed to put out much heat. The result was a constant search for new sources of fuel. They scoured the woods for fallen trees, though taking them was illegal. Some of the guys even cut them down. Farrington, Jerry had informed them, bought an ax from a nearby farmer. The officers' barracks apparently weren't any warmer. An elaborate system of black market barter had been established with guys who worked at the mess hall or the hospital, which had their own coal supplies. Then there was stealing, slipping past the guards at the supply dumps in the night or paying them off.

"Jerry and I went out on a recon last week," Jack grinned. "Night patrol. But we cannot divulge our sources."

"This is a serious matter, gentlemen," Howard said with exaggerated earnestness. "And frankly, I'm shocked. The commanding officer of this base is compelled to remind you men of the penalties for such covert activity. May I read to you from the station *Bulletin*, 26 October 1944." From a sheaf of papers tacked to the wall by the door Howard pulled a notice and read: "It is necessary that all personnel pay strict attention to the conservation of solid fuel. Coal will not be burned in any of the living sites. It is primarily for use in the mess halls and station sick quarters. . . . Each organization has been notified when to draw coke from the compounds upon authority of the station quartermaster. *Anyone* found removing coal or coke without authority of the station quartermaster is subject to trial by court-martial."

Jerry snapped his Zippo, igniting a bright orange flame in the stove. "A risk worth taking, don't you agree?" he said, his eyes twinkling as the flame jumped and the coal sizzled.

It was a lazy day. Inspired by the arrival of solid fuel, the little stove rose to new heights, radiating a warm glow for at least six feet in any direction. The men lounged cozily around it, writing letters, rehashing the missions. They even talked politics. It was election day at home, Dewey versus Roosevelt, but it was not a very spirited discussion. Only Bob was old enough to vote.

Nobody was in a hurry to leave the hut, so they decided to rest up and get reorganized. They moved their bunks around, straightened up. They even dusted. Somewhere mice were getting into the hut. At night they scurried across the floor, darted under the bunks, and gnawed at everything, even the newspaper that was stuffed under the cotton biscuits on the beds. Somehow they had gotten into a box of month-old cake Nancy had sent, and that was too much. They decided to search out the little bastards.

There was also, Jerry remarked, a distinct odor in the hut. "Like a barn," Howard agreed. "When was the last time you had a shower, Al?" Jack asked. "What month is it?" Al replied. Nobody, they quickly determined, had taken a shower for well over a week. Most of them hadn't changed their long johns or socks. Hadn't had time. Besides, the showers were located in an unheated shed, bearing a sign left by the base's former British occupants. "Ablutions," it read demurely, but it attracted few customers. Standing in the cold spray while the wind whistled through the shed was an act of supreme courage. Most of the guys around the base preferred to go into the Red Cross Club in Norwich, where warm water and indoor facilities could be had. Some didn't bathe at all.

While they were putting things in order the mail arrived, bringing a bounty of letters, and the men settled on their bunks to read. Bob had five from Marie. Bobby, she reported, had been out to a party and he was now proudly sporting a new Halloween costume. Halloween! Bob had utterly forgotten it. When was that? How had it gotten away? He pictured the kids racing from house to house in the familiar Chicago neighborhood, the usual ragtag crew of cowboys, pirates, and fairy princesses, the trick-or-treat bags in their hands. He heard their shouts, their laughter. He shook his head. It all seemed even more remote, more incredible than the election.

As they read the squadron CQ stopped by to tell them officially that the group was standing down due to weather. No squadron meeting today. They were free. Basking in the unusual warmth, Howard stretched out on his bunk. He had not felt so relaxed in days. All around him coat hangers clattered on the racks, clothing and equipment rustled, voices murmured. Jerry had lost his dog tags and had taken apart his bunk, searching. "I think I saw one of the mice wearing them yesterday," Howard yawned. "Good," Jerry smiled, "he can finish up my tour. Just have my mail forwarded back to Manhattan." At the other end of the hut Al and Jack and two gunners from the Hyuck crew had started up a card game. "Red dog," he heard Al saying. Howard closed his eyes, listening to the slick slapping of the cards, the grunts of the bidding, the scuffling of boots along the floor. Outside the window just behind him the wind moaned long and low, and Howard dozed. Borne on a tide of pure exhaustion, he drifted into a deep and dreamless sleep.

He did not know how long he slept or what roused him—a voice, the closing of a door—but as he woke and his eyes slowly focused a figure stood in the half-light of the doorway, just inside the blackout curtain. Howard squinted, propping himself on one arm, still a little woozy with sleep, and a familiar voice said softly, "Hello, old pal."

Howard sprang up from his bunk like a shot. Flinging his arms around his brother-in-law in a rough embrace, he let out a whoop. "Tom, you ol' sonofagun," he yelped. "I don't believe it, I don't believe it. You made it." They slapped each other on the back, pumped hands, laughed, held each other at arm's length, drinking in the sight. Tom was soaking wet. "Come on over by the stove and get the chill out, if you can," Howard said. The card game had broken up and Al had vanished. Bob and Jack lounged on their bunks, while Jerry, mirror in hand, clipped his mustache. Tom looked around.

"The accommodations look pretty familiar," he said.

"We could use a radio," Howard said.

"Yeah," Jack piped up, "otherwise we gotta listen to gramps over here singing." He nodded toward Bob.

"These sorry specimens," Howard said, "are what pass for a crew." He introduced them.

"Oh, God," Jerry groaned theatrically, shaking hands with Tom, "another one that sounds just like you, Howard."

"Hillbillies, hillbillies," Jack chimed in. He broke into a chorus of "Pistol-Packin' Mama," with an exaggerated nasal twang.

"See the trouble I'm in with these clowns, Tom?" Howard laughed, "I'm surrounded by Yankees."

"Well, there's a war on," Tom added in mock earnestness. "We all have to make sacrifices."

Tom sat down on Howard's bunk and stared at him, smiling, shaking his head slowly in disbelief. He had been overseas for over a year, with no prospect of getting home anytime soon, and here before him was a living, breathing piece of home, not a V-mail, not a card, not a photograph. "I was so glad to see him," Tom wrote home to Trunk Street, "that I couldn't say anything for a long time. I just sat there and looked at him." They talked quickly, excitedly, about Tom's trip up, about the 466th, about Tom's base, about Howard's two missions. Mostly they talked about home, about Mildred and James, about Nancy and the folks. Tom had brought a recent picture of James taken at the university. He was standing on the sidelines at a football game, dressed smartly in his drum major's uniform. Beside him a majorette clutched a large bouquet of mums. She beamed out at the camera. Behind them in the stands a sun-splashed crowd, the men in their hats, coats, and ties, shielded their eyes against the glare. There was not a uniform in sight.

"I believe the young doctor is doing okay for himself," Howard said, running his eyes over the picture and grinning. "They'll have to lock up those coeds," Tom agreed. Howard handed him a snapshot of Mildred made sometime during the summer. Wearing a light summer dress with white buttons and puffed shoulders, she sat on the glider on the front porch at Trunk Street, smiling. Tom recognized the dress and the heart-shaped locket she wore around her neck, a present from him when they were dating. Tom had never seen the picture, and he studied it greedily. Howard tried to bring him up to date, told him about Mildred, about the trip home in September. Barely two months ago, it seemed like a lifetime. Tom hung on every word, every bit of news, every detail Howard could relate. "He told me all about home," Tom wrote later that night, "and it really made me homesick. I would give anything to see you all. It's been an awfully long time."

In spite of the raw wind and the intermittent rain, Howard showed Tom around the base. In the jeep they drove the winding roads that snaked among the huts, past the squadron ops, past the bomb dump, and out to the flight line. With the group grounded all the planes sat hunkered down on their hardstands. They stopped at the mess hall for a quick bite to eat. Tom had a long drive in the dark ahead of him, over fifty tortuous miles of narrow, hedge-lined roads back to Framlingham. Over a plate of baked beans and brussels sprouts, Tom reminisced wistfully about eating on the back porch at Trunk Street, everyone seated along the large white table, the bugs thumping against the screen on hot summer nights. "I sure would like to put my feet under your mother's table and sit down to one of her dinners," he said, glancing over at Howard. "When I do get home, I'm going to eat fried eggs, bacon and ham and hot biscuits, French fried potatoes and pork chops, steak and veal tips, with lots of iced tea and cold sweet milk." His eyes had a dreamy look, and Howard smiled. "Some hot corn bread and butter, I'd like that, too, and a big dish of banana pudding and a slice of devil's food cake and ice cream and then go drink a big chocolate milk shake." He went on and on, and Howard could only laugh. "You stay here long enough on this godforsaken island, old pal," Tom said glumly, sipping the scalding black coffee, "and you'll know just what I mean."

Outside, the rain had picked up, gusting across the field. The branches of the trees rattled, and the light, already dim, began to fade. It was time for Tom to hit the road.

"I ought to get a pass around the beginning of next month," Tom said, as they surveyed the sea of mud outside the mess hall.

"We ought to be due then too," Howard said.

"Let's meet up in London," Tom said, zipping up his jacket. "I'll show you the sights—Rainbow Corner, Big Ben, Piccadilly, the works. Howard, you aren't going to believe London. It's the damned craziest place you ever saw."

"I'm ready," Howard said, shaking his head. "We haven't been off this base since we got here."

"I'll write," Tom said, hunching his shoulders against the wind as they slogged through the mud toward the jeep. He climbed in and turned the key. The motor sputtered, started.

"You be careful, old pal," Tom said, grabbing Howard's elbow firmly.

"I'll do it," Howard said.

They waved, and the jeep slithered through the mud toward the road, found its traction, and sputtered away past the huts toward the main gate of the base.

"Today was my happiest day since I have been in the army," Howard wrote home that night. "Tom came over to this base . . . to see me, and, Mother, he really . . . wants to get home something awful. He looked so good. He isn't very far from here and we should see a lot of each other. Boy, he was happy, no kidding."

On November 8 high winds and heavy clouds lingered over the base, and the 466th stood down again. Nobody flew. The entire Eighth Air Force was grounded. The crew had risen late again and after breakfast had gone to the squadron dayroom for the daily crew meeting. The weather was dismal, but reports were that it would break sometime during the night. High pressure was moving in, and the Farrington crew was alerted again. The boys dispersed. Bob had stopped by the mail room and Harry had disappeared, but Howard and the other enlisted men decided to walk back to the PX. The rain seemed to be trying to stop, and Jerry insisted they walk. As they trudged along the narrow road leading away from the WAAF site Jerry said casually, "You notice anything about Harry?"

"Yeah," Howard said, "What's gotten into him?"

"He won't talk to me about it," Al said.

"Then you've noticed it, too?"

"Sure," Al said. "The guy's tight as a drum. I can't get two words outta him."

"Well, something's sure as hell bothering him," Jack said, "You hear what he did to Bob?"

"What's that?" asked Jerry.

"Says Harry jumped him."

"Come on," Howard said incredulously.

"I'm serious," Jack said.

"They were on their way back to the hut after chow after the Sterkrade mission. Just chewing the fat. Talking about the mission, you know. Bob couldn't remember exactly what he said to set Harry off. They were bone tired, just walking along. Suddenly Harry stops and turns on him. He pokes his fist into Bob's chest, tells him 'to shut the fuck up. He don't want to hear any more about that goddamn mission or about that plane.' Bob hadn't even mentioned that plane, you know, the one that went down. Bob just stared at him. Didn't say a word. Then Harry gives him a shove, not kiddin' around, you know, a real shove, almost knocks him down. Then he stalks off."

Nobody spoke. They ambled along in silence, dodging the puddles. These things happened from time to time. Guys living on top of each other, lots of tension, tempers frayed. Somebody lost too much at craps or drank too much or got a bad letter from home, somebody said the wrong thing, said anything, pushed somebody. They might wrestle around, throw a punch, burn off a little steam. Usually not much damage was done, and it was quickly forgotten.

But this trouble with Harry was unsettling. Harry was always on the quiet side, a loner. He rarely joked or joined in the horseplay in the barracks. He kept to himself, minded his own business. But he was easy to get along with. He knew his job and did it. He didn't bellyache, and he never caused trouble. In the States he had gravitated naturally toward Al. "The Armenian brotherhood," Barrett called them. They went drinking together. They talked. Harry had introduced Al to his mother when she came east to visit him at Mitchel, but he gave away little about himself.

But after that first mission, in fact after the first practice mission in England, Harry had grown moody and irritable. He sulked in the hut. He sat quietly at chow, and although he tagged along with the gang, going to the movies or the Aero Club, he seemed preoccupied, remote. Just after their second mission he had picked a fight with a guy at the mess hall, a cook, roughed him up badly. Then, when Al tried to pull him off, he took a swing at him.

"It's just nerves," Jerry said at last, shooting a quick glance at Howard. "Just nerves."

"Yeah, he'll be all right," Howard said, but he did not sound so certain.

At briefing on the following morning, Farrington and his crew learned that they were bound for eastern France. In fact, the briefing officer explained, the primary was the same heavy concrete gun emplacement near Metz they had tried to hit on November 5 before going on to Karlsruhe. All three bomb divisions would be bombing tactical targets in the area, so the air space would be tight, and American troops would be close to the bomb line, so extra caution was in order. Farrington would be flying high right in the lead squadron, carrying four giant 2,000-pounders.

The mission began well but deteriorated over the continent. Due to dense cloud cover over the primary and a malfunction of the radar equipment on the lead plane, the group moved to the secondary, the marshaling yards at Saarbrücken, just across the German frontier. Nothing went right. On the bomb run the radar equipment continued to malfunction, and strike photos, developed that night at the base, would reveal that the first two squadrons had dropped their bombs ten miles northeast of the target. The trailing squadron, without any radar, was unable to keep up with the first two and could not establish visual contact to see when the leader dropped his bombs. With a 10/10 cloud cover and the front so close, they chose not to drop on a target of opportunity and instead brought their bombs back home. There were a lot of complaints at interrogation. The brass was upset, and nobody was happy about the results, but for the crews it was one more mission behind them.

Farrington and the boys didn't have much time to mull over the day's events. They were awakened again before dawn for a mission that would take them back to Germany, to an airfield just east of Frankfurt. The route in would be tricky, dodging known antiaircraft installations at Koblenz, Limburg, Giessen, and the flak belt around Frankfurt itself. The Luftwaffe could be expected to show up, possibly in numbers. It had all the makings of a rough mission. To everyone's astonishment—and relief—the mission proved to be a milk run. They took off at 0900, and the weather held up all along the route. There were no enemy fighters, although Barrett, riding in the top turret, spotted the contrails of a jet at forty thousand feet, and, most amazingly, no flak rose to greet them at the target. After the fiasco of the day before, the group operations officer declared the results of the bombing excellent. Writing up the mission narrative, group HQ reported no casualties, no aircraft missing, and no battle damage. "Just the kind of mission I like," Jerry said, riding in the truck back to the hut.

After four missions in six days everyone was spent. "At this rate," Jack said, "we'll be done by New Year's. You'll be popping the cork at the Waldorf, Jerry." Exhausted, they were relieved to discover that although the group was alerted for the following day, their names were not on the list. That relief turned to elation when Farrington stopped by the hut to inform them that they would be free to go into town then. Nobody wanted to stay in the hut. Jerry and Bob decided to go to the movies at the Opera House. *Tampico*, with Edward G. Robinson and Victor McLaughlin, was playing. Jack and Al had hooked up with a guy in the 785th, who was going to take them to the pub just down the road, The Dog. They had been talking about it for days. Now they would get to see it. They would slip off the base after dark, out the back of the WAAF site. They had bikes.

For days, it seemed, they had seen nothing but the inside of a Nissen or a B-24, and the hut emptied quickly. Standing at the side of his bunk, Howard ran a comb through his short hair and splashed some cologne on his cheeks. He could no longer distinguish the smell of sweat in his clothes, but on some days the odor of the rubber oxygen mask lingered in his nostrils, haunting him for hours after he pulled it off. The cologne was the only thing that worked against it. He had not had a shower in two weeks, but he would get one tomorrow at the Red Cross in Norwich. What he needed now, he thought, was some time alone, away from the crew. Maybe he would head over to the Aero Club, listen to some records, read this week's *Yank*, write some letters.

As he turned toward the door Howard discovered that he was not alone. His eyes shut and an unlit Lucky Strike dangling from the corner of his mouth, Harry lay sprawled on his bunk. In spite of the cigarette, Harry remained so utterly motionless Howard thought he might actually be asleep. Howard studied his profile. For all the hours they had spent together in the plane and in the hut, Howard barely knew him. They had worked out together in the gym at Westover, even sparred a little with the gloves, but they had never really spent any time alone, had never really talked. Harry was the last thing he needed right now, Howard thought, but maybe this would be a good time to sound him out. Without the others around, maybe he would loosen up. "Hey, Harry, how about you and me going over to the Shamrock, listen to the music?" Howard said casually, tucking his tie between the second and third buttons on his shirt. "It's dance night. The Liberty Run girls will be coming in." The Shamrock Tavern was just across from Special Services, not far from the hut. Harry did not answer. "Come on, we'll get a start on the weekend."

Thinking about it, Howard realized that Jerry was right. Something had been wrong since they began flying on this side. Harry was the chief armorer on the crew, but on the last two missions Howard had discovered Al quietly double-checking the guns, making sure that Harry was paying attention to his job, checking the sights and the solenoids in the plane, oiling them, storing them carefully in the burlap when they got back. Things seemed okay, but it made Al nervous.

After a little coaxing Harry listlessly agreed to get up, and together they wandered over to the Shamrock Tavern, found a table, and ordered a beer. Harry was quiet.

"Hey," Howard began, once they had settled in. "You see where they're going to have ten bouts of boxing on Sunday, right here on the base. I saw the notice for it over at the dayroom. They got guys coming from all over the ETO, all star boxers. They're going to hold the fights in the combat mess hall."

Harry ran his fingertip across the rim of the glass.

"You know, the base has a boxing team," Howard continued. "You ought to go out. You'd be a cinch." The Andrews Sisters were belting out "Rum and Coca-Cola" on the radio. Harry took a sip of beer. He did not speak.

"What gives, Harry?" Howard said at last, trying to hide the mounting exasperation he felt.

"Nothin'."

"Something's eating you. Why don't you spill it?"

"Mind your own business."

"Harry, you all right? The guys are getting a little worried about you."

"Fuck them."

"Come on, Harry, give yourself a break. What's on your mind?"

Harry stared down into his beer.

"Look, we're all scared," Howard continued. "I'm scared to death every time I climb in the ship. You aren't alone, you know."

"Who says I'm scared?"

"Well, something would be pretty wrong if you weren't."

"Is that what Farrington thinks, that I'm yellow?"

"No, no, honest, Harry. We're all scared, Jerry, Al, everybody."

For the first time since they had sat down, Harry looked directly at him. His face was pale and blank, but in his eyes Howard could see a dull flicker of pain. For a moment, a split second, Howard sensed that a door had opened, however slightly, and that behind it, Harry was there, listening, accessible.

"Just do your job," Howard implored. "Stop worrying about it. Stop thinking about it." He leaned back in his chair. "It'll be okay, Harry. You'll see."

The Andrews Sisters had finished, and Peggy Lee was purring "How Long Has This Been Going On." The Liberty Run girls, rounded up in Norwich and the nearby villages, arrived, and Howard swiveled in his chair to look them over. "Not bad," he said, "not bad." When he turned back, Harry was gone.

At 12:45 the next day the 6 × 6 stopped with a jerk in front of the Aero Club for the afternoon Liberty Run into Norwich. Howard and Jerry, Bob and Jack were waiting, their uniforms neat and their expectations high. They had not been into town since they arrived. All they had seen of England had been from the air or out the tailgate of a truck or sliding through the country darkness on the way to a pub. Now, their first pass in hand, they were ready for high adventure. The 6 × 6 halted again at the mess hall and Al jumped in. Nobody had seen Harry. The truck was jammed with men decked out in their class As, smelling strongly of aviation fuel. Dry cleaning—French cleaning, the English called it—was impossible in wartime Britain, so the boys dipped their wool uniforms in tubs of aviation fuel, then hung them out to dry. The cleansing effect of one-hundred-octane gasoline was impressive. So was the lingering aroma. No one seemed to notice.

Some were armed with forty-eight-hour passes and were off for London

or Cambridge. Some carried the names of hotels and dance halls, of pubs
with Irish whiskey, of girls they had met, of sisters of girls met by a guy in
the barracks. One guy was heading for Liverpool and a girl he had met
during combat orientation. He passed her picture around. Nice, everybody
agreed. Some hoped to make it to the Red Cross Club at the Bishop's
Palace. It was at the cathedral and served good, hearty meals, cafeteria
style, had clean bunks, and, most important, provided hot showers. Another
guy, a radio operator from Virginia, told them about a lady out in Falkland
Street who rented rooms to Yanks. The rooms were modest, but her home-
cooked breakfasts were something else. There were even sheets on the
beds. It was away from the crush of the Red Cross Club. You had to bike to
get there, the radioman warned them, but that was no problem. Just rent one
from Dodger, the local bike man. They'd find him, no trouble. There was
much kidding about the Piccadilly Commandos, the blackout, the beer.
Mostly there was relief. None of these men would be flying today.

The truck rumbled along through the soggy countryside until the rural
lanes vanished and the road broadened. The 6 × 6 slowed, and the boys
lifted the canvas flap at the rear to peer out into the gray afternoon light. The
truck had stopped at Larkman's Corner, the first outpost of the town, and
several boys jumped down eagerly. No one could remember just how this
unlikely neighborhood had become such a favorite of the 466th, but the pub
on the corner had acquired such standing among men in the group that the
Liberty Run, by popular demand, had begun stopping there. On some
weekends, when the weather was particularly bad and the groups around
Norwich stood down, the smoke-filled pub trembled with the twangs of the
Texas hill country and an English voice was as rare as a sunny day.

As the truck wove through the narrow streets, the gaunt silhouettes of
bombed-out buildings closed around them, a tangle of twisted metal and
crumbling brick facades. Shells of buildings, the chalky traces of rooms no
longer there etched on their walls like fossils, lined their passage. The
skeletal remains of roofs rose above windowless ruins below, and through
empty casements, like the hollow sockets of a skull, birds swooped and
dove in mournful arcs. Norwich had not been attacked for almost a year, but
the scars of those early raids lingered on a landscape of shattered buildings
and rubble-filled lots, sudden voids in a row of whitewashed houses or
shops, like a missing tooth. In the early years of the war, they were told, the
city had suffered forty-four raids, though most of the damage had come in a
deadly series of attacks in April and May 1941. Still, an occa-

sional Luftwaffe pilot, following the RAF back from a raid, would come roaring low over the city, drop his bombs or strafe aimlessly in the darkness below, and vanish. Nobody seemed to pay them much mind.

The buzz bombs were another matter. Throughout the summer they had chugged periodically across the sky. In the streets and shops the people would stop and stand and listen. They would look up, even if they were inside, hoping that the "doodlebugs" would putter on to the west. Usually they did. In September, though, when the giant V-2s had begun to rain down on London, one slammed into an area just outside the city, creating a crater ten feet deep. Was it just off course, or was Norwich back on Jerry's target list? The papers didn't report much about the new rockets, but there was fear that Hitler's new V—for vengeance—weapons would find Norwich. Inside the Liberty Run truck nobody was worried about V-2s.

The truck slammed to a halt at the Thorpe station. Norwich was the hub of the Second Air Division, with a dozen bases within twenty miles, and all around the sandbagged entrance to the station, through the dusty red brick hall, along the bleak platforms in the dull light of the blackout lamps, GIs stood in clusters, waiting for the 14:12 train to London or the Liberty Run back to Rackheath or Tibenham or one of the other bases. The Snowdrops, the white-helmeted, club-swinging MPs were there, too, patrolling the parking lot, sweeping up the drunks, curbing the unruly. Today they had little to do. But it was early yet.

Barrett unfolded the map, and after getting their bearings they pushed off toward the center of town, following several groups of GIs who seemed to know what they were doing. High above them, in the middle distance, they could see the squat, crenellated hulk of the castle and beyond, to the right, the spire of the Norwich Cathedral.

Following the gentle incline of the Prince of Wales Road, they climbed the hill from the station. They wandered up narrow, meandering streets, past cobbled courtyards and brick alleys. They stared in at the stark shops with their sparse wares, the shelves grim with the privations of five years of war. A chemist, a tobacconist, a tailor's shop, founded in 1834, specializing in military uniforms, a news agent, a bookshop, a movie house. Barrett clung to the map and they occasionally consulted it, but nobody cared much about navigation. The goal was vaguely to see the sights—the castle, the cathedral—and hit the pubs. And here they were treading the gray streets in their finest class As, frisky as college boys out on a panty raid, ready for whatever Norwich had to offer.

Up Bedford Street they wound their way along cobblestone passageways, through a maze of ancient timbered buildings with mullioned windows and leaded glass. Like ships caught on a swell, the soot-stained shops listed out onto narrow, undulating streets, their gables looming like giant prows above them. The men turned through an archway, climbing steadily, until at last their way opened onto a public square and the portals that marked the entrance to the castle. A light rain was falling over the city, and through the low wispy clouds the view was striking. Below to the east they could see the silver cupola of the railway station, to the west the ornate steeple of St. Peter Mancroft and the giant clock tower of the new city hall. To the north, beyond a sea of black slate rooftops, broken by an occasional swath of orange tile and a jumble of chimney pots, rose the graceful spire of the great cathedral.

While they paused to get their bearings, Jack pulled a neatly folded sheet of paper from his breast pocket. He had a map with the best pubs listed by a guy in the 785th, and he was determined to sample as many as possible. Shielding it from the drizzle, he turned the small scrap of stationery on its side, deciphering the scrawl along the margins.

"Back's Public House," Jack read, "says here Back's is the largest bar in Norwich. Everybody knows where it is. Sits almost directly opposite the marketplace. Has a front entrance, a side entrance, and a rear entrance that comes out into a little alley known as White Lion Street. When the MPs come busting in the front, everybody rushes out the side."

"Let's find it," Al said.

They pushed off across Castle Meadow. Skipping down a flight of steps, slippery now in the gathering mist, they turned left and followed a series of twisting streets that led them gradually downward. Rounding a corner, they found themselves on a busy thoroughfare—Gentlemen's Walk, Jack's map told them—filled with men hurrying home from work, clerks darting out of offices, soldiers and solicitors jostling along the crowded sidewalks. The feeble afternoon light had already begun to fade, and the blackout would be in effect soon. "Hey," Jack said, "this must be the market." To their left a sea of black canvas-covered stalls stretched out across a large square, huddled in the shadow of the massive city hall. The stalls bustled with activity, and a greasy scent of fried fish filled the air. They sauntered among stalls selling hats and handkerchiefs, odd bits of hardware, dog-eared travel books, stamps and rare coins, knickknacks. Somewhere an accordion played. Howard stopped to examine a sample of faded doilies—"Not

French," the fat, red-faced proprietress told him with surprising vehemence—and, at another stall, a collection of lead soldiers, slightly battered, caught his eye. No toys, the old gentleman perched on a stool told him, had been produced in Britain since 1942. He browsed, but there was not much to excite interest, no souvenirs to send home.

Circling back onto Gentlemen's Walk, Howard found Bob leaning against a red phone box. Al and Jack, Bob reported, had gone in search of the pub and would meet them later. Jerry had struck up a conversation with an English girl in front of the movie theater, and Bob wanted to find the Sampson and Hercules dance hall.

They agreed to meet later at the dance hall, and Howard headed across the market. He would grab a bite to eat at the Red Cross, take a hot shower, and then he would find the Sampson and Hercules. As he ambled casually along the rain-slick cobblestones, pausing occasionally to listen to the muffled gurgle of laughter and song that eddied beneath the blackout curtains of the pubs, it struck him that for the first time in months he was actually alone, away from the crew, from the army, from the war. It was a dreamy, luxuriant feeling, this fleeting sensation of solitude, of privacy, a sensation that belonged to another lifetime, like the simple, sensual steam of a shower.

It was pitch black when he found his way into Tombland Street and, turning left, walked along the ancient flint-work walls that guarded the grounds of the great cathedral. The wall was pierced by a series of gates, stately Georgian houses and red brick shops, and as it descended along the wall, the street broadened, opening onto a square that even in the darkness was teeming with activity. Everywhere he looked, Howard saw GIs. GIs standing in small clumps of olive drab outside the Maid's Head Hotel, GIs darting across the square, dodging the 6 × 6s that rumbled by, GIs hovering around the entrance to a large gabled building just opposite the main gate to the cathedral. Music throbbed from the building, and between the grinding of the trucks and raucous chatter of the GIs the insistent beat of "Tuxedo Junction" carried across the square to where he stood. Howard smiled in recognition.

Stopping a group of GIs, he asked directions to the Bishop's Palace. "Just follow this wall on around to the side of the cathedral, Mac," they told him. "You cawn't miss it." They guffawed drunkenly and plunged into the square, weaving toward the music.

Ahead of him in the gloom, Howard could make out a cluster of trucks parked in the middle of the street, twenty, maybe thirty of them, stacked two and three deep at a wide spot in the road. This must be it, Howard thought, the enlisted men's pickup for the Liberty Run was at Palace Plain. Then the wall gave way to a gate, and turning in he followed an airman along a gravel path that led to an imposing stone structure lurking in the very shadow of the cathedral. Like a castle or a chapel, Howard thought, as he stood before an arched portal beneath a set of ornate clovered windows and between two massive stone buttresses. Following the airman, he pushed open the heavy door, brushed aside the thick blackout curtain, and entered.

The room—a large entrance hall, actually—was brightly lit, and for a moment Howard could only blink. The ceiling above him was lined with age-blackened beams, and a young man, a British civilian, sat at a reception desk across a small, shiny swath of parquet floor. Just to the left and down several stone steps lay a large vaulted room. Howard peered into it. He could smell French fries and caught the steamy scent of cabbage. A string of GIs, trays in hand, were edging along a small cafeteria line.

"Checking in with us, are you?" the young man at the desk asked pleasantly.

"Just thought I'd get a shower, if I could." Howard said. "Maybe a bite to eat. Am I in the right place?" he asked, looking around. "The Bishop's Palace?"

"Righto," the young man said. "The showers are just upstairs and down the corridor. Towels and soap are provided. Food is just here," he nodded, gesturing toward the vaulted room.

"Looks kind of like a crypt in there," Howard said.

"Exactly what it was before the bishop signed the place over to the Red Cross for the duration. Created quite a stir when it first went in, you know, the cafeteria. Quite a novelty, your hot food and your sweet served at the same time—and on a tray."

Howard signed the ledger, claimed a worn white towel and a bar of soap, and made his way up the stairs. He stood in the shower for a long time, the warm water coursing over him in steamy, voluptuous bursts. Lathering up with the small bar of soap, he realized that he hadn't seen his own body for weeks. It was mushroom pale, and lean, and his thin white legs and the dark matted hair that clung to them seemed to belong to a stranger. Only his hands looked familiar. Closing his eyes, he hummed to himself, quietly at first, then louder, a few bars of "It Had to Be You." Snatches of songs that he and Alice had danced to in the smoky, crowded clubs in New York came to

him on the lush and throaty voices of Dinah Shore and Peggy Lee and Jo
Stafford and that girl who sang with Harry James. They harmonized with
him on the sultry torch songs he loved: "Deep Purple," "I'll Get By," "My
Devotion." There were other men in the shower room, but Howard hardly
noticed them. They stood languorously beneath the hissing nozzles, each
utterly oblivious to the others, lost in that strange inner solitude produced
by a prolonged lack of privacy.

Dazed by the rush of pleasant sensations, Howard dried himself and
dressed slowly. He was warm and clean and suddenly very hungry. They
were serving meatloaf in the cafeteria below, and while it wasn't great it was
okay. He ate slowly and sipped a cup of coffee. Pushing his tray away, he
stood up, pulled on his jacket, and grabbed his cap. He would visit the
dance hall across from the cathedral, back on the square. He asked the guy
across from him, a tech sergeant with flyer's wings, about it. "Oh yeah," the
sergeant said, drawing heavily on a Camel, "that's the Sampson and Hercules. Great place. Some of the guys call it 'Muscles Hall.' You'll understand when you see it."

Retracing his steps along the wall, Howard found his way back to the
square. "Ah ha," he said aloud, as he saw the two gigantic carved figures
who flanked the entrance, holding up the portals. Sampson, a lamb slung
across his massive shoulder, clutched the jawbone of an ass, while Hercules wielded a mighty club and carried the carcass of a lion. Passing
between them, Howard paid, entered, and joined the line. "No alcoholic
beverages, gents," a matronly lady just inside the door reminded them. "No
flasks, no bottles." All along the line GIs raised their arms as she frisked
them. "I carry mine in my pants, honey," the guy in front of him said. "Not
back there," he added, as she gingerly ran her hands along his backside.
"Up front." Unfazed, she passed her hands up the insides of his thighs and
patted his crotch. "I'm afraid you're wrong, ma lord," she said. "There's not
much there at all." The line erupted in laughter.

Passing through the blackout curtains, the noise, the smoke, the smell
had stunned him momentarily. The cavernous room was hazy and hot with
the press of bodies. Raucous laughter, shouted conversations, whoops and
whistles mingled with the music, rattling the senses. Gradually Howard got
his bearings. Edging his way through the crowd, he watched as couples
surged onto the dance floor, clasping each other tightly to "We'll Meet
Again," and "Moonlight Cocktails," bouncing, jiving, jumping to "Chattanooga Choo Choo," and "Little Brown Jug." The band wasn't bad. He

looked at the girls who milled around at the fringes, chatting, laughing, unattached girls, who danced first with one guy then another. Weaving his way along the cusp of the crowd, he wandered over to a small, plumpish girl, her plain dark hair pulled back in a buoyant wave, and, almost shouting over the din, asked her to dance. She gave him a quick, noncommittal look, a hint of a distracted smile playing on her bright red lips, and followed him out onto the crowded floor. The band eased into "You'll Never Know," and as they embraced, Howard inhaled the faint scent of perfume rising from her soft white neck. It was a sweet dime-store fragrance, cheap and cloying, but it staggered him like a blow, unleashing a spasm of half-forgotten sensations, memories, images of another life. They moved awkwardly around a tiny fragment of the crowded floor, bumping into other couples, stumbling, smiling. The girl was not much of a dancer, and when she tried to say something, her lips pressed against his ear, it was impossible to hear. He nodded, smiled foolishly. He had no idea what she was saying, but it didn't matter.

After another dance she asked him if he would like to walk her back home. Dad was working in London and Mum would be asleep at the aunt's, but Howard couldn't. Had to make the Liberty Run back to base, he explained. The band struck up "Twelve O'Clock Jump," and out of the corner of his eye Howard caught sight of Bob. Relaxed and happier than Howard had ever seen him, the old man of the crew really cut loose, jitterbugging across the floor. His partner did her best to keep up, trying to follow him as he bounced and swayed, but she was lost. He spun lightly on his toes, pivoted, and twirled her suddenly beneath his outstretched arm, swinging his shoulders, his hips with abandon. His feet slid smoothly across the floor, his arms and legs swirling in a blur of frenetic energy. Looking up, he caught a glimpse of Howard, smiling at him from only a few feet away. Howard grinned impishly at him and winked. "Careful, old boy," he called out in the lull between songs, wagging his finger like a metronome. "Not as young as you used to be." Bob laughed, dancing away into the crowd.

At around 10:30 the crowd began to thin, as the GIs, some staggering, some with women clinging unsteadily to them, drifted out into the black rain-slick streets to find their pickup points. The Liberty Run trucks would be pulling out at 11:00. It wouldn't do to be late. Outside the Maid's Head Hotel Howard caught a glimpse of Jerry Barrett as he embraced a woman a full head taller, gave her a lingering farewell kiss, and broke away, joining the throng headed for the trucks. The square teemed with the shadowy forms of men in a hurry, surging toward Palace Plain. There the trucks, maybe sixty of them, idled, dousing the damp air with a greasy splash of diesel. As they groped along in the crowd, trying to locate the 466th's trucks, Howard could see that the MPs—the Snowdrops—were out in force, their white helmets bobbing like bubbles of foam on the dark wave of moving men. Along the sidewalk a GI was doubled over, emptying his guts into the gutter, while two buddies, none too steady themselves, tried to hold him up. Oblivious to the passing throng, GIs pressed their dates against the walls of the cathedral, while just beside them a row of men decided to take a piss, their steam rising into the chill mist. A scuffle broke out somewhere between the trucks, and the Snowdrops scurried forward. It was pandemonium.

Howard climbed into the truck after Bob and Jerry and slumped back in his seat. They had not seen the other guys from the crew, Al or Jack, but they would show up. Jerry lit up his pipe and sighed contentedly. Howard was humming. They had made their first Liberty Run. They had done the town. And tomorrow they would not be flying.

CHAPTER V

IF ONLY
IN MY DREAMS

Dick Tracy was in trouble. The beautiful, tormented Snowflake Falls had been slipped an amnesia drug, and now Shakey and his mob had abducted her, snatching her at gunpoint right out of police headquarters. "Stand right where you are, coppers. These guns don't kid." They had given Tracy the slip and only Junior, on the way to his afternoon job at the drugstore, could help him find her. Terry Lee was in trouble, too. On a flight from the jungles of Burma to Calcutta, Jap flak and fighters had blinded the pilot and killed the copilot of the storm-tossed B-25. With the radio dead and both motors spitting smoke, Terry had to pull them through. "Gosh, I've never flown a two-engine plane before." Refusing morphine and struggling to stammer out instructions, the blinded pilot talked Terry through the controls. They were still lost somewhere over the mountains, but it looked like Terry would make it.

Howard turned the page. He hadn't seen the funnies in the *Stars and Stripes* for over a week. Some joker had taken the Thursday issue, but he could see in Friday's paper that Tracy was on Shakey's trail, closing in. He was trying to remember the details of the love triangle in *Terry and the Pirates*, but couldn't quite manage it. Why was Terry Lee going to India anyway? Not much was happening in *Male Call*, but he looked as usual at the slinky women in their clinging dresses. Must be the models for the guys who do the paintings on the planes. He glanced briefly at the war news. All the way across the world the big naval battle at Leyte Gulf was going well. A Jap carrier had been sunk, the Imperial fleet was routed. A large map with converging arrows and dotted lines showed it all. He studied it for a moment. It might as well have been on Mars.

The Russians were making a push for Budapest and were approaching East Prussia. Königsberg, Insterberg—where were those places? He should know. Maybe the war would be over by Christmas—a lot of the guys seemed to think so—if the Russians kept at it. Howard tried to visualize the map in the briefing room. He had not seen it for days. They had not flown a mission for almost two weeks, not since the Saarbrücken raid. The group had gone out twice but the Farrington crew had stayed put, flying practice missions, attending more ground classes. They had made a cross-country flight, two locals, and a night flight. No combat. They had been alerted twice, but the missions had been scrubbed, once before briefing and once as the planes were taxiing out for takeoff. Howard sipped his Coke. In another part of the Aero Club, beyond the popping of the Ping-Pong paddles and the tinkling of glasses, Doris Day's velvet voice purred through the static of the Armed Forces Network (AFN). She was crooning "My Dreams Are Getting Better All the Time," and Howard hummed along absently. He had brought a few V-mail forms, thinking he might write some letters, but there was really nothing to report. He looked at Saturday's paper. The Luftwaffe had been up in force for the first time since early September. As many as four hundred Jerry fighters had been sighted over Germany. Four hundred. They had not seen a single enemy plane, not one, unless you counted that jet contrail that Barrett saw on the Frankfurt mission. He was not complaining.

"I have a few minutes," he wrote at last, "and thought I would tell you all I'm okay. It is cold as can be here and I wish I could see some good old Tennessee sunshine. . . . I'm just fine, Dad, but a little bit tired of England." The weather in early November had taken a sudden turn for the worse, although that didn't seem possible. The usual squalls had turned to sleet and freezing rain, peppering the windows like buckshot. It was impossible to stay dry or warm, and everybody's nerves were as raw as the weather.

Although the group had stood down for days on end, the crews had been repeatedly alerted, awakened in the frozen darkness, and briefed, only to have the mission scrubbed at the last minute because of weather. And the trouble with Harry lingered like a sore, souring their life in the hut and on the plane.

The folks at home didn't need to hear about this. Howard sealed up the letter and took another sip of his Coke. Mail call had brought him a slew of letters, twenty-five in all, and he had stuffed them into his musette bag to read here in the Aero Club armchair where it was passably warm. The letters always seemed to come in flurries. For days on end there would be nothing, as if the world outside the air station, outside the war, had ceased to exist. Then he would be buried in an avalanche of V-mails from his folks, from his brother, James, from Mildred, and long airmails from Nancy—and from Alice.

Alice. A package from her, wrapped in coarse brown paper, was among the stack of mail he had shoved into his bag. He could hardly believe it. She was so exotic, so glamorous, so utterly unlike anything in his experience. She was the stuff that dreams are made of. When he had shipped out Alice had promised to write, extracting a similar pledge from him, fervent promises made at wartime partings, every day on every front. The war was full of brief, frantic romances that evaporated like steam when the troop train pulled out of the station. He was under no illusions. But shortly after he had settled in at Attlebridge, the letters from Alice began arriving, day after day, regaling him with tales of her life in New York. He was astonished, perplexed, flattered. Howard had sent a snapshot of her home, not to the folks, but to his kid brother. "James, she is the prettiest girl I ever laid my eyes on. She worked at Mitchel Field and that's where I met her."

Howard carefully tore open the large envelope, sliding an 8 × 10 photograph free of its wrapping. Faintly tinted and softly focused, the portrait had been done professionally. Alice's upturned face glowed in the gauzy light, her eyes shining brightly. She was simply stunning. "You ask what I hear from Alice. Well, she is strictly on the ball. I'd like to tell you all about her," he wrote, "but it would take an awful long time. She is really beautiful, James, and she has the nicest personality of any girl I know of. She is twenty-one and is a model for some fashion store in New York . . . and, gosh, she is on the ball." He looked up, smiling to himself, surprised at his own gushing enthusiasm. The radio was throbbing with "Green Eyes," and he tried to remember what color Alice's eyes were. Blue, he decided. "I hear from her almost every day. You know Hedy Lamarr. Well, she is Hedy made over, except much nicer. Wish you knew her. She is tops." He didn't know where to put her in his life, what to make of his feelings or what role she was to play in his future. But the future was something that he didn't need to sort out, not now. Like everything but the war, it was on hold, suspended.

A low wolfish whistle rang just above his ear.

"What a doll," Bob whinnied, nodding his head in approval.

"It's that gal from New York, isn't it?" Brennan asked, patting Howard on the shoulder in approval. "The one you were with all the time at Mitchel." The two of them stood behind Howard's chair, leaning over to admire the picture. They had been to the base barbershop, and Howard could smell the talcum. He nodded, grinning sheepishly. He folded the letter to James, slipped the picture of Alice back into his musette bag, and stood up.

"He's got one in every port," Jack said, nudging him. "I just don't understand what they see in you."

"It's that southern charm," Bob volunteered.

"It's that athlete's body," Jack said, striking a Charles Atlas pose.

"Well, it can't be money," Jerry Barrett said, strolling up to the group. "He still owes me for that dinner in town the other night."

"Speaking of dinner, it's time for chow," Jack said. "They're serving turkey and all the fixings tonight," he added. It was the first Thanksgiving for the 466th in the ETO, and the mess hall, the boys had heard, was planning a real feast.

"Looks like this will be another Thanksgiving, Christmas, and New Year away from loved ones," Bob wrote to Marie that night. Their anniversary was less than a week away, and they would be spending it apart for the third year running. Three years of the army, three years of the war. "Seems like I keep getting farther from you every anniversary," he wrote. "One thing sure is we should be together again in 1945, and I hope out of the army. . . ." Still, the day had "turned out to be rather nice. Slept till 10 A.M. Then went to chow—then formation—then haircut—then show, *Lady in the Dark*—then evening Thanksgiving turkey. Cranberry sauce, candy, apples, tomato juice, coffee, sweet potatoes, cheese, pumpkin pie, and beans." To top it off, another low pressure system had settled over East Anglia late in the day and the group was standing down again. They would not fly combat the next day. That seemed to be the pattern these days. Either

England was socked in or clouds hung over the continent. "I sure am thankful . . . to be alive," Bob concluded. "Looking forward to peace on earth and an early return to your arms. . . . Hope Bobby and Arthur don't forget me." He held up the newly arrived snapshot of Bobby in his Halloween costume and admired it. "Sort of a strange world," he mused, "I like children yet I have had so few moments to enjoy my own."

"Your target for today is Bielefeld," the S-2 said tersely, his pointer tapping a spot midway between the eastern tip of the Ruhr and Hannover, "specifically, a railroad viaduct approximately two and one-half miles from the town. The bridge is 384 yards long and 72 feet high. A major bottleneck for German troops and supplies heading west to the front, it is first on the transportation priority list and has not been attacked before." Bielefeld, the purple gray target maps revealed, was a small city in the rolling hills of Westphalia, about forty miles east of Münster, and the red ribbon on the giant wall map indicated that their route would take them past Amsterdam and Osnabrück, skirting as much as possible the great flak concentrations of Westphalia and the Ruhr. Each of the group's thirty-seven planes would be carrying a heavy load, eight 1,000-pounders, and the men shuffled their feet uneasily at the news. A full bomb load and fuel for a trip into Germany always ratcheted up the anxiety level for takeoff.

The escape and evasion officer went through his usual spiel on the articles of war, the name-rank-and-serial-number-if-captured routine that they all knew by heart, but on this bright cold morning he reminded them pointedly that the Nazi government had declared all Allied flyers *Luftgangsters* and Goebbels was now officially urging German civilians to take vengeance on all downed "terror flyers" wherever they found them. "If you have to bail out over Germany," he stressed, "avoid civilians if you can. Wait until dark to move about. Use caution in approaching farmers or even clergy. If you must contact civilians, slip into a Catholic church after dark."

The Farrington crew was flying in the low element of the high-right squadron, and as they convened at the hardstand the pilot seemed confident and upbeat. This would be their deepest penetration into Germany, but at least it wasn't the Ruhr again and he liked their position in the formation. Arriving late from the bombardiers' briefing, Manners grumbled that whoever dreamed up trying to hit a narrow railroad bridge from twenty thousand feet should have his friggin' head examined. This was a job for light bombers flying at low altitudes, or even fighters. "P-47s could dive-bomb the damned thing," he groused as they stood beneath the wing of the plane. "Curly," Jack Regan said, one long, lean arm draped over Manners's burly shoulder, "we're sending you as our representative to Eighth Bomber Command to express our objections to this mission. You have my permission to commandeer that jeep over there on the double. We'll wait here." "Ah, screw you, Jack," Manners mumbled as he squatted to climb into the plane. "Curly, you look like a bear trying to waddle into a cave," Farrington laughed, as Manners squirmed awkwardly into the nose wheel well. Everyone seemed surprisingly loose.

The mission passed without incident. No fighters hung in the contrails and no black smudges soiled the azure blue sky on the bomb run. They slipped through a thin veil of flak near Osnabrück and two planes in the low squadron later reported some serious battle damage, but for the Farrington crew the trip was uneventful. The bombing was to have been visual—radar assisted, if necessary—but a 5/10 cloud cover at Bielefeld threw a patchy haze over the narrow viaduct. From bombing altitude the giant span blinked only intermittently into view, no more than a gossamer thread woven illusively into the gauzy fabric of clouds and countryside below. The group dropped 245 1,000-pound general-purpose bombs through the haze, but at interrogation nobody seemed sure about the results. Strike photos later revealed that Curly was right. The closest bomb fell three thousand feet from the bridge, and three days later the 466th was ordered back to Bielefeld.

They would go without the Farrington crew. The November 26 mission to Bielefeld was the crew's fifth and qualified them not only for the Air Medal but also, according to group practice, for their first pass. They were now officially a veteran crew. During the Eighth's first year of combat, when only 28 percent of all bomber personnel survived a full tour, 37 percent were lost before completing even three missions. Those numbers had improved dramatically during 1944, but the first five missions, when crews were adjusting to the harsh realities of combat in the ETO, remained the most perilous. The crew was happy about the Air Medal, glad to get the first five behind them, but it was the prospect of a pass that really excited them. For the first time since they had arrived in England they would be free to travel beyond Norwich, to see some of the country and to get as far away from flying as they could.

Just after chow the next morning Howard and the other enlisted men eagerly collected their passes at the squadron HQ and hopped a truck that would take them over to the base's main communal site. Showered, their shoes shined, and their clean class A uniforms smelling only slightly of aviation fuel, the boys stopped by the base hospital. Before leaving the station on pass the enlisted men were required to report to the flight surgeon's office, where they were read the riot act about venereal disease. They had seen the ghastly scare films almost from the moment they had entered the service, and Doc Hoff reminded them sternly that a case of clap was grounds for court-martial. He needn't have bothered. The barracks were full of advice about London. "Man, them Piccadilly Commandos will give you such a dose, it'll peel the pecker right off you," a tail gunner from Little Rock warned them cheerfully. "Just keep those 'French letters'—that's what the Limeys call 'em—handy and you'll be all right. Don't worry if you run out, it's easier to get a rubber in London than a bar of soap. Hell, the newspaper boys on the corner sell 'em— sell more of 'em than newspapers, I'll bet. I wouldn't be surprised if they didn't sell 'em with fish and chips," he chuckled.

They had all heard about wild and wicked London, about the pubs, the cavernous dance halls, the hotels, with real sheets and warm baths. Then there were the girls—the Piccadilly Commandos and the Hyde Park Rangers, about whom they had heard so much—pros, who prowled the nighttime streets, turning tricks in doorways, in cabs, and under park bushes; there were the nice girls, too, girls who, after dinner and drinks and dancing might, if you were lucky, lead you back to their flat for a weekend away from the war.

"It's my experience," Doc Hoff related to them with a worldly sigh, "that crews returning from pass are rarely in an improved physical state." He paused to wipe his glasses. "All the hurry and rush involved in traveling, usually to London, the alcohol usually consumed, and the loss of sleep sustained in practically all instances, tends to lower the resistance of the flyer to the future rigors of operational flying." He looked at each of them individually, a quick, knowing look. "A short stay in a rest home is infinitely more valuable than any number of ordinary passes or leaves." They all nodded. The Wehrmacht, he knew, couldn't keep them from London. "You boys be careful," he said finally, and they were out the door.

The afternoon express to London was jammed. GIs poured from the dusky platform into the ancient train, swamping it, spilling over into the narrow corridors. The distinct odor of aviation fuel, leavened by sweat and a tinge of aftershave, filled the tight compartments as the men elbowed their way along the platforms and shoehorned themselves into threadbare seats. The unlucky and the tardy stood patiently waiting, pressed against the windows in the clogged corridors, prepared to stand all the way to London. No one was going to wait for the next train. Some of the cars were the quaint Victorian carriages with doors that opened directly onto the platform, and GIs hung from them or leaned from their windows waving, yelling, or just taking in the scene until the conductor's whistle blew and a cloud of steam hissed from the engine and the train ground slowly out of Thorpe Station.

Crowded into one compartment Howard, Jerry, and Al sat knee to knee, facing Harry, Jack, and a dead-drunk mechanic from the 467th, as the landscape of East Anglia slid by beyond the windows, a blur of moist ochre and brilliant green. Somewhere in the train the officers had climbed aboard. They had lost track of one another at the station. Maybe they would link up in London. As the train picked up speed, they hurtled past ancient farm-houses and rural villages with their Norman churches and sleepy commons. Sheep grazed in the gaunt Norfolk countryside, and across the rich, flat fields an occasional farmer mounted behind a horse rode an antique piece of farm equipment. The train stopped all along the route, disgorging hand-fuls of thankful civilians, and along the platforms of the small stations neatly dressed GIs from the nearby airfields eagerly awaited it. In Suffolk the billiard-table terrain gave way gradually to gentle hills and hedge-lined fields. A card game—there was always a card game—got under way in the next compartment, and over the steady clattering of the rails they could hear the bidding and shouting and swearing. A bottle materialized. Scotch. Jack and Al took big swigs, smiling.

Sitting in the cramped compartment, the boys were filled with excite-ment and anticipation. The pass was for thirty-six hours, not forty-eight, as they had expected, but it was still thirty-six hours away from the base, away from flying, away from the biscuits and the cold showers, away from the war. They were ready for the sights—Rainbow Corner, Piccadilly Circus, the Stage Door Canteen, Big Ben, the Tower of London, the hotels, the girls. "Stay at the Strand Palace," a waist gunner in the 787th had advised, and the boys had dutifully written down the address. They carried with them the names of pubs, the names of hotels, the names of women, the names of buddies, the names of restaurants. Howard had made plans to meet Tom, and Al's brother, whom Al had not seen in two years, was also going to leave his address at Rainbow Corner. The old hands lamented the frenetic Wild West days of preinvasion London, when more than a million soldiers of every Allied nation roamed the streets, filled the buses, the dance halls, the pubs, speaking in every tongue imaginable. Still, the city held its marvels, and the boys were determined to see them all.

Norwich was two hours behind them when the rural countryside began to melt gradually away and the clusters of stucco cottages along the track thickened into settlements, spreading almost to the horizon in a vast delta of plaster and stone. Past Clapton the last, lingering marshy flats gave way to a dismal industrial landscape of somber factories and drab warehouses and mammoth railroad sidings. An occasional church steeple jutted from the maze of clotheslines and yellow-brick terrace houses, puncturing the bluish haze that hovered in the air like an approaching storm. The train rumbled past once-prosperous Victorian buildings, their ornate facades now soot stained and shabby, past block after block of neat row houses, their columns of identical bay windows and single dormers aligned as if on the parade grounds at Sandhurst. Slowing in Bethel Green, the train crawled on elevated tracks over acres of bleak tar-paper rooftops, through a sea of chalky gray brown tenements that might have been the south side of Chicago or the Bowery. No more than twenty feet away the sooty windows of dingy flats flashed suddenly by like frames on a roll of film, offering up a flickering tableau of faded wallpaper and threadbare chairs and a white-haired woman in an overcoat pouring tea at a kitchen table. Then the train plunged suddenly down through a series of short tunnels, rose again gently, and braked, gliding to a steamy halt under the vaulted steel canopy of Liverpool Street Station.

Pigeons cooed among the girders far overhead, swooping through the empty steel frames that before the war had held panels of the frosted glass roof. The boys jumped down onto the platform, stretching their legs, yawning in the clouds of steam that rose from the tracks around them like a sigh. After the rhythmic clatter of the train the clamor of the cavernous station jarred them. Horns hooted, loudspeakers echoed unintelligibly, conductors' whistles trilled, and people bustled along the crowded plat-forms toward the front of the train. The boys were swept along in the stream of passengers and groaning baggage carts. Past the barrier where the tickets were collected British soldiers in their battle-dress brown, home on leave or returning forlornly to duty, sat surrounded by piles of equipment, their saucer helmets and rifles slung over their shoulders. From every booking window and every concession booth, at every phone box and newsstand long lines of people wavered into the dusky terminal, waiting, always waiting.

As usual Jerry seemed to know what to do. Weaving quickly through the throng, he got his bearings. He pointed to a line of ancient cabs waiting at the side entrance. Pushing resolutely through the milling crowd, their khaki musette bags slung over their shoulders, the boys followed Barrett as he led them hurriedly toward the taxis. Stepping to the curb, he raised his hand with the commanding presence of a born New Yorker, and all five of them piled roughly into the quaint black taxi that jerked to a halt directly in front of them.

"Where to, Yanks?" the cabbie asked as he snapped down the For Hire sign on the dash, " 'otel?"

"Strand Palace," Jerry said. He gave the address.

"Righto," the cabbie responded, and the taxi swung around, sped up a short ramp, and rumbled into a canyon of gray brown buildings. It was late afternoon and raining, and the wipers sloshed energetically as the taxi wound its way through a maze of dark, narrow streets, past offices and pubs and blocks of flats. Bright red double-decker buses crawled along a wider street, stopping, starting, sliding again into the sparse traffic. Along the crowded sidewalks black umbrellas bobbed like seals in a heavy surf, and on the corners men in greasy caps hawked papers with thick headlines proclaiming the latest war news. The Germans were in full retreat on both fronts. The war looked good. Through the rain-streaked windshield the dome of St. Paul's loomed up before them, the first landmark Jerry recognized. From the front of the cab, where he was engrossed in conversation with the cabbie, Jerry pointed it out to them. Then Fleet Street, London's newspaper district, he explained, and finally the brown and gold awning that marked the entrance to the Strand Palace. Before they untangled themselves and tumbled out onto the wet pavement, Jerry had arranged for the cabbie to stop by the next morning at ten o'clock. He would give them a proper motor tour of London.

At the reception area a young woman in a brown uniform with faded gold braid on the sleeves informed them that, terribly sorry, there were absolutely no rooms available. The hotel was totally booked. Howard was ready to leave, to find the alternative hotel she suggested or to press on to one of the Red Cross clubs, but Jerry persevered, chatting amiably with the receptionist. Howard wondered if Tom had made it. His brother-in-law was scheduled for a pass, and they had arranged to meet at the enlisted men's Red Cross Club on Charing Cross Road, not far from Piccadilly Circus. Howard felt a tug at his sleeve. Jerry stood beside him, smiling. In his hand he held two keys. "Don't ask," he said merrily, and they quickly collected the boys, who prowled the lobby or sat slumped in the giant, overstuffed chairs. On the way to the elevator they stopped to peer into the hotel restaurant, where white linen tablecloths muffled the tinkle of cups and saucers and a roomful of civilians—a striking sight—sat at tea. Piling into the cramped elevator—why was everything in this country built so damned small? Jack asked—they found their way to two tiny rooms joined by a bath. A bath! They pressed in to have a look at a tub as big as a bed.

The bath would have to wait. Dumping their bags in the rooms, they rode the elevator back to the lobby, and, getting directions from the doorman, they left the Strand for Piccadilly Circus. Tom had written that he would leave a message for Howard at the Eagle Club on Charing Cross Road. With little trouble they located the club, but at the reception desk Howard found no message from Tom. He had not checked in and there was nothing on the message board. Howard scribbled a note for him, giving the Strand Palace address, and they headed off again for Piccadilly Circus.

They wandered along in the gray twilight, turning, on instructions from the Red Cross girl at the Eagle, into Coventry Street at Leicester Square. Gawking at the endless clutter of shops and pubs, restaurants and cinemas, burlesque houses and tattoo parlors, they joined the thickening throng that bustled toward Piccadilly Circus. Like tributaries flowing into a pool, the streets emptied into a gigantic rotary, an oval of rounded six-story buildings whose cluttered facades bristled with a chaos of colorful signs and bright letters—Gordon's Gin, Bovril, Schweppes Tonic Water, and, in a concession to the ubiquitous presence of the Yanks, Wrigley's Gum, for Vim and Vigour. A beaming female face, the size of a boxcar, smiled down on them, urging them to try Bile Beans, for Radiant Health and Fit Figure and beneath the hands of a mammoth clock marking Guinness Time, they found the reassuring message that Guinness Is Good for You. Antique black cabs, crowded double-decker buses, and jeeps filled with white-helmeted MPs scudded past around the rotary. In the midst of the hubbub the famous statue of Eros stood, boarded up now and sheathed for the duration in panels of concrete that rose to a smooth, rounded point, "like a big nipple,"

Jack said aptly. On the steps around its base soldiers lounged, waiting to meet their buddies, to pick up girls, or just to take in the passing scene.

They jogged across the street to the base of the monument and wandered around it, gawking in the fading light at the surrounding buildings, the scurrying pedestrians, the traffic. Howard never ceased to be astonished at how suddenly night seemed to seep through the frail afternoon dimness in England, like spilled ink spreading on a page, and as the feeble twilight vanished they stood for a moment at the center of Piccadilly, motionless in the pitch black. All along the crowded sidewalks dark forms moved purposefully through the blackout, flares of light beaming down at their feet from handheld torches. The buses and cabs still darted around the Circus, hardly slowing down, following the narrow shafts of light from their hooded headlights. The men decided to find Rainbow Corner.

Located on the corner of Shaftesbury Avenue just off Piccadilly Circus and operated by the American Red Cross, Rainbow Corner was legendary among GIs. While the pubs closed their doors at ten, Rainbow Corner was open twenty-four hours a day. It had recreation rooms with pool tables, pinball machines, juke boxes. Its two gigantic dining rooms could seat two thousand men, and a meal set you back just twenty-five cents. A snack bar in the basement, set up like a sandwich shop back home, dished out thousands of hamburgers, waffles, doughnuts, and bottle after bottle of Coke. Entertainers, from Danny Kaye and Betty Grable to local London hopefuls, performed there, and dances were held five times a week. The staff organized sightseeing tours of the city, obtained theater tickets, rented out bicycles, and even mended shirts and sewed on stripes. GIs could get a bed, take a shower, get a hair cut, or sleep one off there. Just beside the first-aid room was the Where Am I Room, offering succor to those who discovered after a night at the pubs and the after-hours clubs that beer and scotch and gin were a more potent blend than they had thought. In the lobby across from the reception desk a sign offered directions, one arrow pointing toward Leicester Square, only a few feet away, another pointing toward New York, 3,271 miles to the west, and another, less popular, toward Berlin, 600 miles.

Outside Rainbow Corner they dispersed. Jerry and Howard walked toward Leicester Square. They would stop by again at the Eagle Club for Tom, then proceed to the dance hall. A cool drizzle was falling as they stumbled along in the blackout, but the night around them was alive. In doorway after doorway couples clung together in the darkness, pressed against the walls. In one entryway, no more than three feet from them, they spied a faint shadow of a figure crouched on her knees, her head buried in the crotch of a soldier. The man wore an Australian bush hat, and his pants were at his ankles.

" 'owbout it, luv?" A voice cooed from nearby as they passed. A pencil point of orange flame glowed in a darkened alcove, and when they paused, a torch flickered down to reveal a parted overcoat and a startlingly short skirt. Two fine legs. High heels. Howard and Jerry were startled. Neither spoke.

"How much?" Jerry stammered at last.

"Two quid, ducks," the voice said.

"Two pounds!" Jerry said with mock indignation. "We came to save your ass, honey, not to buy it."

"For the both of you, dearie," she explained patiently.

"No thanks," Howard laughed, "we're just window-shopping."

They were everywhere, the Commandos, wandering the dark streets, waiting in the doorways, hovering by the entrance to the Underground, plying their trade. Howard and Jerry ran the gauntlet happily.

They made their way again to the Eagle Club, dodging the squads of sodden soldiers shouting and singing in Polish and French and Texan, but Tom still had not checked in. They wandered back onto the street and located the Underground station at Leicester Square. They checked the giant diagram of the subway system, discovered that Covent Garden was only one stop away, and bought tickets. Plunging through the stiles, they glided down bank after bank of wooden escalators so long and steep they seemed like ski jumps. Through a maze of brightly lit tile corridors they followed the signs for the Piccadilly line, stepping carefully around the people who had bedded down there for the night. Families of two and three, small children and elderly women, homeless victims of the V-1s and V-2s, slept on rolls of blankets or pallets, their meager belongings spread among them. They did not look up as Howard and Jerry passed.

The dance hall at Covent Garden was filled with fox-trotting couples moving, as if in formation, counterclockwise around the crowded floor. Neither Jerry nor Howard had seen anything like it. Men in uniform danced with women in uniform, RAF blue, American olive drab, Canadians, Australians, Free French, British Land Army girls, WAAFs, Waves, Wrens, civilians, the works. The orchestra, a British imitation of Glenn Miller with a little Tommy Dorsey thrown in, was pretty good, and eventually they danced. An American Red Cross girl from Indianapolis asked Howard—it was the custom here, she explained, and she had gone native. Jerry got a chance to demonstrate his version of the Lindy Hop with a Land Army girl from Portsmouth. "It's just wizard!" she exclaimed, watching in helpless admiration as Jerry gyrated around the floor. They danced, they chatted, they watched.

It was late when they left Covent Garden, exchanging addresses and taking telephone numbers from partners they knew they would never see again. Jerry was intent on having a drink at the Savoy, and after another quick and fruitless stop at the Eagle Club they made their way there. Neither Jerry nor Howard were drinkers—their near abstemiousness was a source of endless kidding on the crew—but they had to see the Savoy, Jerry insisted. It was, Jerry explained, one of the most elegant hotels in London. Once inside the posh lobby Howard was not so sure that this was the sort of place for two GIs on a thirty-six-hour pass. But Jerry was undeterred, brushing airily past the doorman and striding into the restaurant-bar as if he were an old regular just back from a stint in the colonies. Awestruck, Howard followed him. Jerry knew how everything worked, Howard thought in amazement—the cabs, the trains, the Underground, the money, the hotels—he knew them like he knew the airplane. He knew every nut and bolt, every cable and wire, how they functioned and how to fix them. He was never at a loss, whether tethered to a rubber oxygen mask twenty thousand feet over Frankfurt or with a glass of sherry perched in front of him at the mahogany bar at the Savoy. "Your health," Jerry smiled, raising the delicate glass to his lips. Howard took a sip, wishing he had a Coke.

Jack and Harry were hungover, and the kippers and powdered eggs and weak coffee at breakfast didn't help. The long hot baths they had taken had started the morning right, but they had had a big night and now they were paying the price. Al had not returned with them last night. He had found his brother and gone off with him, arranging to meet the crew at Madame Tussaud's between one and two. At ten o'clock sharp, shaved, bathed, and spruced up in their class As, the boys were assembled in the lobby when the cabbie from the day before arrived at the hotel to take them on the sightseeing tour Jerry had arranged. He had done this many times, he explained, taken a cab full of Yanks around the city, and he had his routine down pat. They began by skirting Trafalgar Square, with Lord Nelson perched high above the giant bronze lions at the column's base. "They roar every time a virgin passes," he told them wryly. Past Whitehall they drove along the Mall, with its row of colonnaded Georgian houses, past St. James's Park, where, in the heart of London, sheep grazed lazily in the fluorescent green grass. They whisked by Buckingham Palace—the king was in, but not expecting them, the cabbie said—and so they passed on to Westminster, to Big Ben and Parliament. At Parliament Square they scrambled out to wander through the hushed vastness of Westminster Abbey, gaping at the statues, the chapels, the cloisters. They drove along the Thames toward Tower Bridge, watching through a fine chalky mist as barges plowed sluggishly through the gray choppy water and barrage balloons bobbed in the stiff breeze overhead. At the Tower of London they climbed out, and wandered around the grounds until lunchtime. They ate at a pub close by, Jack finding in his two pints of bitter the hair of the dog that bit him, and then, fortified with their shepherd's pie, they made their way to the Underground that would take them to Baker Street and Madame Tussaud's exhibition.

Al and his brother were waiting for them at the wax museum. It was a favorite haunt of GIs in London, a "don't miss," and after waiting in the inevitable line, they filed in to stare at Henry VIII with his six wives, the death of Nelson, and the royal group—the king, queen, queen mother, and assorted dukes and duchesses, only slightly less animated than normal, clustered in dignified splendor around the throne. Jack saluted General Eisenhower, and, as Jerry said later, "was so hungover he thought Ike saluted back."

Then it was time to go. Jerry carried the train schedule, and they had just time to get a bite to eat and then grab a cab for Liverpool Street. It was hard to believe. Their thirty-six hours had flashed past them like a dream. Just beyond Marble Arch, while Jerry and Jack settled into a wedge-shaped tea shop, Al and his brother ducked into a little studio specializing in postcard photographs, developed on the spot, that they could send home to Brooklyn. Al pulled Harry and Howard into the studio, and the four of them pressed together in the brilliant white light for a group photo. The picture came out well, Howard thought, slipping his postcard, stamped November 28, 1944, into his musette bag. Looking at Al and his brother, he wished that Tom had made it, that he could have been in the picture. They would have loved it at home. Outside, Jack, a greasy newspaper cone of fish and chips in his hand, stood at the curb, motioning anxiously to them. Jerry had flagged down a cab. It idled noisily in the drizzle, waiting to carry them back to the station, back to the war.

The trip to London did not soothe Harry's nerves. On pass he tagged along in the cab, ate quietly in the snack bar at Rainbow Corner, never said much, never stepped out of line. A shadow. But the tension was still there, the mouth still drawn in a tight, colorless line, the eyes still pale and anguished.

After sulking for weeks, snapping at everybody who came near him, he had seemed to calm down a bit after the Saarbrücken mission. Maybe he was going to be okay. Then, without warning, he took a swipe at Al, slapped him sharply on the side of the head, a compact pop with his open hand that left Al's ears ringing. They were alone in the hut. Al had been talking about the turrets—"matter-of-fact, like," he said later—about how once you wiggled into them, you couldn't really wear a chute, and with your legs wedged into place you could never get untangled to get out. He worried about it every time he climbed into the plane. He was searching through his duffel bag as he spoke, muttering as much to himself as to Harry, and he did not see it coming. Suddenly Harry began to scream, long, bellowing shrieks, swearing at Al. Leaping over the bunk like a wild man, Harry pounced on him, his eyes glaring, and struck. In midswing a flash of indecision seemed to grip him, and the blow came up short, something between a slap and punch. Al rocked back on his heels, stunned. Instinctively, he had taken a step toward Harry, but something in the man's eyes, a savage, frightened look that hinted that worse was waiting to happen, made him back off.

The others were furious when Al told them about it, fed up and exhausted by Harry's sulking and fits of rage. Jerry and Howard agreed to do something about it, and they confronted Harry, cornering him after gunnery practice in the drafty hangar. It was a cold blustery afternoon, bright and dry, and while the mock turrets whined and twin fifties rattled behind them at the firing butts, they pleaded with him, cajoled him, and finally threatened him. If he didn't shape up, they would have to go to Farrington. Nobody wanted that, but Harry had to pull himself together or get help. They wanted him on the crew, they needed him, but he had to get a grip on things. He listened impatiently, alternately ignoring them and glaring at them. No dice. He wasn't having any of it. That same night Jerry and Howard went to see their pilot. Farrington listened. He had seen the problem with Harry building with each mission but had hoped that Harry would pull himself together. Farrington didn't want to ground him or remove him from the crew, not yet, but he agreed to talk to Harry and to consult the flight surgeon.

Cases of nerves were not uncommon, Doc Hoff told Farrington at the station hospital after breakfast the next morning. It could happen to anyone. The doc had been the group's flight surgeon since it arrived in the ETO, and he had seen it all—the bouts of depression, combat fatigue verging on catatonia, self-destructive behavior that endangered a man and his crew. He knew better than anyone on the base the debilitating effects of constant strain, the long hours on oxygen at altitude, the flak, the fear. He read the psychological studies of combat personnel the Eighth's high command sent to him, and he knew the dominant patterns of stress in a tour of duty. He understood the pressures of this bizarre form of war, facing flak over Berlin in the morning, eating at Simpson's in London that night.

Harry's was not an unusual story, he told them. The first five missions were typically the worst in a combat tour, when men saw flak and fighters and the tight formations for the first time, when they came to understand the brutal fragility of their existence. Some became mouse quiet, withdrawn, stumbling through their anxiety in a daze. Others became boisterous, aggressive. They drank too much, got into fights—just another form of denial. These first five missions were almost as bad as the last five or so, the Doc sighed, exhaling the deep blue smoke of his Chesterfield into the medicine-sweet air of the sick bay, when guys had watched too many planes cartwheeling out of the sky or disintegrating in a shower of flame over the target and started the countdown to the end of their tour. In between most fellows settled down. They concentrated on the details of their jobs, hunkering down into the routine, and realized that they could cope with the stress and survive.

Maybe Harry would be okay, Farrington said hopefully. Maybe their pass to London would snap him out of it. He was still doing his job. Harry might settle down yet. He might. Howard hoped so, but he was not so sure.

"A time bomb," Jerry said to Howard as they watched Harry in London, "just waiting to go off." When the crew reassembled after the pass, Farrington took Harry aside and spoke to him. Harry went to see Doc Hoff, and Farrington was encouraged. But Jerry was right.

"No takers?" Jack called out. "Come on, you guys! Let's go! We can make it to The Dog in twenty minutes. Al, you can ride on the handlebars. Gonna have some smooth Irish whiskey tonight, they tell me." He had spent the afternoon at the Shamrock and he was feeling no pain. Nobody was listening. Exhaustion hung in the room like a bad odor. They had been awakened at 0200 and briefed for a target in southwest Germany. They had trucked out to the hardstand, preflighted the plane, and assumed positions for takeoff, when a red flare from flight control signaled that the mission was scrubbed. Everybody hated to see a mission scrubbed—all the anxiety of waking in the frigid darkness, the tension of briefing, and then gearing up mentally for the mission—all for nothing. Although they were not alerted for tomorrow, everybody in the hut was on edge. Everybody but Jack.

"Well, if you fellas are just gonna hang around here, I'm going." He zipped up his jacket. "Last chance."

He waved. "Adios, amigos." As Jack weaved uncertainly toward the door, his foot caught on the bed frame. He wheeled dizzily, lurched to his right, and stumbled headlong into Harry's bunk.

"Goddamn it," Harry barked. In a flash he was on his feet. Wheeling around quick as a cobra, his small white hands curled into fists, he blocked the door and beckoned threateningly.

"Watch where you're goin', you clumsy sonofabitch," he bellowed.

Jack rose sloppily from the bunk. He squinted down at the disheveled blankets and the biscuits, strewn now on the floor. With comic difficulty he brought them into focus, and smiled peacefully. "Hey, where'd that bunk come from?" he laughed. "Tie that thing down, wouldja!"

"I said watch where you're goin', you dumb prick!"

"Quiet, children," Jerry muttered, not looking up from his book. He was propped up in his bunk smoking his pipe.

"This ain't the fuckin' New York Public Library, Barrett," Harry hissed. Startled, Jerry looked up for the first time and turned his head toward Harry. Standing in the doorway of the hut, Harry was quaking with rage. The pallor of his face, so stark it seemed to have been dipped in chalk, loomed grotesquely in the grainy yellow light like an African war mask. His fists were cocked.

"Hey, take it easy, Harry," Howard said, rising cautiously from his bunk.

Not very steady on his feet, Jack tried to edge his way around Harry, making for the door. Harry spun quickly and swung. The short right jab grazed Jack's cheek, but the left that followed it like a tracer caught the bigger man squarely in the gut. The force of the blow sent Jack sprawling back over the bed, crashing onto the floor. Letters, photos, sheets of newspaper flew in a shower from the clothes rack, and an explosion of dust rose in the pool of yellow light between the bunks.

Howard took a step forward.

"Stay outta this, Goodner," Harry snarled.

"Easy does it," Howard said smoothly. He was no match for Harry, and he knew it.

Dead sober now, Jack climbed uncertainly back to his feet. Keeping his eyes on Harry, Jerry eased out of his bunk and stood beside Howard. Harry glared at them menacingly.

"You wanna be next?" he shouted at Jerry. Barrett did not move. "What about you, Goodner? You want some?"

"Calm down, for Chrissakes," Al muttered. "Everybody just calm down."

No one moved.

Keeping one fist cocked, Harry bent over his bunk and fumbled for his jacket. His hand was trembling. Glowering at them, he backed slowly toward the door, pushed the blackout curtain aside, and was gone.

For a moment they stood in stunned silence.

"Good God," Jerry exhaled at last. "What was that all about?"

"You all right, Jack?" Howard asked. Brennan slumped down on his bunk. "Swell," Jack answered. "Just swell." He was pale, and beads of sweat had broken out on his forehead.

That was it for Harry, the final straw. Later that night, when he returned to the hut, they were waiting for him.

The next morning Jerry and Howard cornered Farrington outside squadron headquarters. The sun was shining weakly and the group had gone out before dawn to hit a railroad yard in Germany. The crew was scheduled to do some work with a mobile training unit that traveled from base to base. Farrington was shocked by what they told him.

"What happened when he came back?"

"The fellows jumped him outside the hut," Howard said without hesitation, "dragged him down into the air-raid shelter, and tried to shake a little sense into him."

"Sweet Jesus," Farrington exclaimed.

"The boys have had it with Harry," Jerry said evenly. "They can't live with him, and they won't fly with him."

"Was he hurt?"

"No," Howard said, "but he's not in a very good mood today."

Farrington did not say another word. He turned and walked briskly back into the squadron dayroom. When the crew returned from their training exercises with the mobile trainer, Harry's bunk was empty, the biscuits were neatly stacked, and the blankets had disappeared. Harry's clothes, his oxygen mask, everything had been removed from the rack. He was gone. The flight surgeon, they learned later, would examine him, make an evaluation. Maybe Harry only needed a rest, a reprieve from combat. Maybe he would fly again, but it would not be with the Richard Farrington crew. The trouble with Harry was over.

With Harry off the crew, the tension eased. The crew settled in again to the routine at the base, went to ground classes, and waited for their next mission. On AFN Christmas songs heralded the arrival of the holiday season, and *Stars and Stripes* began a series on how to order presents for loved ones in the States. The station *Bulletin* announced plans for GIs to spend Christmas with British families, and group Special Services promised a host of festivities to mark the season. "Christmas time is coming near," Bob wrote on December 6. "This will be number three away from home. Seems to me we have been separated more than any couple should be. We will really appreciate each other when we can be in each other's arms every day. . . . Sure no fun to sleep in an army cot and reach for you . . . and find cold space. It will be heaven to have you by my side and be near you when I say goodnight. . . . Next Christmas will surely be ours together."

To Bobby, who at six could hardly remember a Christmas at home with his dad, Bob wrote, "They keep me busy flying over Germany. I sure hope the war ends soon. It would be more fun home playing with you, Arthur, and Mom than flying in a bomber. I hope you have a nice Christmas. Hope Santa Claus brings you a lot of nice presents and Arthur some, too. You sure look swell in your new suit. Bet you are the best-dressed boy on the block. Good-bye for tonight, Son. Be a good boy and take care of Mom and Arthur."

During the lull in flying Bob and the other enlisted men moved into a new barracks. It was not far, just down the lane in the WAAF site. Since arriving at the station in October they had shared the drafty Nissen hut with the six enlisted men of another crew. Now they moved into a much larger barracks housing the enlisted personnel from four crews, twenty-four men in all. The new barracks was crowded, with even less privacy than before, prompting Bob when he first saw it to comment wryly, "I don't think I'll have any trouble becoming a civilian again. I'll really appreciate the status." On the other hand, it did have its advantages. "Our new barracks is concrete entirely and much warmer than the former," Bob wrote to Marie when they settled into their new quarters. "It's very comfy here—inside—always damp outside."

The damp, of course, was no surprise, but as December arrived, the air turned startlingly cold and great mountains of lead-gray clouds drifted ponderously across the bitter sky like ice floes. Frost formed on the wings of the planes at their hardstands, and blades of rime sliced through the clouds like a scythe. The group flew missions on December 2 and 5, battling bad weather on both trips, and on the sixth, the Second Air Division made another fruitless attempt to hit the viaduct at Bielefeld. On the seventh, the Farrington crew was awakened and briefed for a target in Germany, but the mission was scrubbed due to a lingering weather front over the primary.

It was Pearl Harbor Day, and back in the barracks, trying to coax more heat out of their one lone stove, the boys reminisced about where they were on that unforgettable day three years before. Howard remembered the Friday night before that fateful Sunday, when the high school football banquet was held in the Cherokee Hotel. Seven stories of brick and ornate limestone trim, the hotel was by far the largest building in town, dwarfing the picture show next door, the bus depot across the street, and even the cupola of the red brick courthouse. It was the pinnacle of small-town elegance, the site of every special occasion, every local gala for the Lions' and Elks' clubs, the Rotary, and the high school. Its restaurant and meeting rooms hosted reunions and wedding receptions and political fund-raisers. A smile flickered across his face. How sophisticated they felt that night, dressed to the teeth and bounding up the steps under the elegant green awning to the brightly lit lobby. How secure they were in their comfortable cocoon of innocence on that December Friday night a thousand years ago. People were dying by the hundreds of thousands from Manchuria to Shanghai, by the millions across the plains of Russia, but for Howard and Nancy and their friends the autumn of 1941 meant only that the team had gone undefeated, whipping even the big schools from nearby Chattanooga.

It was a wonderful night, carefree and enchanted. His teammates, buddies he grew up with, were lighthearted and proud, dancing with their dates on top of the volcano. Nancy went with Howard to the banquet, a corsage he had bought at Schugart's Florist clinging to the breast of her stiff formal dress. Later they rode in Buddy McLeod's '37 Ford out to Curley's Bar-B-Q for a black-and-white malted, and the world was sweet and full of promise. He thought of those boys now, scattered across a world convulsed by a war that had seemed so impossibly remote on that night. Buddy was in the Air Corps, maybe on his way to the Eighth, Ralph Chancey and Jack Manis were in the army, and Nancy was at home, working, waiting.

The Farrington crew flew their sixth mission on December 10, bombing the marshaling yards at Bingen on the Rhine. It was an uneventful trip, with little flak and no fighters. They did not see the target, bombing by radar through a 10/10 cloud cover, but HQ judged the results to be good. It was the crew's first combat mission in almost two weeks, their first without Harry, and they felt confident, relieved that the waiting was over. Battle damage had been light for several weeks, and the group had sustained only one combat casualty in a month—a tail gunner who died of anoxia when his oxygen system malfunctioned. Although the Allied drive toward Germany had slowed, everybody remained optimistic. It was only a matter of time. "Everybody here is working hard as usual," Howard wrote, "and, Dad, things look good over here. . . . We're hoping they stay that way." They didn't.

Two days later the crew was alerted for a mission, but the dawn broke raw and wet as a new bad weather front swept across Britain and settled over the continent. Temperatures plunged and heavy snow fell over northwestern Europe. Throughout eastern England the rain and fog turned to sleet, encasing the planes, the huts, the wires, the trees in a crystalline coating of ice. Outside the barracks the world looked as if it were made of glass. Britain's coldest winter of the century was settling in, and the entire Eighth Air Force stood down. The headlines in *Stars and Stripes* that morning, December 16, brought good news—Patton Smashes into Germany—and that evening when the men gathered in the Aero Club to listen to the Glenn Miller Sextet on AFN, the world news program reported briefly that units of the American First Army had engaged German units south of Aachen. The road to Berlin, as AFN liked to call it, was opening. The war was entering its final phase.

It was not until the eighteenth, after three days of dense, swirling fog had grounded the Allies, that dispatches from the front at last made clear that the Germans had launched some sort of counterattack against American positions in Belgium. On the nineteenth, U.S. radio correspondents were reporting heavy fighting along the Belgian frontier, and later in the day

Allied Supreme Command imposed a blackout on battle-line reports of operations along the length of the First Army's front. The next morning *Stars and Stripes* revealed that German units had driven twenty miles into Belgium. Although news remained sketchy, the scale of the German operation gradually became apparent. On the morning of December 16, ten German Panzer divisions had poured out of the Reich into the the thick hilly woods of eastern Belgium, slicing through the weak and disorganized American resistance in the Ardennes forest. Protected by a vast cover of dense fog and low clouds that lingered for a week, the Germans pressed relentlessly forward, hoping to split the Allied front and drive to the crucial port at Antwerp. While the fierce German offensive hammered out a salient in the overextended American front, all over England the bombers sat motionless on their hardstands.

Like virtually every group the 466th stood down for day after agonizing day, and in the barracks and mess halls and hangars of the fogbound base the men helplessly followed the German advance. They listened to the grim news dispatches, the intelligence briefings, and the usual rumors, but they did not need S-2 to tell them that as the bulge in the American lines deepened, the war whose end had seemed so near would now grind on and on and on. Three times the crews were alerted and briefed, only to have the mission scrubbed during preflight. On December 19 Farrington and the crew were awakened at 0200 and briefed for a mission against a railroad junction just behind enemy lines. The trucks carrying them to the hardstands edged their way tentatively around the perimeter track through fog so thick and billowing it seemed alive. The crews were at their stations before 0700 and waited first in their planes and then in the tents beside the revetments until 1100, when the mission was at last scrubbed. Twice more, on the sixteenth and eighteenth, the planes had actually taken off on instruments, climbing through ice-laden clouds as thick as cream, only to be recalled before reaching the target. With each alert and scrubbed mission morale tumbled and tension on the base mounted. "Another night," Bob wrote to Marie, "and anxiously or nervously awaiting the dawn. Who knows, maybe I will see the continent again."

On Christmas Eve the cold morning sky trembled with the thunderous roar of engines. Howard heard them on the runways just after dawn, as he crawled deeper into his blankets, trying to ward off the cold. The CQ had come through the barracks hours before, waking two crews scheduled to fly. He had heard them fumbling in the darkness with their clothes, then he had drifted back into something like sleep. The barracks stove had burned out during the night, and it was bitterly cold. Sitting on the edge of his bunk, his teeth chattering, he could see his breath materialize before him, tiny puffs of steam heaved into the darkness. Pushing aside the blackout curtain behind his bed, Howard peered out at a bright, sunlit morning. He had slept in his clothes, as he had for days now, and he slipped on his boots and jacket and stepped outside. All around him bright sequins of frost drifted through the clear, calm air, glittering in the cold sunlight.

Squinting against the harsh glare, Howard looked up. High above him the sun shimmered off formation after formation of silver planes droning eastward toward the continent. He started counting but quickly gave up. An intricate layered chain of glinting aircraft stretched from horizon to horizon like an ancient suit of mail wound loosely around the sun. Later he would learn that it was the largest single raid of the war, with over two thousand bombers hitting targets close to German lines.

After breakfast the crew reported to squadron ops, where the duty officer informed them that their forty-eight-hour pass had been canceled. They had been planning a trip to London, had talked about it for days during the stand-down, but nobody was surprised at the news. All flying personnel, the officer explained, were restricted to the base. They wouldn't be seeing London again for the holidays, as they had hoped, but as they scanned the alert list for tomorrow's mission their mood improved. The Farrington crew would not be flying on Christmas Day.

In the afternoon they dropped by the Opera House to see Don Ameche in *Wing and a Prayer*. Nobody liked the song—too cornball—but the movie wasn't bad, and anyway, it was warmer than the barracks. After the movie they stopped in at the Aero Club, where one hundred children from the area had arrived in trucks, invited for a special Christmas party. The guys stopped just long enough to warm up, but Bob lingered on. Leaning against the wall, his arms crossed placidly on his chest, he drank in the scene, mesmerized by the soft, sweet sound of the children's voices, the colored paper, the small, scrawny Christmas tree. He watched them closely, the little boys Bobby's age, their scrubbed creamy faces beaming above the neat bow ties and heavy woolen sweaters. They gobbled up their turkey and dessert and drank their Cokes. They chewed stick after stick of gum. They laughed and shouted and between the games and songs they greeted the arrival of Father Christmas, who was remarkable, they must have felt, for his pronounced Alabama accent. "I don't know what to say as to telling

Bobby about Santa," Bob wrote later, musing on the scene. "I think I was seven or eight. Use your own ideas on the subject." He thought again of the children's faces. "Believe I would wait till after next Christmas so I can enjoy one day with the boys before they grow up."

That evening the barracks emptied quickly. Al and Jack went along with Bill Deal, a veteran gunner from Philadelphia who occupied the bunk next to Jack's in the new barracks. Jack's uncle lived in Philly and ran a saloon at Sixteenth and Susquehanna, and the two boys, both big, easygoing, and Irish, had hit it off right away. Deal was the top turret gunner on the Bob Moore crew, a lead crew in the 784th Squadron, and since neither was scheduled to fly the next day they decided to celebrate the yuletide in fine Irish style. They would stop by the Shamrock Tavern for a pint or two or three and maybe slip off the base for a touch of something at a nearby pub Deal knew. They would try to make it back for midnight mass. Bob decided to go along, and, bundled against the cold, they headed out just after chow.

Howard and Jerry passed on the Shamrock and for a while lounged around in the hut, writing letters, talking, stoking the fire. Jerry had found a steady supply of bomb rings, heavy, wax-impregnated cardboard collars placed around bombs for shipment, and when they went into the little pot-bellied stove they sent out a brief burst of warmth that took away the chill for several precious minutes.

"Guess who I ran into this afternoon at the mess hall," Jerry said, as Howard sat on the edge of the bunk trying to warm his hands.

"Santa Claus?"

"Not hardly," Jerry said. "He's been grounded for the duration." Using a short metal rod salvaged from one of the tech sites as a poker, he prodded the sizzling lump of wax and paper and coke. "I saw Harry."

"Harry Gregorian?"

"The one and only," Jerry nodded. "Ran into him leaving the mail room."

"Did you talk to him?"

"No. He wasn't much interested in a chat—especially with me—but I heard from a guy at squadron ops that Harry's back on combat status."

"He's flying again?"

"Yes, but not with a regular crew. He's a spare—flies whenever a crew is short a gunner."

"Well, what d'ya know," Howard said, shaking his head. They all had heard that Harry had been grounded since late November. He had been medically evaluated, given the usual psychiatric tests. If the doc determined he was unfit to fly or if he refused a board would be convened and he could be reclassified or even sent home in disgrace. Howard tried to picture their nose gunner—in his combat gear, in his boxing gloves, in his A-1s ready for the Liberty Run—but the image was a curious blur. They had flown together for months, but now he was off the crew, out of the hut, out of their lives. Replacement gunners, a different man every time, had flown with the crew in the nose turret since Harry left. He already seemed like ancient history, and their world, Howard thought with an odd sense of detachment, had shrunk down to this, to the crew, to the men immediately around them, and to the dream world of home, nothing more.

Later in the evening Howard decided to join a couple of guys from the barracks who were heading back to the Aero Club to hear the group's glee club sing Christmas carols. Glancing down at his watch at a little after nine, he thought the folks at home were probably converging on the house on Trunk Street. Maybe they were already clustered around the radio in the parlor listening to the war news, waiting for the Jack Benny program. In October his father had decided to leave his job at the TVA to work for a new, high-security government project in Oak Ridge, and his folks had taken an apartment in nearby Knoxville. They would be coming down, and Mildred would already be there taking care of the house. His sister Sibyle and her husband, Charles, would be driving across the mountains from middle Tennessee, bringing their daughter, Elizabeth Ann, and James would be home from the university. He wondered what Nancy was doing on this Christmas Eve. She would probably stop by to say hello, exchange a few small gifts and news about him. He thought, not for the first time on this day, that he had not been home for Christmas in two years, and the old familiar songs, even the jingling, cheerful ones, left him wistful and quiet. He turned in earlier than he had planned.

On Christmas morning the sun rose over a cloudless horizon and a thick layer of frost covered the barracks, the trees, the hedges, the wires, everything. "Hey, you guys, take a look at this," Al shouted from the doorway, "We've got a white Christmas." They had slept late, buried under their blankets, and they piled out of bed to have a look. The wind was biting cold, and, as Bob wrote later, "the frost . . . so heavy that it [was] nearly like snow." They dressed slowly, layering up against the frigid wind on what would be the coldest English Christmas in one hundred years.

"Hey," Jack called out as he pulled on his jacket, "where is Deal? Is he already at the mess hall?" He looked around. There were several empty bunks.

"Hey, where is everybody?" Jack asked.

"Didn't you hear them last night?" Jerry said. "The CQ came in around one and rousted them out. The Moore crew flew today, flew lead with another group in the wing, I think I heard the CQ say."

Jack shook his head in sympathy. "Those poor bastards," he sighed. "They must have just hit the sack."

Howard nodded. During the night he had heard the door of the barracks snap open, heard the frozen grit of the CQ's boots grinding against the concrete floor, and through a haze of slumber he had seen the men struggling groggily into their clothes, shivering in the bitter cold darkness, while the beam of the CQ's flashlight swept across the ceiling like a searchlight. "But we're not alerted," one of them grumbled. "We're not supposed to fly today," the voice muttered over and over again. "There's gotta be some mistake." Outside a truck idled. "No mistake, Sergeant. Let's go, we gotta step on it." Howard had felt a ripple of cold as the door opened and the men, shadowy figures gliding past in the darkness, filed out. He had drifted back to sleep. It might have been a dream.

"Twenty-three friggin' degrees Fahrenheit," a cook at the combat mess complained when Howard and the crew stumbled in out of the blinding white for breakfast. The large Nissen hut was full and festive. They ate heartily on this day: fried eggs, bacon, bread, butter, jelly, and orange juice, and a special dinner, served from 2:00 to 4:30, consisting of turkey, potatoes, corn, asparagus, tomato juice, apple and pumpkin pies, cheese, apples, and hard candy. An amazing feast. Someone even said that lemons had been passed out to the early birds, but nobody could confirm the rumor.

In between they stopped by the Aero Club to listen to records and the AFN news. There was a special Christmas broadcast, a program with Bob Hope and his troop of regulars—Frances Langford and Jerry Colonna and Joe E. Brown—clowning and singing from somewhere in the South Pacific. Guy Lombardo's orchestra played from a ballroom in New York, and through the whine of Atlantic static Bing sang "I'll Be Home for Christmas." The war news remained grim. The German offensive had driven almost fifty miles into Belgium, and the American First Army was taking a beating. The Eighth was at least flying again, and the group's crews, back from the day's raid, reported that the mission had gone well. The giant high pressure system—a Russian high, the weather boys called it—was holding over all of northern Europe, and it looked like good flying weather for tomorrow.

It was evening when the crew arrived back at the WAAF site. A stop at the squadron had confirmed that they were not alerted for the next day's mission, and everyone was feeling cheerful. All in all it had been a good day. They jumped down over the tailgate of the frigid truck and swung open the barracks door.

"Hey, pop, think you can spare some of those raisins you're hoarding?" Jack prodded Bob as they pushed away the blackout curtain and stamped the wet frost from their feet. A package with nuts, raisins, gum, and assorted candies had arrived the day before from Bob's folks in Illinois. Most of the guys in the barracks had received packages from home, and crumbling pieces of stale cake and cookies as brittle as phonograph records had passed from bunk to bunk for days.

"Jack, are you *always* hungry?" Jerry asked.

"Come on, pop," Jack said, "Where's the old holiday spirit?"

"Merry Christmas, Jackie boy," Bob said, tossing a small red box toward Jack.

Jack did not try to catch it. It bounced off his chest, falling to the floor. He stood motionless beside his bunk, staring.

"What's the matter?" Howard frowned, stepping around the bunk bed toward Jack. Then he saw. Five bunks had been stripped, the biscuits folded neatly on top of the metal frames. The shelves behind them had been swept clean, the clothes packed, the pictures removed. Nothing remained of Bill Deal, Harry Tootell, Arthur Parks, Mel Robinson, and Jim Brenner. The Bob Moore crew had bought the farm.

CHAPTER VI

LUCK IS A LADY

The coin, a worn English penny, floated into the air. As it fluttered lazily toward the ceiling the smooth copper caught the light from the desk lamp, and the three men watched it fall.

Farrington knew something was up when the major asked him to report to squadron headquarters that afternoon after chow. It was a frosty day, like every day since mid-December. The crew had flown two missions in the week after Christmas and two more in the first frigid days of the new year. The missions had been in support of the American counteroffensive in the Ardennes, which was now going well. They had hit railroad junctions in southwestern Germany, trying to cut off supplies and reinforcements to the Wehrmacht in Belgium. At least that's what they had said at briefing. Enemy opposition had been meager, but on each mission the temperature at altitude had plunged to fifty below zero and the wind had sliced through the ship like a razor. Shortly after takeoff on the twenty-eighth, division had radioed all ships in the formation to exercise their bomb doors to keep them from freezing over the Channel. They had flown in the *Hard Luck*—Al's plane, Barrett had quipped—and at twenty-two thousand feet crystal beads of ice had bubbled like blisters on the Plexiglas turrets. The sky on these missions had been a canvas of clear cold chrome, and wisps of bone white clouds had swirled across the snow-carpeted terrain far below them.

Farrington had spent the morning in the Link trainer, practicing instrument flying in the bone-numbing cold of the hangar. Just a couple of days ago seven inches of snow had fallen in East Anglia, and four hundred men had been rousted out of their huts to clear the runways at AS 120. It seemed to snow every night, sleet in the morning, and then thaw in the afternoon, turning the base into a vast quagmire of mud. Trudging through the slush up the barren knoll to the 787th HQ, Farrington rehearsed what he would say. He knew what this meeting was about, he thought, and he had his objections.

The squadron headquarters was crowded as usual, but the orderly signaled him directly into the CO's office. The major greeted him heartily, motioning him toward a chair. Seated at the other edge of the major's desk was Earl Beitler, another pilot from the squadron. A thickset man from California, Beitler sported a dapper mustache. He nodded at Farrington. They knew each other well. Their crews had arrived at the 466th at the same time and been assigned to the 787th on the same day, and their officers lived in the same barracks. They had flown the same number of missions, and both crews had earned a good reputation around the squadron, attracting the attention of both the group and the squadron commanders. The major wasted no time getting to the point. "I have to make a recommendation to transfer a crew to the 784th for training as a lead crew." In July the 784th had been transformed into the group's elite squadron, made up exclusively of lead crews. Commanders of the group's other three squadrons made the recommendations, selecting their most promising crew after it had completed ten missions or so. "You've both compiled excellent records," the major continued. "You've both got top-notch crews. It's got to be one of you."

Beitler and Farrington glanced quickly at one another. This was what they had expected, but still, confronted with the situation, neither knew what to say. Neither man was eager for the job. Being a lead crew carried with it prestige and rank. The aircraft commander would be promoted quickly, and his crew could expect a faster increase in rating. Being chosen for lead was an acknowledgment that the crew had proven itself in combat, that the men, from the pilot to the tail gunner, had done their jobs well, that

The Richard Farrington Crew, March 1945. Kneeling, left to right: Bob Peterson, Jack Brennan, Jerry Barrett, Howard Goodner, Albert Seraydarian. Standing, left to right: John Murphy, Jack Perella, Jack Regan, Richard Farrington, George Noe, Christ Manners.

Howard Goodner, Westover Field, 1944.

Bill Deal of the Bob Moore Crew outside the enlisted men's hut at AS 120.

Inside the officer's hut, John Murphy sitting at center, Jack Perella standing at right.

Crews waiting for the Alert List at 787th Squadron Headquarters.

Howard (in white t-shirt) at home on pass, September 1944, with friends.

Mildred and Tom at the house on Trunk Street, August 1945.

The Petersons at home in Chicago, June 1944: Marie, Bob holding baby Arthur, and Bobby.

Louis Wieser and father, on last leave home, March 1944.

The officers of the Farrington Crew on the way to the flight line, December 1944, left to right: Mel Rossman, Neil Gobrecht, Jack Regan, Richard Farrington, and Christ Manners.

On pass in London, November 1944, standing left to right: Howard and Harry Gregorian; sitting left to right: Albert and Robert Seraydarian.

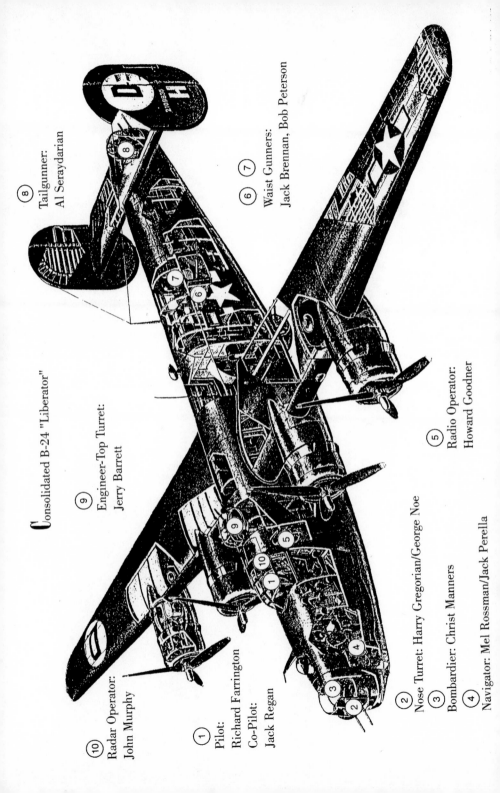

Consolidated B-24 "Liberator"

(8) Tailgunner:
Al Seraydarian

(6) (7) Waist Gunners:
Jack Brennan, Bob Peterson

(9) Engineer-Top Turret:
Jerry Barrett

(5) Radio Operator:
Howard Goodner

(2) Nose Turret: Harry Gregorian/George Noe

(3) Bombardier: Christ Manners

(4) Navigator: Mel Rossman/Jack Perella

(10) Radar Operator:
John Murphy

(1) Pilot:
Richard Farrington
Co-Pilot:
Jack Regan

The 466th over target.

The Black Cat, late 1944.

The 466th Bomb Group
en route to target, 1944.

A room filled with color.

they made an excellent team. It also carried with it a staggering responsibility. Lead pilots and copilots had to be talented, unflappable men, men
who could not only handle their own plane but maneuver an entire formation. The lead navigator and bombardier had to be sharp and dependable. If
the navigator missed a checkpoint or miscalculated speed or windage, the
entire formation would be off course. The bombardier had to be able to read
the terrain, locate the target, and put his bombs "in the pickle barrel." All
the planes in the formation would toggle their bombs on him, and if his
calculations were off the entire mission would be a failure.

All of this meant considerable pressure—and additional training. Lead
crews carried an extra man, a radar operator—the mickey man, they called
him—and a second navigator to assist with visual navigation. Coordination
among the pilot, navigator, mickey man, and bombardier was imperative in
flying lead, and the crew would have to put in hours of practice in the air
and on the ground to develop the essential teamwork. On top of that lead
crews did not fly as regularly or as often as other crews in the group. They
flew only in lead positions, and given the responsibility and the danger—
they would be first over the target and a prize target for both flak and
fighters—they might fly only every sixth mission or so. It could extend their
tour by as much as a month, maybe two, given the weather. After completing
their training they would first fly several missions as squadron lead, then
they would lead the group, the division, and, maybe, even the entire Eighth
Air Force. It was a big job.

Outside the sleet had turned to light snow, though the sun kept trying to
peek through. As they sat in front of the major's desk, the room turned light,
then dark, then light, and through the window Farrington could see the
passing shadows of the clouds glide across the gnarled shrubs and frozen
gravel. The major ground out the stub of his cigarette in the metal ashtray in
front of him and eyed the two pilots, waiting. He was not in a rush. Neither
pilot spoke.

"Well," the major said at last, "what say we flip a coin?" Since neither
pilot answered immediately, the major fished the penny out of his pocket.
The three men stood up. "Heads, it's you, Lieutenant," he said, nodding at
Farrington, "tails, you, Beitler."

Up it floated. The major caught the coin in his right hand and, without
looking, slapped it onto the back of his left. The men leaned over, staring
down at the penny. "Heads," the major said, turning to face the two pilots
standing in front of him. "Looks like you're it, Dick."

Farrington shook his head. "Yes, sir." He took a deep breath. "I'd like to talk it over with the boys," he said.

"Fine," the major said. "Report back to me tomorrow before formation."

Farrington called the crew together after chow. Howard rounded up the enlisted men, and they arrived at the combat-crew library by bicycle and truck. No one was late. Farrington laid it out for them, the pros and cons, without tipping his hand. He had seen it coming, and so had the crew. They had arrived from phase training in the States with a high rating, and with each raid Farrington's skill in handling the B-24 had become increasingly apparent to the crew as well as to the squadron commander. They had faith in his judgment and his ability, and with each mission their confidence had grown. They *did* work well together, and with Harry gone they got along. They trusted each other. They were close. Still, it was a big step, and one with profound implications for them. No one wanted a snap decision.

"It will mean an extended tour," Regan said in his calm, earnest voice. He weighed his words carefully, as he always did. "It will take us a lot longer to get our missions in, flying lead."

"Yeah, but it's thirty missions, though, instead of thirty-five," Manners put in.

"We'll have a lot of practice missions, first." Farrington reminded them. "We may stand down from combat for as long as a month."

"A month!" Al exclaimed. "The war may be over in a month."

"Don't bet on it, Brooklyn," Farrington said. "The Germans are still in Belgium."

Round and round it went until the men broke up for the night. Howard and Jerry and the other enlisted men were full of confidence and ready to do what Farrington thought best. Flying lead would make little difference to the gunners or the engineer. Their tasks would remain largely unchanged, but in the tail turret Al would have to monitor the formation, reporting who was lagging, who was too high, too low, and as radioman Howard would have much more responsibility. Throughout the mission he would maintain communication with headquarters, alert for any change in plan. He would also send coded messages on the mission's progress, reporting just after the bomb run the results of the raid. Before they broke up for the night, stamping out into the icy cold, it was clear that they would follow Farrington's lead.

The officers continued to talk it over as they trudged back to their barracks. A ghostly, ice-laden mist huddled close to the ground, swirling around their knees and obscuring the path. The movie at the Opera House had just ended, and men drifted reluctantly out into the frozen damp, swearing, as always, about the weather. Farrington was lost in thought. Several lead crewmen lived in the barracks with them—Dave Bridgers, a lanky, slow-talking pilot from Mississippi, and his copilot, Henry Hiter, a fellow Mississippian, slept just beside them, and there were mickey operators from several lead crews, too. Farrington had watched them, Bridgers and the others, awakened an hour and a half before the regular crews for the prebriefing meetings of the lead crews. He had seen the pressure and the strain etched in their faces at interrogation. He knew all the arguments for and against flying lead. They had been kicked around in the barracks by different men, confronting the choice he now faced. He had anticipated this moment for some time, and yet he was no closer to a decision than he had been earlier.

Sometime before dawn, Farrington rose. The CQ had come quietly into the hut an hour or so before and awakened the crews scheduled to fly on this dismal morning. Beside him Jack Regan was also awake.

"We aren't going to make it," Farrington muttered aloud, sitting on the side of his bunk.

"What's that?" Henry Hiter, stretched out in the bunk next to him, asked. He thought he had heard wrong.

"I don't like it," Farrington sighed, rubbing his hand across the stubble of his unshaven face. "I have a bad feeling about this."

Regan rolled over on his side, staring through the cruel half-light at Farrington. The small stove sat cold and forlorn a few feet away, and the scent of burnt coke lingered in the damp air. Like his pilot he had confidence in the crew, in himself, but nobody liked to change. They had been lucky so far, eleven missions without a scratch. They knew their jobs, performed them well. They were on a roll. And now this. "I don't know," he said. "I don't like it much either."

"What about you, Curly?"

Manners had climbed out of the sack. He had slept fully dressed. He put on his jacket as he sat down on the foot of Farrington's bunk.

"Well, I'm not crazy about it either. We can do it, I know that, but I'm not crazy about it."

Rossman joined them. A blanket was draped around his shoulders and he wore his fleece-lined flying boots. "You think we really have much choice?"

"I don't know, Mel," Farrington said, exhaling a shot of steam into the hut, but in the instant he said it, he realized he had decided. He would turn it down. He would refuse. He would tell the major. The boys would understand. They would back him.

Farrington dressed quickly and shaved. Outside the barracks he climbed aboard a truck that wound its way carefully across the base between the huts and hangars, depositing him outside the 787th HQ. It had snowed during the night, and the roads were treacherous threads of ice. He bounded up the gravel path, past the mounted dummy bomb with 787th Squadron painted on it and into the orderly room. Only a handful of men hovered near the stove, and a lone typewriter clicked erratically. The major was at his desk. He had been at the control tower when the group departed, and he had only just returned. A mug of cold coffee stood untouched on his desk.

"Good to see you, Lieutenant," he said. "Didn't think they were going to get off in this sleet. Supposed to clear by the ETA. I sure as hell hope so."

Farrington cleared his throat, ready to speak, but the major continued. "I'm glad you stopped by, Dick. Yesterday afternoon we cut orders moving Mel Rossman to a lead crew in the 784th as a pilotage navigator. You'll be getting a good man to replace him, one of the very best. You know him— Jack Perella, Beitler's navigator. He's already flown several missions as a second navigator on lead crews. Everybody seems to think he's the best navigator around." He paused to light a Chesterfield. Farrington's head was spinning. "You should be getting the schedule for lead crew training by tomorrow morning. As of 18 January you are standing down and will report for training to the 784th."

Farrington was speechless. His mouth was dry, and his eyes refused to focus. "Let Corporal Harris get you a cup of coffee, Dick," the major said, smiling. "You look like you could use one." Farrington took a step back and reflexively gave a quick salute. "And, Dick," the major said, casually returning the salute, "Congratulations."

"I knew we had a good crew and I think I told you so on my last time home," Howard wrote on January 11. "Well, to back it up we have proved it by making lead crew. Lead crew is something not every crew has the opportunity to be. You have to be darn good to make it, and we have made it. It means more work and more responsibility for me. The bad part about it is that it will take me

much longer to finish my missions. . . . But on the other hand, the good part is
that we get five missions less to do. In other words, I only do thirty missions
instead of thirty-five. So I am now [almost] half-finished."

He had listened to plenty of advice about the perils of flying lead from
Bill Deal and the other enlisted men of the Bob Moore crew, who had
miraculously returned from the dead. Howard had spent New Year's in
Norwich on pass, and when he returned to the base he was stunned to find
Bill Deal, Art Parks, and other members of the Bob Moore crew lounging
about in the hut. They had been officially listed as missing in action and
presumed dead since Christmas, when they flew lead of a squadron in the
467th. At interrogation that day other crews reported seeing their plane go
down after being jumped by a swarm of FW 190s. Some even reported seeing
chutes. But as Deal told him, Moore regained control of the ship, dodged
the fighters, and brought it down at an emergency landing strip in Belgium.
The tail gunner, Mel Robinson, was badly wounded but would recover. The
ship was in such bad shape, shot up by 20-millimeter shells and flak, that
they were stranded in Belgium for days, returning to AS 120 on New Year's
Eve to discover that all their belongings had been boxed and they were
presumed dead. "The ghosts of Christmas past," Barrett joked, but everyone was glad to see them.

The crew was sorry to lose Mel Rossman. He had been with them since the
beginning, since crew training at Westover, and they trusted his judgment
and ability. Now he was gone, transferred off the crew and out of the
barracks. But Farrington and the officers knew Jack Perella, the new
navigator, knew him personally from the barracks they shared and knew
him by reputation. Jack was a handsome twenty-year-old, and he looked
younger. Like so many of the guys on the crew he had been a star athlete,
playing football and basketball at Joliet High School and in his freshman
year in college. Around the squadron his reputation as a navigator was
exceeded only by his reputation as a fun-loving, reckless hell-raiser. In the
air he was all business, with an extraordinary mathematical aptitude and an
absolutely uncanny knack for dead-reckoning navigation. He was calm and
dependable. He knew his job. On the ground he liked to wear his pistol
strapped to his side like a cowboy, and with the trace of a mustache arching
rakishly across his lip, he was ready for a good time no matter where or
when it beckoned.

"Gotta watch this fella," Neil Gobrecht kidded Farrington when Perella was transferred. Gobrecht was Perella's copilot on the Beitler crew and, since crew training at Westover, his best friend. "He's a holy terror."

Perella smiled wickedly, his arm slung around Gobrecht's shoulder.

"Is that on the ground or in the air?" Farrington asked.

"Well, he'll get you home from anywhere," Gobrecht said. "Best navigator I ever saw. He can lead you home from Berlin or back from the pubs around here in the dead of night."

"Trained in celestial navigation," Perella smiled.

"Some of his best missions have been on bicycle," Gobrecht laughed, "after we've bent our elbows a bit."

"Dead reckoning," Perella put in.

"We'll take him up on both," Farrington promised.

Perella was excited about being a lead navigator, but he hated to leave Gobrecht and his crew. They had gone through months of crew training in the States and had completed ten missions together in the ETO. He liked the Farrington crew. He knew the officers from the barracks, where they all lived, twenty-five men in the open bay. He respected them, and he knew they were a good crew. He would fit in well. But switching crews, breaking the pattern, the routine, made him uneasy. He was not alone. In the huts and barracks on every air station in East Anglia, superstition clung to flyers like the omnipresent dampness. If things were gliding along smoothly, nobody wanted to change—change crews, change socks, change anything. Almost to a man they wore lucky hats, lucky scarves, lucky shorts. They carried St. Christopher's medals with their dog tags, rubbed rabbits' feet, pressed four-leaf clovers into their flying clothes. They followed lucky rituals—rising on the left side of the bunk on the morning of a mission, sitting in the same seat at briefing, patting the nose of the aircraft three times as they entered. Luck loomed large in their lives, and change, any change, was bad.

The boys met the other two new men assigned to the crew when they assembled in the 784th Squadron area for their initial orientation. All around them on the hardstands sat the specially equipped B-24Js that the lead crews flew. They had seen them, of course, at the base and on every mission, a large T9 painted near the tail, but they had never crawled inside one. From the outside the lead planes hardly appeared different. Yet on closer inspection they could see just behind the bomb bay a slick whitish dome, the color of a cue ball, protruding slightly from the ship's belly. "Like an ant's egg," Manners muttered. It was, they all knew, the radar. By late

1944 all lead planes in the Eighth Air Force were equipped with pathfinder equipment, radar devices designed to identify terrain features through the clouds. During the first two years of combat operations in Europe the weather, especially the omnipresent cloud cover, had frequently frustrated the American strategy of daylight precision bombing. The answer to the problem was a modified version of the radar system used by the RAF for nighttime navigation and bombing. The H2X—"mickey," the Americans liked to call it—used a retractable scanner mounted in place of the ball turret to reflect images of ground features and flash them to a receiver on the flight deck. The mickey man and his set were on the flight deck, separated from the pilot by a bulkhead on which his scope was mounted. Facing forward at a small table surrounded by navigational equipment, the mickey man spent the mission peering into the brightly lit scope. He worked closely with the navigator and bombardier, providing radar fixes on the terrain below, aiding in navigation and target identification.

The man who would operate the radar was a slender, dark-haired twenty-year-old from West Chester, Pennsylvania. Farrington and the officers all knew John Murphy. He lived in the same barracks with them. He was quiet and pleasant, an unassuming boy with the traces of recent acne still evident on his pale face. At times, sitting in front of the stove in the barracks, talking in his slow southeast Pennsylvania accent, his manner was more that of a precocious student, a member of the high school 4-H or electronics club, than of a radar operator on a four-engine bomber at war.

Murphy had flown with different lead crews, as mickey operators often did, and he was a good man with the scope. In December and January he flew with the Harken crew, which finished up its missions on January 28 with a rough raid on Dortmund. He posed for the crew picture with them beside the plane. They were all smiling, happy, relief dripping from their cold faces like sweat. But he was not finished, and when the Harken crew completed its tour, Murphy joined Farrington. It was good to have an experienced mickey man, someone from the barracks, someone they all knew, Farrington thought. During the next month of flying practice missions they came to have tremendous confidence in his ability to read the shadowy images that would lead them to their target.

At twenty-four George Noe was almost three years older than Farrington and Regan. They had seen him around the base, at squadron formations, in the Officers' Club, and Manners recognized the man with the fair, thinning hair from the bombardiers' briefings. He had enlisted in the

Michigan National Guard in 1941 and had been commissioned in the Army
Air Corps in February 1943. Trained as a bombardier, he had arrived in the
ETO in November 1944 with the Gatlin crew and had flown his combat
missions in the 787th. As the pilotage navigator Noe, and not a gunner,
would ride in the nose turret and assist both Manners and Perella by
providing visual checks on the terrain below. He was essentially a backup
navigator, another check for the lead navigator to rely on in leading the
formation to the target. As a bombardier he had trained to read terrain
features and follow the course visually, and in their first few practices, it
was clear that Noe was good at his job. He was as comfortable as it was
possible to be in the cramped nose turret, and he worked well with Manners
and Perella. Like Peterson, he wrote letters home to a wife and two small
children. They were waiting for him back in Detroit.

The remainder of January and early February passed in a frosty swirl of
ground classes and practice missions. Although the crew stood down from
combat flying, their schedule was rigorous. They were up early and out at
the flight line almost every day, taking off on practice missions after the
departure of the group for the day's raid. Under the direction of the group
operations officer they ran through the exercises and problems developed
for lead-crew training, working in particular on developing the essential
teamwork among Farrington, Perella, Manners, and Murphy.

   In addition to their usual exercises in the Link trainer, practicing
instrument flying, Farrington and Regan devoted much more intensive
work to the automatic pilot, both in the Link and in flight with the bombardier exercising control. On the bomb run Manners would be flying the
plane, using the automatic pilot to line up the target in the crosshairs of his
bombsight, and the timing and trust between him and the pilot had to be
smooth and flawless. Manners also participated in an intensive set of
classes for lead bombardiers, studying the most recent operational information on the Norden bombsight, the C-1 Autopilot, and the H2X equipment.
Between practice flights he sat in classes on target identification, navigation, and bombing techniques using the H2X. Jack Perella was enduring a
similarly intense refresher in navigational techniques and instruments,
especially in the use of the mickey equipment. He had to know how the
H2X operated and how it could be used in conjunction with the navigational techniques and instruments with which he was already familiar. He

would rely on the mickey man to provide him with radar fixes on the terrain below, but he had to understand just how these radar fixes related to his own calculations. So he studied. The pressure on Perella would be intense. The pilot didn't navigate, and neither, in the final analysis, did the mickey man. It would be his job to hit the checkpoints at the right time in the complex and dangerous process of forming up and to lead the formation, however large, to the target, to keep them on course, and to avoid the ugly circles of red on the briefing map.

Between classes they flew. Local navigational exercises, relentless bomb runs, dropping on targets in the North Sea or in the gaunt hills of northern Scotland. They flew in good weather and bad, on clear days when the target barges were clearly visible bobbing in white caps, and on days when coils of cloud lay stacked below them, swaddling the earth with an impenetrable layer of gauze. They flew at night, which they had not done since their first days at the base, climbing through the moonlit clouds into a sky so black and cold and empty they seemed to have slipped beyond the grasp of gravity itself and drifted into limitless space. For the first time since phase training in the States, Perella, peering through the astrodome in the nose, practiced celestial navigation, plotting his course by the bright unblinking stars. On other days, simulating low-level attacks on airfields, they roared along just above the treetops, startling villagers and terrifying sheep. Leaning from the open windows of the waist Jack and Bob waved to aproned women standing at their flapping clotheslines, and Al, sitting white-knuckled in the tail, flinched as the leafless trees and high hedges shuddered in their wake. "Goddamn," Manners shrieked from the nose one afternoon as Farrington buzzed through a valley in the northern highlands, "I got a piece of heather in my teeth," and back at the hardstand on one such day the props were actually tipped with green.

They flew with command pilots, experienced combat flyers who monitored each phase of the crew's operation. These men had already completed a tour of duty and flew in the lead planes on missions, usually sitting in the copilot's seat. After each practice they critiqued the crew's performance. Flying lead, they stressed, there was no room for error. The squadron or group or wing or division was following you, they repeatedly emphasized to Farrington and the crew. Screw up, and the mission will fail. Screw up, and men will die. The pressure, particularly on Farrington, Regan, Manners, Murphy, and Perella, was intense. "After being over here I have no regrets about not being a pilot or navigator," Bob wrote in the last days of January. Since lead ships had no ball turret, he now rode in the waist, back-to-back with Brennan, and he was glad. "I have a much easier time being just a waist gunner."

The schedule was grueling. "Another evening," Bob wrote in late January "and back to base. Seems like we are always landing at another field." They were seeing a lot of Britain, but only from twenty thousand feet. "[We're] having a lot of practice missions," he explained on January 21. "Probably won't fly combat again until after my birthday." He would be twenty-nine on February 12, and there were times, after a night on the town with the boys or hours on oxygen, when it hit home. "I am getting old," Bob wrote. "[and] begin to feel it at times. I do have several gray hairs. Most fellows here take me from twenty-one to twenty-four so I must not exactly look or act my age. Maybe that is because I am in a young man's game. Flying."

Adding to the strain was the weather. The bitter cold that accompanied the German offensive in the Ardennes lingered deep into the new year, and the relentless rain of autumn gave way to a season of sleet and snow. "It snowed last night and all morning," Bob wrote in what became a steady refrain throughout the short, dark days of January and February. "A layer of several inches covers the ground. Everything that was green up to a couple of weeks ago has been frosted and is brown." The brief afternoon thaws, when the weak, watery sun would slink from behind the clouds, did not bring relief. Coke supplies on the base ran low, and coal was nowhere to be found. Everybody was cold. "Been flying today," Bob wrote on January 22, "and it was 50 below up there. After a late formation, etc., it is 9 P.M. and back to the barracks. . . . We rarely have heat in the barracks. It's . . . disagreeable to shiver on the ground and in the air! About the only time I get warm is when I'm in town at the Red Cross. . . . It will take years for me to thaw out after being here."

February 15 was a beautiful day, "the nicest we've had since I got to England," Howard wrote. "The sun actually came out . . . and there wasn't a cloud in the sky." Sitting on his bunk at 1900, Howard had just learned that the crew was alerted for their first mission as a lead crew. "The war is standing kindly still," he ruminated, "but I hope the Russians start again. The war won't end when they reach Berlin, but we all have strong hopes." He looked down at the blue envelope and the blue stationery his mother always used. She wrote nice airmails, reporting on their life in Knoxville, about his dad's work out at Oak Ridge, and about family and friends from home. The letter today was about a classmate of his. He had played in the band, sung in the glee club, and performed in the school theatricals. Howard had not known him well in school. They had not been close pals, but they had been drafted on the same day in March two years ago and reported together to Fort Oglethorpe. They had confronted their first drill sergeant together, slept in their first army barracks together, and gone through the military testing together. Then they had lost touch as they shuttled from camp to camp in the States. Now he was dead, killed in action in the Ardennes. "I'm sorry to hear about Courville," Howard wrote, "because he was a very nice guy. . . ." He looked up, taking a deep breath. In the bunk beside him Bob was writing a letter, and Jerry, turned on his side, his head propped up in his hand, was reading a two-week-old *Yank*. Jack was asleep, and Al was playing cards at the end of the barracks. Howard looked carefully at each of them. "I guess we can't all come back," he wrote at last, "but I'll tell you right now to keep my old room ready because I'm coming back."

At 0345 the CQ entered the barracks to awaken the lead crews. Their reveille was one full hour before the other crews. They would eat together and then attend a prebriefing for all lead crews at 0515 before attending the full briefing scheduled one hour later. When the five lead crews for the day's mission—one for each squadron and two deputies—assembled for the prebriefing, Farrington discovered that he would fly lead of the third squadron. The 784th Squadron commander would be riding with them as a command pilot. Everybody was excited. They had not flown combat in a month and now they would be flying lead. It would not be a deep penetration, fifty miles across the Dutch frontier, but the target, a small synthetic-oil refinery at Bottrop, lay on the northern fringe of the Ruhr. Tension was high as the men gathered at the hardstand.

The weather was terrible, cold and foggy, and conditions over the continent weren't much better. The gin-clear skies of the day before had vanished like a mirage, and as the men went through their preflight rituals a steady rain pattered against the ship. Al offered odds that they would not fly. "No way we can go up in this soup," he stated confidently. Jack took him up on it. Howard studied the communications flimsies in front of him on the table. He reviewed his notes from briefing for the third time; he went through his preflight checks. It was like the first mission. He checked his watch. Fifteen minutes to start engines. His stomach churned. Suddenly he felt a tap on his shoulder. Barrett crouched beside him and was trying to tell him something about the turret when Howard heard the coded message from the tower over his headset. He did not want to hear it, but after a moment's pause the message was repeated: "Mission delayed. Stand by your ships." He groaned, not audibly he hoped, but his heart sank. He relayed the message to Farrington. Jerry looked at him, frowning. "Christ," Farrington sighed, when he heard. He went over the interphone, informing the crew. In the waist, Bob let out a groan. "Not again," Jack yelped, slamming his hand into the bulkhead.

They hoped at first that this would be only a momentary delay, but as they sat listening to the drumming of the relentless rain on the aluminum shell of the ship, they knew they were in for a long wait. Maybe the whole mission would be scrubbed. Nobody wanted that. They were primed, ready to go. To think that all the anxiety of being alerted, the icy tension of the cold, dark hut, the near nausea of breakfast, the nervous strain of briefing had been for nothing was too much. No, they wanted to go. To get it over with. And so they waited, at first in the ship, then, as the minutes turned into hours, on the hardstand, then in the ground crew's tent, then finally in the ship again. They stripped off clothing, tried to catch a little sleep, tried to talk, to joke, but everybody was jittery, and as the hours ground slowly by their nerves frayed and their talk died and the nervous energy that had sustained them throughout the morning darkness drained away in the dim light of dawn.

The weather did not improve, and yet the mission was not scrubbed. The dense fog and intermittent rain that had greeted them at 0300 dissipated only slightly, and a dismal species of timid light settled over the base. Flying conditions remained horrible, "damifiknow" weather, the pilots called it, and a mission on this day seemed remote. Soon a bright red flare would arc across the field announcing that the mission was scrubbed, then the trucks would be coming to carry them back to the locker rooms. They would turn in their gear, their papers. For the first time all day Howard allowed himself to think about the hut, about his bunk. He was exhausted. A wave of weariness washed across him. He dozed.

He was not sure if it was the sputtering of the trucks that woke him or Jerry tugging at his sleeve. He was slumped over his table, but he snapped wide awake.

"Better have a look at this," Jerry said calmly. He was standing on the flight deck, peering through the rain-streaked windshield of the cockpit. Farrington and Regan were gone, probably in the tent or stretched out in back of the plane. Howard rose and peered out through the Plexiglas. Along the main runway a stream of vehicles—ambulances, wreckers, fire engines, the radio truck, and a command jeep—trickled through the wispy fog toward the far end. "There go the meat wagons," Jerry said. "Looks like we're in business." Through the copilot's side window Howard watched as a jeep pulled up at the hardstand. Emerging from the tent, Farrington spoke with the driver. Manners and Perella were already climbing back into the ship. Howard could not hear them, but Jack Perella was clowning around, nudging Manners in the ribs as Curly squatted by the nose wheel well. Perella was irrepressible. "Spagetts," Manners had taken to calling him, and the name stuck.

Farrington appeared from the bomb bay. "Looks like it's on, Howard," he said hurriedly as he climbed into the pilot's seat. "Start engines in fifteen minutes." Throughout the plane the men scrambled to their stations. Howard swung around on his stool. The mickey man's station was just behind him, and he watched as John Murphy methodically checked the radar screen. The command pilot, a major who would ride with them today, settled into the copilot's seat, while Regan stood in the engineer's position on the flight deck between the major and Farrington. The cockpit seemed crowded. Between the figures of the pilots Howard could see nothing but a billowing blanket of gray beyond the windshield. It seemed impossible to go up in this mess. Howard shot a final glance toward the runway. Patches of mist still hung like gauze across the field. He could not see the end of the runway, could not even see the grim line of emergency vehicles that had, he knew, assumed their positions alongside it, waiting for disaster.

The men again adjusted their flying clothes, tested their electrical suits, and went hurriedly through their preflight checks. The air was supercharged with excitement. The aircraft fairly bounced with tension. Everyone was wide awake, alert. Everyone was scared. They were flying their first mission as lead, and Farrington would be making an instrument takeoff. Nineteen planes would be lifting off into the murk before them and nineteen after them. It would be plenty crowded. Howard chose not to think about it. He looked down at his small radio table, vibrating as first one engine, then another and another and another choked, churned, and finally revved into an earsplitting roar. The dense odor of aviation fuel and exhaust surged through the aircraft. He closed his eyes. He tried to pray, but he could not concentrate.

Somewhere in front of them the long line of silver ships inched toward the main runway, and above the idling of the engines they could hear the planes, one by one, thundering into the soup. The pounding roar of 160 engines revving, idling, then revving once again sent shock waves through the ground like the spreading tremors of an earthquake. "Jesus," Bob thought, "an instrument takeoff." He closed his eyes, feeling the sweat trickle down from his flying helmet across his forehead. Braced against the bomb-bay bulkhead with his knees drawn up against his chest, he sat shoulder to shoulder with Brennan and Brooklyn. Jack crossed himself, as he always did at takeoff, and Bob, fighting back a surge of nausea, reflexively followed his example. His hands seemed to be made of lead. Haltingly, the plane crept forward along the perimeter track, bobbing roughly as Farrington braked, then eased forward, braked, and then eased forward for what seemed like hours.

Peering through the wipers as they slapped furiously at the sheet of mist before them, Farrington could scarcely make out the dull gray forms lifting off at the end of the runway. He watched the ship in front of them as it swung onto the tarmac, barely stopping before throttling up to full power and rumbling down the runway. It disappeared into the overcast, a faint blur of running lights blinking from its wing tips. Rolling into position, Farrington revved up the engines until the entire ship shuddered in a spasm of suppressed power. Then with a steady graceful motion he released the brake and the plane pitched forward, roaring headlong into the sheet of all-enveloping gray. At his table Howard could see nothing. A blanket of featureless murk unfurled beyond his tiny window, and the yellow tips of the props spun iridescent halos of moisture as the ship struggled upward. Within seconds they were swallowed up in a mountain of cloud.

Unable to see beyond the nose of the ship, Farrington watched his instruments intently, following the briefed course as the group struggled to form up in the impenetrable froth. Somewhere out there, they all knew, beyond the sonorous droning of their own engines, thirty-eight planes, each one utterly isolated in the heavy cloud, were flying blind as they climbed and turned, climbed and turned for what seemed like an eternity. No matter how many times they went through the ordeal of forming up in heavy weather, they could never get used to it and they never failed to feel the extraordinary sense of astonishment and relief when at last they broke through the thick belt of cloud into the stark, sunlit firmament.

On this day the clouds below them did not break as the formation droned eastward across the North Sea, joining with the other groups of the Ninety-sixth Combat Wing. A 9/10 cloud cover blanketed the continent, stretching like a vast, tattered cloak from the Dutch coast to the Ruhr. On the interphone Howard could hear the calm voice of John Murphy, seated just behind him, calling out coordinates, radar fixes, for Perella down below them in the nose. Perella stood in the cramped nose compartment, poring over the charts on his small worktable. It was impossible to sit on the tiny fold-up seat on his left, and so he worked in a perpetual crouch, facing backward. He had to be careful not to step on Curly. Manners was stretched out, peering through the Plexiglas at the slab of cloud below them. Perched in the nose turret, Noe could see nothing, just rippling folds in the rumpled sheet of cloud. But they were on course, Perella claimed. He sounded confident. Nothing to worry about.

Just before the IP, the coded signal to scrap the primary target crackled over Howard's headset, and almost instantly the formation began a series of laborious turns that would take them north of the Ruhr to the marshaling yards at Osnabrück. Hitting the secondary meant new headings, new target coordinates, new calculations, and Murphy and Perella worked feverishly. They would make the computations themselves, not relying on the squadron before them. Farrington began his turn. If he turned too quickly, some planes on the inside of the turn would be forced to down throttle, risking a high-speed stall, while those on the outside would have to accelerate just to keep up. Farrington handled the big ship with skill, making the turn at the IP and then at the secondary so smoothly that all the planes in the squadron could maintain their position in the formation without difficulty.

At last the bomb-bay doors rolled open, and ahead of them, above the fleecy whiteness, a scattered pattern of dark smudges appeared off to the left. The flak was not bad—it was what the interrogation officers would later describe blandly as "moderate and largely inaccurate"—but after a month away from it the sight of it, the muffled thudding sound of it sent a shiver through the ship. The formation shifted into position for the bomb run, and over the static of the interphone they could hear Manners and Murphy, their voices oddly calm, detached, lining up the target. With the automatic pilot tied to the bombsight, Manners was flying the plane.

Curled over the bombsight he knew that all through the squadron the bombardiers were peering intently at him, straining to see the bombs spill from the lead ship before toggling their own. Squinting through the sight, he could see nothing below him but a coarse carpet of white, but his instruments told him they were over the target, and Murphy's voice confirmed that they were on course. "Bombs away," Manners whispered hoarsely, the ship heaved suddenly upward, and they began a long, banking turn.

They had dropped their bombs through the clouds, never actually seeing the target, never actually seeing the earth. They had flown for hours above a thick canopy of cloud, glimpsing only fleeting, indistinct traces of the landscape below them—not the North Sea, not the Dutch coast, not the marshaling yards at Osnabrück. But Manners and Murphy were confident about their position, confident that the bombs were on target, confident that they had done their job.

Along the route out a squadron of Mustangs cavorted far off to both sides of the formation, black dots in the bright glare on the Plexiglas. Somewhere over the North Sea they disappeared, bound for their bases along the English coast. It was late afternoon as the formation began to ease down, sliding through the watery sunlight toward the heavy clouds. The weather over England had remained nasty all day, the fog and rain turning first to sleet, then light snow. The field was socked in, and on the approach the formation dispersed in the murk. The radio buzzed as ships peeled off, diverted to other fields with better visibility, but Farrington, flying on instruments, was determined to set the plane down at Attlebridge.

They dropped into the clouds. Waffling in the choppy turbulence, the ship shuddered and pitched as Farrington eased it down through the icy mist. They had lost their wingmen. Were they in this cloud bank too, just behind them, above them? How many planes were in this soup, slogging their way toward the field? Were they on course? Perella and Murphy said so, but they could see nothing. Regan watched the altimeter dropping steadily—two thousand feet, fifteen hundred, one thousand. He called out the numbers. They were almost on the deck, and still the plane was wrapped in a veil of limitless white. "Five hundred feet," Regan said tensely. They were still dropping. "Jesus," the major whispered. Suddenly the white diminished, the air around them turned dark, and through the last traces of wispy cloud the shadowy forms of a village and a copse of trees lurched up at them, so near, it seemed, they could reach out and touch the rusty weather vanes. Their altitude was no more than three hundred feet, but beyond the village and the rain-darkened checkerboard fields, the blue runway lights of AS 120 blinked through the gloom less than a mile away. The landing gear whirred, and the ship dropped quickly. They were coming in too high, too fast, but in this fog they could not risk going around again.

With the flaps fully extended and the wind screaming around them they hurtled past the edge of the runway, dropping fast. The wheels slammed into the tarmac with a savage booming groan, bounced heavily, and bounced again. Skittering on the slick surface like a rock skipped across a frozen pond, the plane careened wildly down the runway. They weren't going to stop in time, Farrington thought. They would fishtail, slide off the runway, and plow into the tents and sheds and half-frozen fields beyond. The gasoline would ignite. They were finished. The brakes shrieked and the left wing dipped, and for an agonizing second the plane seemed ready to flip into a deadly ground loop. Staggering like a drunk toward one edge of the runway, the ship slowed, righted itself unsteadily, and swerved back toward the opposite edge. Slowing, slowing at last, it skidded to a jerking halt at the very end of the runway, leaving long black smears of rubber along the tarmac.

At the hardstand the crew climbed shakily from the ship, ignoring the hoots of congratulations from the ground crew, who converged around the hatches. As they stood stiffly under the wing of the plane, their gear piled around their ankles, waiting for the truck to carry them to interrogation, the major patted Farrington on the shoulder. It was an impressive beginning for a lead crew, he said, nodding at Perella and Manners. It was a good landing under horrible conditions, a tough bit of flying, a good job all around. In fact, the whole mission was a success. The crew had performed coolly under adverse circumstances. They had taken off in the soup, located and bombed the target using radar, and landed in the fog on instruments. The major was impressed. Good work, he said, smiling grimly at them all. They stared back in silence. Behind the tail, at the edge of the revetment, Bob vomited into a mound of mud-spattered snow.

"Have a few moments so I decided to let you know I'm still perking," Howard wrote that night in the barracks. "I'm fine and doing okay, I guess." He was exhausted. After interrogation and chow the crew had received the oak-leaf cluster, "a gold leaf which shows that you have been presented with a second air medal," he explained. He did not mention the events of the day. He never wrote about flying, about the missions when he wrote home, but what he had seen that day was on his mind. "Dad, to you and Mother both, I want to tell you that I have always wanted you all to be proud of me and I want to tell you that there has never been a guy who has come overseas and tried any harder to get back okay than I have. So don't ever worry about me because I'll be okay and one of these days I'll ring the doorbell and that's what I want."

In the following week the crew was alerted twice but did not fly combat again until the twenty-first, a rough mission to Nuremberg. The entire Eighth Force—over one thousand heavy bombers—swarmed over the city, hammering the marshaling yards. The crew flew lead of the second squadron of the 466th. They had never seen so many aircraft. The sky was thick with planes—B-17s and 24s, Mustangs, Lightnings, and Thunderbolts filled the heavens—and the smoke from the burning city rose through the wreath of heavy clouds that lay draped over the area. Over the target, bouncing through a wall of flak, they watched a Liberator take a direct hit in the number three engine, watched the long, tapered Davis wing fold in an instant and the burning plane tumble in a steep, sickening spin. There were no chutes. A week later, on March 1, they flew another long mission to Ingolstadt in southeastern Germany, the crew's deepest penetration. The route in took them south of Munich, along the craggy foothills of the Bavarian Alps. Miraculously, they saw no flak at the target and no enemy aircraft rose to meet them. It was a milk run, but they were in the air for over nine hours, on oxygen for seven.

In early March the crew flew two more missions, one to Soest, just east of the Ruhr, on March 7, and four days later a long flight to bomb the sub pens at Kiel. Farrington flew deputy lead for the group on the mission to Kiel, a seven-hour mission that took them into Denmark. Between raids they attended briefings for lead crews and flew practice missions on an almost daily basis, honing their skills. It was a rigorous schedule, but life on the ground had at least improved. The officers had been promoted and were now first lieutenants, and the enlisted men also moved up a rank, Howard and Jerry to tech sergeant, and the other enlisted men to staff.

Pass was coming regularly now, too, at least six days each month. They looked forward to the passes, to the time away from the base. The crew was still close, but as time passed the men tended to pair up or go their separate ways when they went on pass. Al and Jack were fond of London, and although they sometimes took the train out to the pier at Great Yarmouth, to an amusement arcade where they played the game machines and watched the rough surf and drank at the pub next door, they usually spent their passes in London. Howard and Jerry went to London, too, but in February and March Howard spent two of his passes with his brother-in-law Tom and since January he had been on the 466th basketball team. The team traveled around East Anglia playing squads from other bases, so Jerry frequently found himself alone in London. Bob hung out with the gang on the base, going with them to the movies, to the Aero Club dances, and occasionally into town, but he preferred to spend his passes in Norwich, alone. A married man with two children at home, he occupied a different private universe. "Brennan is sort of halfway engaged back home," he wrote to Marie. "His girl is just seventeen and he's just nineteen. They are kids yet. . . . We go to town together at times but when he dates I go to the Red Cross or to a movie."

There were parties and dances on the base, too. Twice a month the girls arrived in Liberty Run trucks from Norwich and the surrounding villages. Land Army girls, WAAFs, locals. "The squadron party [on March 3] was quite a success," Bob reported. "They had an orchestra and a bunch of WAAFs here. The WAAFs are the girls of the Royal Air Force. Quite a few were good dancers but their looks???—There wasn't a good-looking one in the group. I danced several dances. They had barrels of beer for all. Ice cream for the girls. I didn't drink very heavy and so had a pretty good time listening to music and dancing. However, there were quite a few headaches this morning."

No headaches for Howard. He was busy playing ball. In December the station *Bulletin* announced tryouts for the group's basketball team, and about forty hopefuls showed up at Blackfriars' Hall in Norwich for the first practice. The gym was not really heated, and between the thumping echoes of the ball and the shrill squealing of their black tennis shoes on the hardwood floor, the sleet lashed against the high gloomy windows. There were the usual assortment of aspirants—the high school hotshots, the self-styled athletes, and a handful with some college experience. In January the team was reduced to a squad of ten and began its season. The base had no indoor court so the team played its home games in town at Blackfriars', just up the hill from the Sampson and Hercules and the Bishop's Palace. The home games were not well attended, but on the road, playing at base facilities, they played to packed houses, sometimes with an audience of a thousand rowdy GIs hooting and cheering.

They practiced when they could, between missions and ground classes, and, Howard thought, were not half bad. Despite the constant fatigue and strain of combat flying, the exercise was a welcome escape, a release. The familiar feel of the leather ball, the stop-and-start sprints up and down the shining court, the singing swish of the net were sensations from another, happier world. Even the smell of the sweat was different, sweet and invigorating, as he ran and ran and ran. It was not the clammy sour sweat that seemed to seep from his bowels on the missions, hanging in his oxygen mask for hours, but a sweat born of simple exertion, a sweat free of fear. "I just got back from playing basketball and I had a great time," Howard wrote on February 12. "We won by a score of 66 to 58, and last night . . . by a score of 59 to 39. I got fifteen points tonight and twenty-one last night. I'd give anything to have you see me play, James, because you wouldn't know it was your brother. I've improved considerably."

As the season progressed, Howard and the crew's copilot, Jack Regan, quickly emerged as the stars of the team. Both had played basketball in college, Howard at Western Kentucky and Regan at NYU, and it showed. "I have enclosed a picture of our basketball squad," Howard wrote on March 10. They had just won the consolation finals of an Eighth Air Force Invitational tournament in Norwich and were looking forward to a big Red Cross tourney. During the course of tryouts and practices and trips to the games Howard had gotten to know his copilot much better. He had seen him toss a baseball around in the States and had played pickup basketball games with him at the gym at Westover. Howard loved to watch him shoot, long, graceful jump shots from the left side that were just deadly. Between Howard and Regan and Dick Chapdelaine, a feisty tail gunner from the Westbrook crew, the 466th's team looked pretty good. "They are a fine bunch of guys," Howard wrote on the night before the mission to Kiel. "We are in a Red Cross tourney starting on the 18th," he concluded, "so wish us luck."

They would need all the luck they could get on March 18. At the prebriefing for lead crews at 0300 the string on the giant wall map slanted across Holland north of Amsterdam, passed southern Westphalia, and slashed straight across Brandenburg before plunging into the largest splotch of red on the entire map. Prebriefing for the four or five lead crews usually lacked the theatrical air of the larger, later briefing for the group, but on this morning there were groans when the men saw the map. They were going to Berlin.

Big B, they called it. The city itself was enormous, the group operations officer told them, the third largest in the world, sprawling across nearly nine hundred square miles of the flat Brandenburg plain. It was not only the capital of Hitler's Reich, but an industrial and communications center of the first magnitude. It had been bombed relentlessly during the past year, though the Eighth had not launched a major raid on the city for over two months. Despite the appalling punishment the city had absorbed, it remained the most intensely defended target on the continent. As the field order on March 18 emphasized, over a thousand heavy guns were concentrated in and around the city, covering an area of approximately fifty miles. Flak in the target area would be both radar aimed and barrage types. They could expect it to be intense and accurate.

The men listened with a mounting sense of foreboding. They studied the target maps, the aerial photographs, the formation diagram, the routes and times. They asked questions. They would not be lonesome in the skies over Berlin on this March morning, the briefing officer explained. Every group in the Eighth Air Force was dispatching planes to targets in Berlin. With over fifteen hundred heavy bombers and their fighter escorts, it was to be a maximum effort. It would be, he said, the largest daylight raid on Berlin in the war. The target for the 466th was a tank factory in Tegel, an industrial district in the northwest corner of the city, and the group would be leading the entire Second Air Division, over three hundred aircraft. The Farrington crew was flying lead of the second squadron.

Al was the first to reach the plane. He had become chief armorer-gunner, and while the others attended the main briefing he went directly to the hardstand. He picked up ship's guns from the armaments shed and installed them in the plane. Then he searched the squadron area for planes not flying the day's mission, slipped inside, and took the flak jackets. Tossing them into the jeep he raced back to his aircraft and carefully lined the waist and tail with the heavy lead aprons. He had seen too many of the gaping, jagged slashes left in the thin aluminum skin of the B-24 by flak to leave anything to chance. Sure, you had to have luck, but the flak vests were an insurance policy. They improved the odds. He worked quickly.

As the truck stopped and the men dropped onto the hardstand, a sliver of watery light already edged the treetops along the dim horizon and beams of pale amber arced dully upward across the dark sky above them. In the dew of the gathering dawn, shimmering trinkets of light glittered along the fuselage like strings of tinsel, broken toward the nose compartment by a dark painted figure. A panther stretched from the bomb bay to the navigator's window, leaping above Oriental-style lettering straight out of *Terry and the Pirates* that spelled the ship's name: the *Black Cat.*

The crews were at their stations at 0700, and the planes, their outboard engines whining shrilly, lumbered out onto the perimeter track for the main runway an hour later. Takeoff and assembly went without a hitch, and the weather cooperated all along the route out. Noe picked up the visual checkpoints at Zwolle in Holland, at Celle, at Dummer Lake near Osnabrück, and at Stendahl, less than fifty miles from Berlin. As the vast formation droned onward the contrails, great expanding swaths of gray, spread across the sky, pointing like an arrow toward Berlin. The prop wash was the worst Farrington had ever encountered, and the plane bounced and wallowed in the turbulence for hours. Fighting the controls all the way, Farrington was drenched with sweat long before they began their approach to the IP.

Things began to go wrong as they neared the turn for the target. The thin band of clouds that had stretched beneath them across northern Germany began to thicken, and far ahead through the gathering overcast they could see a wide, drifting smudge rising from the earth. The sky around them was teeming with planes, and from the waist Peterson and Brennan spotted bandits, far out of range, following along the route of the formation. Focke-Wulfs, Me 109s, they thought, but they were not sure. Just after the IP Perella's voice echoed over the interphone. The lead squadron was drifting off course. He gave the headings, and Murphy confirmed. The approach was wrong. On this heading, he said, they could not hit either the primary or the secondary. Voices crackled over the command set, but the lead squadron continued on with no correction, and within minutes the formation was swallowed in the maelstrom.

All around the ship flak bursts erupted, like a sea of black umbrellas popping suddenly open on a crowded London street. It didn't seem possible not to be hit—like running through the raindrops, Howard thought—but the plane plowed on, through the flak so close he could hear its eerie whumpfing sound over the droning of the engines. Below, through the light clouds, a raging inferno rose from the stricken capital. Towering plumes of black smoke roiled upward from the gray brown city, broken by a succession of brilliant red orange flashes, then clouds of billowing gray, sprouting like mushrooms on the blighted urban landscape miles below them.

"B-17 going down," Bob's voice rang out on the interphone. "Three o'clock."

"I see it," Regan said. "Two engines smoking, number one and . . . oh God!" Hardly breathing, he pressed his face to the glass and stared out through the bursting flak at a ragged oily smear in the sky where only an instant before a Fortress had been. Bits of debris, none larger than a cigar box, showered crazily down through the formation. They saw no chutes.

Like beads of water freezing on a windowpane, seconds stretched with agonizing languor into minutes, and for what seemed like hours they called out planes in trouble, planes going down, counting the number of chutes, while Murphy desperately stared into his radar screen, searching for the lakes on Berlin's western fringes that would orient them toward the target. They were lined up on a canal or a river, running north of Berlin, and through his bombsight Manners thought he could see it. Through the billowing smoke and drifting clouds, it looked like the target. Noe agreed, and, with flak still bursting all around them, the bombs were away.

Interrogation at AS 120 and subsequent aerial photographs revealed that the mission was a disaster. The first squadron had indeed gotten off course and had bombed Ulzen, a target of opportunity between Lübeck and Brunswick, and the third squadron lead had held his bombs through the Berlin area, dropping them on the marshaling yards at Wittstock, fifty miles north of the target. The remainder of the third squadron had jettisoned their bombs at various points on the route home. Only the second squadron, led by the Farrington crew, had dropped its bombs in the Berlin area, on the target, they believed. The strike photos, developed that night, told a different story. They revealed that the second squadron had not hit Tegel at all but Oranienburg, ten miles north of the primary. Twenty-one of the group's twenty-seven aircraft sustained class A battle damage, but—and it was the only positive result of the mission—there were no casualties. For Farrington, Murphy, Perella, and Noe, it was a sobering experience.

Al sat on the stool, grinning hazily up at them. His new battle jacket was tossed carelessly on a coarse straight-back chair just beside him and his sleeve was rolled up above the elbow. His collar was open, his tie pulled askew, and dark patches of sweat arced down his sides. The air in the close, cluttered room was sour with cigarette smoke and as humid as a green-house. "Jeez," Al grimaced, squirming in the chair. " 'old steady, mate," the man said testily. Howard and Jerry, their faces beaded with perspiration, watched in fascination. "Have a drink," Al said placatingly to the man, offering him the half-empty bottle. "When we're finished 'ere," he said, pausing only to take a drag on a foul-smelling cigarette. He stood facing Al, bent over his left side, like a dentist. Al took a long swig himself. The needle moved through the thick dark hair of his forearm with an electric hum, giving off a faint odor of burnt cotton.

"Just almost finished 'ere, Yank," the man rasped, pausing to spit a cough of phlegm into a handkerchief.

"You're next, Jerry," Al said.

"You bet, Brooklyn," Barrett replied, "the three musketeers."

"All for one and one for all," Al beamed. His voice sounded a little husky.

They had been at the Bull and Terrier all evening. It was Al's pub, the place he went to in London on pass. He had gone there with his brother in November, and since Christmas he had become a regular, showing up in the little Soho pub every chance he got. He stood at the same spot along the bar, chatting pleasantly with the barmaid. He lost a little money playing darts, but he didn't care. Brennan usually came along. Al had worked out an arrangement with the barmaid. He paid her a little something, and she agreed to keep a bottle with his name on it. Into it she poured leftover scotch, cognac, Irish whiskey, whatever remained from drinks or the bottoms of other bottles. The taste was a bit unpredictable, but with wartime rationing you couldn't be too picky, Al agreed. This way, regardless of shortages, there was always something waiting for him when he hit town. Jack thought it was a great idea.

They felt like celebrating tonight. Earlier, as they walked along Piccadilly Circus, Jerry let drop that he was engaged. He said it casually, almost in passing. She was English, an actress, and he had met her on pass in London just over a month ago. Jerry had told Howard all about her, had shown him a snapshot. Howard knew that Jerry spent his passes in her small flat whenever he could, but he was still surprised. Guys did it, of course. He knew that. The army frowned on it, but more than forty thousand GIs had married English girls, Jerry said. They would make it official when Jerry finished up his missions. That would be in May or June it looked like.

The pub closed at ten, and they were making their way through the

crowded streets to a private club Jerry knew when they passed the seedy
tattoo parlor, and in a moment of inspiration, Jerry insisted they pop in.
They should get tattooed together, he suggested, the three of them. They
had lost Jack somewhere along the way. He fell in with a WAAF at the pub
earlier in the evening and disappeared, saying something about a dance. So
here they were, the three musketeers, comrades, blood brothers forever,
Jerry sang out. Matching tattoos, Howard agreed.

"You go first, Brooklyn," Jerry suggested, and Al readily agreed, dropping into the chair and rolling up his sleeve. It wasn't so bad. Stung a little
bit, but the scotch helped. He took another draw on the bottle.

"Aw right, Yank, you're all done."

A little woozy, Al rose unsteadily to his feet. He looked down at the
bruise-colored figure on his arm, straining to focus. As he did, the door
swung open and a blast of cool air swept into the shop.

"You're next, Jerry," he said, glancing up. But Jerry and Howard had
disappeared. "Hey," Al shouted, shoving the man aside and stepping out
onto the pitch-black street, "what gives?"

A few yards away Howard and Jerry stood in the darkness, doubled over
in laughter.

"Your turn, Jerry," Al called, a note of suspicion creeping into his voice.
Neither Jerry nor Howard moved.

"Come on back here!" Al yelled after them.

"Maybe next time," Jerry laughed. "Besides, I can't stand the sight of
blood."

Al glared at them in disbelief. "You four-flushing SOBs," he shouted,
standing on the cool sidewalk in his shirtsleeves.

"Be reasonable, Al," Jerry soothed, "What would Howard's mama down
in Tennessee think if her baby boy showed up with a tattoo? We'd have to
answer to her."

"You sorry sacks of shit," Al bellowed, "I'm not flying with youse any
more!"

"Come on, Brooklyn," Howard laughed, his face full of childish mis-
chief. "Let's get you a drink."

"Bums," Al grumbled. "Rotten bums." He stared at his two crewmates,
his voice brimming with injury. They thought it was a great joke. "Oh, what
the hell," said Al finally, pushing open the door. "Next time, though," he
insisted, "next time we're in London, next pass, you guys gotta go through
with it."

"Absolutely," said Jerry.

"Scout's honor," promised Howard.

In the grainy yellow light of the tattoo parlor, they peered down at Al's forearm. Rising from just above his wrist to his elbow, a series of reddish purple lines the color of a birthmark coursed through the dense, dark hair in the form of a horseshoe. Sitting astride the horseshoe, her long bare legs draped over its curves, rode a shapely woman. Her naked breasts peeked pertly above a garlanded scroll bearing the script "Good Luck." Jerry couldn't contain himself. He burst out laughing. "Well, Brooklyn," he said, patting Al affectionately on the shoulder, "I can't think of anybody who needs it more."

As time passed and the missions piled up the strain, rather than dissipating, mounted. Everyone found a way to cope. Al and Jack played and drank and chased girls. Jerry was engaged and spent his time in London. Bob dreamed. He lived in the dreams now. They were with him every day. He went with the gang to the movies, he clowned around in the hut or at chow, he rode in the waist of the B-24, but that world, he had decided, was not real, and he slipped through it like a sleepwalker. More and more he resided in a quiet, tranquil inner space, in a landscape of dreams—dreams about life with his family, about life after the war, dreams more real to him than the points on the briefing map or the flak or the shrieking winds at twenty thousand feet.

"I dream all kinds of things," he wrote shortly after the Berlin raid, but gradually his dreams had become fixed on a particular place, as far removed from the cold and stress and danger all around him as he could make it, a dreamscape he could share only with Marie. He would build a house for them in the mountains, in Arkansas, where he had visited once as a boy, or in the wide open spaces of Texas, where he had trained. He dreamed about "the mild climate, blue skies, bright stars, romantic moonlight, and the smell of the pine woods," and on pass in Norwich or sitting on his bunk in the hut he drew floor plans, sketched blueprints, and filled his letters to Marie with his dreams.

For Howard, the basketball helped to relieve the tension, helped him to ease away from the world of oxygen masks and flak vests and frostbite. Seeing his brother-in-law helped, too. In late February he spent a weekend with Tom at the 390th in Framlingham, and shortly after the Berlin mission

Tom traveled back to Attlebridge. "Tom was over day before yesterday," Howard wrote on March 25, "and we had quite a time. He looks great but is homesick, of course." They spent a forty-eight-hour pass together, talking about home, about cars, about food, about the future. They joked about opening a drugstore together in Chattanooga when the war was over, with Howard as pharmacist and Tom as manager and James, the young doctor, funneling them business. They rode the train to London for a day, did a little sightseeing, and planned to get together again in early April. "Wish you all could have been there with us," Howard wrote, "or better still that we could have been home."

The letters from Nancy arrived daily, bearing the familiar hometown postmark, with reports on their friends and families and hints about their life together after the war. She sent him monogrammed stationery for his birthday—on March 2 he turned twenty-one—a shaving kit, cookies, and cakes. She was the future. But Alice continued to write regularly, too, a never-ending source of wonder and confusion to Howard. "Heard from Alice today," he wrote to his brother on March 28, "and I sure would like to see the old girl and that convertible. . . . She is still after me, and if I get home and she finds it out she says she is going to take a trip south, etc. She is really a beautiful girl and . . . you'd love her, James. By the way, you should see her sister. She isn't bad either."

Howard particularly looked forward to James's letters and their enthusiastic accounts of college life. James wrote regularly about girls, about sports, about his classes, about the fraternity he hoped to pledge. They were bulletins from a world as far away from AS 120 as could be, and Howard relished every detail. "I was glad to hear that you made some good marks on your tests," he wrote. "I realize the studies are hard, but dig in and stay after them. You don't realize how lucky you are that you can keep after your schoolwork. There are about a million fellows who would give their left arm to swap places with you, so don't give it up. . . . James, I don't know what to do after the war," he admitted. "I'm positive I'm going to continue school but I don't know what to study." He was thinking of Georgia Tech or Penn State. Maybe he could play basketball or football there. It seemed so far away. "I'm not worrying about it because it will be quite some time yet. . . . Glad you sent me a picture of the frat house. Wish I was there to enjoy it with you."

Writing to his parents, he urged them to keep after "the young doctor." "I guess I didn't realize it before I got into the army but now I would give anything to be [in school] again. . . . I hope and pray that James won't have to come into service. It's fun at first," he added, thinking about his days at Miami Beach, about the college atmosphere at Scott, about the easy friendships of crew training, "but the fun doesn't last. . . . I have two gray hairs in my head." He was also losing weight, not surprising considering the stress. "I have lost fifteen pounds," he wrote in mid-March, "and am getting skinny as a rail."

They all looked tired and a bit drawn in the crew picture, made on a 784th hardstand after a routine practice mission in the last days of March. Even the irrepressible Jack Perella seemed surprisingly somber, and the little mutt who lived under Barrett's bunk—G-String Junior, Howard called him—wore a hangdog expression. "It didn't turn out any too good," Howard observed, "but it is as good as could be expected under the circumstances. Still," he concluded, "this is the best crew in England, and I'm not kidding. The old war looks good and maybe it won't be long."

With each passing day the war in Europe ground nearer to its agonizing but inevitable conclusion. The Russians were on the Oder, less than fifty miles from Berlin, and in the west, American and British troops had at last crossed the Rhine. It was only a matter of time now, and the crew followed the war news closely. They listened to the upbeat reports on AFN and followed the diagrams of the advancing Allied armies in *Stars and Stripes*. Any day might bring the big breakthrough, any day might bring internal revolt and surrender in Germany, any day might bring the end of their war. "James," Howard wrote, "the Russians are only forty-five miles from Big B, which to us is Berlin. I hope they keep it up because things really look good. Maybe I can be home sooner if only the old boys keep it up."

Just after dawn on April 4 the 466th dispatched thirty-eight planes to attack a fighter base at Perleberg, a small town in northern Germany. It was the crew's first mission since a March 31 raid on Brunswick, and Farrington was again flying lead of the second squadron. The target lay roughly a hundred miles northwest of Berlin, and Second Air Division did not anticipate significant flak at the target. This was to be a visual raid, the operations officer emphasized at briefing. No bombs were to be dropped by radar.

The crew looked a little different as the men gathered on the hardstand after briefing. Jack Regan had sprained his knee in the group's last basketball game and was grounded, so Henry Hiter would fly on this day as copilot. Hiter lived in the barracks with Farrington and the crew's officers and they knew him well. He was an experienced copilot who had missed several missions because of a burst eardrum. While he was recuperating his crew finished up its tour, and now he was filling in with different crews. He was a good man, but it was the first mission the crew would fly without Jack Regan, and, like any change in the routine, it was unsettling.

The weather had been unstable for days, and on this morning it was no different. A thick band of cloud blanketed the ground all the way from the coast and did not thin as the formation neared the target. They had seen no flak but had spotted enemy aircraft all along the route—more than a dozen Fw 190s and the 262s, all staying out of range, just trailing along ominously. The clouds did not lift, and as the formation moved onto the bomb run the group's command pilot, waiting until the last possible second, hoping for a break in the overcast, finally abandoned the mission. Without visual sighting they could not drop; he gave the signal, and the group began to bank away for the return to base. It was then that the antiaircraft fire opened up. The barrage was not intense, nothing like what they had seen over Berlin or Nuremberg or Brunswick only a few days earlier, but as the second squadron approached Perleberg the sooty smears that had streaked the sky off to the left and below seemed to ride right up to them, as if gliding upward on a department store escalator.

It was on them in an instant, all around them, in front, below, above. Bone-jarring concussions from exploding shells shook them, and in the midst of the sooty turbulence the plane suddenly shivered, lurching abruptly upward. Out his window Farrington could see a small plume of smoke escaping from the number two engine. In an instant Barrett, riding in the top turret, was on the interphone, his voice calm. "We're losing number two," he said, "I'm coming down." As Howard spun on his seat, he felt Jerry sliding down out of the turret, scrambling toward the fuel transfer panels behind him. Quickly Farrington feathered number two, cutting the fuel supply and turning the prop blades outward to prevent the propeller from windmilling and tearing free of the wing. The thin oily smoke stopped, but the plane was losing altitude.

They swung out of the flak, still slowly dropping, and continued their turn away from the target. "We've blown a cylinder on number two," Barrett announced. The aircraft sagged left as Farrington fought to trim the plane, compensating for the lost engine. The group was swinging around, returning to base on the briefed route, but Farrington could not keep up. They began to slide back through the formation. They droned on, falling farther behind, still slowly descending.

"Bandit at three o'clock," Brennan shouted suddenly. Far off to the right and above them he could see the black dot. It was not a Mustang, not a Thunderbolt. It was moving far too fast. It was an Me 262. "He's coming around."

"I see him," Noe called out from the nose. He hunkered down in the turret. The jet was making a classic pursuit curve toward the nose. He would come in from twelve o'clock high. George Noe was a trained bombardier, now a pilotage navigator. He could operate the turret, he had had some training, but he prayed the 262 would not make a frontal attack, not right at him. Barrett was still down at the engineer's station monitoring the gauges. He scrambled back up into the top turret, swinging it forward, straining through the glare of the Plexiglas to find the fleck that was the 262. Far out in front he could see it. The jet was turning toward them, still out of range. Its closing speed was awesome.

"Here he comes," Noe said. His voice seemed to gurgle through the static, sounding to Howard as if he were underwater. Sitting at his tiny table, unable to see, all Howard could hear was his own shallow breathing.

"He broke off," Barrett fairly yelled. The jet, still out of range, had suddenly swung up above and away from them. Were there Mustangs out there?

"Anybody see any friendlies?" Farrington asked.

"Nothing," Barrett said, swiveling his turret.

They waited and watched. The turrets hummed. Through their tinted goggles the gunners peered out into the bright mica sky. With the number two engine feathered, the usual guttural hum had given way to an erratic rasping, and the aircraft was still slowly losing altitude. Something sounded wrong somewhere.

"He's coming around again," Al barked from the tail. The 262 swung past them, off to the right, climbing at an unbelievable rate. "Heading your way, Nose," Peterson called out.

Noe squinted. He could barely see through the blinding glare. Somewhere out in front of him, heading directly toward him, was the jet.

"Twelve o'clock high," Hiter spat out, his slow Mississippi drawl suddenly as clipped as new-mown hay.

Noe opened fire, squeezing off a long, deafening burst. From up above

Barrett fired too, and a cone of tracers shot forward. The spent cartridges clattered on Howard's table, ricocheting onto Murphy's shoulders.

"He's still outta range," Hiter said, "still out of range."

"Where is he?" Noe called out. "Where is he?"

There was silence as they searched for the jet.

"He's gone."

"Where the hell did he go?" Al coughed.

They could not find him. Had he broken off again? Chased away by little friends they could not see? The jet simply vanished.

"Brooklyn," Farrington said, "You see anything back there?"

"Nix," Al answered. He was drenched in sweat. "He's gone."

While the gunners stared, unblinking, into a sky as clear and white as porcelain, Murphy fed Perella a steady stream of radar fixes and Farrington, struggling to hold the ship steady, made some quick calculations. Barrett had wiggled down from the top turret and was monitoring the fuel gauges. They were still losing altitude, dropping slowly toward the unbroken layer of clouds below. At this rate, Barrett told him, they would not make it back to base, but they could make it back across friendly lines.

"Navigator, give me a heading," Farrington said, his voice almost bland, matter-of-fact, "a friendly field on the continent."

"Well, the closest," Perella said from his station in the nose, "is Sweden." Only yesterday, on a mission aborted over Denmark, a 466th aircraft had landed there. The Baltic coast was not far, and neutral Sweden just a short hop across the sea. It meant internment for the remainder of the war, which couldn't be very long.

There was silence from the flight deck. Then Farrington said, "Anybody want to try to make Sweden?"

No one spoke.

"No takers for Stockholm?" he said.

Silence.

"All right," he said at last, "let's try to coax this thing home."

They lumbered along just above the cloud line for some time. Although the 262 had not reappeared, everyone was still jittery, watching. Howard pulled off his oxygen mask and inhaled deeply. They must be under ten thousand feet now, he thought. The clouds were rising up toward them, their smooth contours dissolving into a range of craggy summits and narrow, wispy chasms. The air was thin and cold, tinged with the lingering odor of cordite and the strong scent of his own sweat. He stripped off his heated gloves and rubbed his hand, still encased in the white nylon, across his face. Over his headset metallic coded signals beeped like a troupe of tap dancers. He made an entry into his log. Suddenly the rough droning of the engines changed pitch, and the plane seemed to stutter. Howard could hear the props behind him—number one and number two engines—choke, then roar, a wild sputtering whine that sent a ripple of terror through him.

The plane swung erratically. Its left wing dropped. "Prop governors in number one and two are running away," they heard Hiter say flatly. "Number four turbo running away," he added a moment later. They were losing power in three engines. Dropping faster now, the plane slid into the clouds. Behind him Howard could see Barrett working feverishly at the fuel transfer panels. He shot a quick glance to his right, toward the bomb bay, where he would jump if they had to bail out. The huge bombs, fully armed, still hung in their racks. He did not want to jump. In the waist, Bob and Jack edged back toward the escape hatch, just three feet from where they stood. Al swung out of his turret onto the little platform where he kept his parachute. It was too tight to wear it in the turret. Crouching on the platform, he snapped it on.

As they emerged from the clouds, Farrington somehow righted the plane, leveled it out, and held it steady. "We've got some power again in number two," Barrett said briskly, and glancing over his left shoulder Farrington could see it, could feel the uneven but unmistakable surge of power. The wing rose. They had a chance, but it was clear they would never make it back across the Channel.

"Navigator," Farrington said calmly, "find me someplace to put this thing down." They were no longer over Germany, Perella reported from the nose, and after a quick conference with Murphy he said, "We should be able to reach a field in Belgium." He studied his map. Barrett was frantically working the transfer pumps, moving fuel to the two good engines. "At this rate—and with a little luck," Perella said, "we might just make it to B-58. It's an air service command base near Brussels." He relayed the coordinates to the flight deck. Howard noted them in his log, wondering how far away they actually were.

The engines whined and sputtered, and the ship swung awkwardly across the brown landscape. In the back the men still stood poised over the escape hatch, ready for the abandon-ship signal, and in the nose, Manners sat with his feet extended into the wheel well, prepared to slide out when the bell rang. But Farrington did not push the bail-out button. They were on course, Perella assured him, and Barrett, monitoring the fuel, seemed confident. They could make it. The engines miraculously held, and after sweating it out for almost two hours, their ears alert for any sound, any change in the rasping whine of the engines, they prepared for an emergency landing at Brussels. On their approach they dropped down over the river Scheldt and jettisoned their bombs. The visibility was good, the field was clear, and at shortly after 1300 the wheels bounced on the tarmac at B-58. They had come in, Jack sighed, on a wing and a prayer.

They spent the night in Brussels, wandering around the city where the women were refreshingly stylish and the children wore wooden shoes and two packs of American cigarettes could get you a bottle of champagne. They ate in a small restaurant, drank the cheap wine, and browsed in the little shops, which even after five years of German occupation seemed brighter and better stocked than their counterparts in Norwich or London. When they climbed into the C-47 transport the next morning, leaving their B-24 behind, their flight bags bulged with bottles of champagne and ashtrays and pairs of brightly painted wooden shoes—souvenirs for the folks at home.

Arriving at Attlebridge exhausted, they found the base bustling with raucous energy. The 466th was preparing to celebrate its two-hundredth mission with a gigantic two-day bash, and a carnival spirit prevailed in the huts and hangars and mess halls. The program was posted all around the base, and despite their fatigue the crew looked forward to the festivities. April 6 was declared Enlisted Men's Day, with the officers pulling KP. They ladled out the food, washed the dishes, and cleaned up the mess hall. In the afternoon contestants for the bicycle pub race convened on the ball field before a large crowd of hooting spectators. Ten barrels of beer stood like sentinels, spaced about three hundred yards apart around the field. The contestants were required to drink three pints at the first pub, or barrel, then ride to the second barrel, where they would down another pint, and then on to the third and one more pint. Then they were off to the home pub on their bikes. Of the forty-two contestants, only three finished the round, as bicyclists wheeled into the crowd or crashed into the barrels or simply slumped somewhere in between.

While the pub race was under way Mustangs and Thunderbolts soared overhead in an aerial circus, flying formation, swooping into long, looping rolls and wingovers before finally roaring down over the field just feet above the runway. In the early evening the enlisted men's dance got under way at the north hangar. The Flying Yanks and the Second Air Division band provided the dance music, and several hundred women from nearby villages and towns were trucked in, along with fifty cases of Coca-Cola and four hundred gallons of punch. Between sets a lottery was held, with prizes ranging from seven-day furloughs to forty-eight-hour passes to Paris.

Howard and the boys left the dance at 2300, walking through the fragrant spring night back toward the barracks. The last strains of "Elmer's Tune" thumped from the hangar, mingling with the muffled hum of laughter and shouting. The music and the happy voices carried across the flat expanse of the field, borne on a gentle breeze. The crew had a forty-eight-hour pass for the following day, but Al and Jack had decided to stick around the base for another day of the party—a beer bust in the afternoon, a band concert, and a floor show in the Aero Club at night. "Planning on winning the Big Bond Lottery, Brooklyn?" Jerry kidded him. Al had bought a sheaf of tickets. Jerry planned to leave for London to see his fiancée, and Bob would be going into Norwich and the Red Cross Club. Trucks ground slowly past them in the dark, and the shadowy silhouettes of men—armorers and ordnance men and engineers in their fatigues—trudged resolutely along the road. The music and the faint laughter of the party still wafted on the clear night air when the first engine turned over. It was far away, in the 787th's area. Then another engine caught, then another, and another, rumbling from different revetments around the field. In the dark ground crews were already working on the aircraft that would be going out the next day. There would be a mission in the morning.

Howard heard the planes leaving just after dawn, bound for a target in Germany. He would not be there when they returned. He was leaving on pass, not for London but for the group's rest home at Mundesley. He could use the time alone away from the crew. Everything was okay, he told himself, he was fine, just tired. But, trying to make change in a shop in Brussels, his hands had trembled so badly he had dropped the coins all over the floor. When he had tried to pick them up, he couldn't. No one had seen it, but he needed to get away, to rest. The 466th operated its own hotel—the "flak house," the men called it—in a small village on the sea north of Great Yarmouth. Standing high on a promontory that jutted sharply out into the North Sea, the old hotel, with its massive walls of cobblestone and concrete, had the aspect of an ancient coastal fortress. It had been closed down over the winter months and had reopened on April 1. According to the brochure Howard had read it was "a soldier's dream." Its rooms were spacious, furnished with "downy beds with thick mattresses and soft, silky eiderdowns." The floors were carpeted, and the bathrooms had plenty of hot water. Its dining room held individual tables for four, gleaming in white and silver. "No chow lines, no mess kits, no bare tables and benches. Enlisted men and officers all eat in the dining rooms together, share bedrooms, and spend their leisure time together. There is absolutely no consideration allotted to rank. The men might wear their uniforms or civilian clothes, some of which are provided." The hotel offered horseback riding, bicycle trips into the countryside, and a nine-hole golf course. The men could play volleyball, Ping-Pong, or pool. The sole prohibition was that women were not allowed in the hotel. "The biggest problem we have here," the manager remarked when Howard checked in, "is that some guys are trying to live their whole lives in three days."

Howard loved it—three days of sleep, listening to the radio, long, solitary walks on the beach. He rode a bike into the village, played darts at the pub, even tried his hand at croquet. They issued him a heavy fisherman's sweater to wear, and for almost seventy-two hours he looked something like a civilian. It was just what he needed. "I just returned from a rest home," he wrote on April 8, "and, boy, did I enjoy it. The food was the best I've had since we got into the army. The beds were tops, and the weather was just fine. A rest home, by the way, is a place where crews are sent just to sleep, eat, and play. The idea is to get your mind off of war, airplanes, or any worries you might have. It is really a wonderful place. . . . All the fellows said to tell you hello and we are all safe and okay. Just hoping the war ends soon . . . and we can all get home again."

April 12 was a warm spring day, and all afternoon the bulletins from AFN brought encouraging news from the front. The windows of the barracks were flung open, and the news, between Dinah Shore and Dick Haymes, washed like sunbeams over the men as they sprawled in their underwear on the scattered tufts of mangy grass. Howard sat in his shorts and T-shirt, gazing at the swallows that wheeled and dove over the fields just beyond the barbed-wire fence of the WAAF site. Yesterday he had watched as a farmer hunted rabbits, sending a small, slinky animal—a ferret, Jerry said—down into the holes that pocked the budding field of brussels sprouts. Al and Jack had placed bets on the ferret's rate of success. Al, as usual, had lost.

"James, you ask how much I lack being through," Howard wrote. "Well, that is something I never discuss or say. You see, I'm superstitious and so are all the other guys who fly combat." He paused. A butterfly, the first he had seen all spring, fluttered onto the feeble grass just beyond his reach. "You'll know when you see me next, so don't worry about me because I'm . . . all right and when you see me I'll be through." From the open window of the barracks Dinah Shore was singing again, a soft Tennessee voice. "Just don't worry, Jim."

Chapter VII

THE BLACK CAT

They were not supposed to fly. They had flown two missions in three days, and they were dead tired and ready for the seventy-two-hour pass that was coming tomorrow afternoon. Their names were not on the alert list at the morning meeting of lead crews, and they spent the day resting. But in the early evening an orderly from squadron operations stopped by to tell them the news. Another lead crew, set to fly tomorrow's mission, had come down with the measles, and Farrington was back on the list.

Bob had already written his daily letter to Marie when the orderly strode into the barracks and barked out the news. Until that point it had been a good day—no flying, no classes. They needed the rest.

On April 13 they had flown to Belgium, ferrying fighter personnel to forward bases on the continent. Then on April 16 they flew group lead for the first time. It was a long, arduous mission to attack the railroad yards at Traunstein in the vicinity of Salzburg. Because of bad weather at the target the colonel, flying with Farrington as command pilot, decided to move to the secondary, the marshaling yards at Landshut, fifty miles northeast of

Munich. It was a long haul for the crew. The CQ shook them awake at 0200 for the prebriefing, and after eating breakfast, attending the main briefing, claiming their flight equipment, trucking to the hardstands, and preflighting the aircraft, they took off at last at 0928. When their plane finally touched down again at Attlebridge it was early evening. They were in the air for more than ten hours, on oxygen for eight, wedged into their cramped positions at temperatures that hovered between twenty and thirty below zero. There were no combat casualties, but as the formation droned peacefully along over Belgium an aircraft right behind them suddenly lurched upward in the prop wash, slicing into the plane just above it. Al and Jack and Bob watched, speechless, as the plane started down and ten parachutes—they thought it was ten, you could never be quite sure—blossomed out of one of the planes, while the other, with one propeller ripped free of the wing, struggled to stay aloft.

The next day they rested, buoyed by a headline in *Stars and Stripes* proclaiming, "Strategic Air War Ends. Spaatz Says It's Tactical From Now On." According to the paper's account General Spaatz, commander of the U.S. Army Air Forces in Europe, announced late in the evening of April 16 that the strategic air war in the ETO had been won "with a decisiveness becoming increasingly evident as our armies overrun Germany." All units would now "operate with our tactical air forces in close cooperation with our armies. . . ." The front lines were so fluid that high-altitude raids were increasingly dangerous, and besides, there were few strategic targets left to bomb. The Farrington crew had flown twenty-two missions, and over half the targets they had hit were now in Allied hands. Spaatz called on the air forces to "continue with undiminished effort and precision the final tactical phase of air action to secure the ultimate objective." The end of the strategic air war was not a rumor—it was official now, embodied in the general's order of the day to all units of the Eighth and Fifteenth Air Forces. The boys read the story eagerly, but just what it meant for them was not clear. For days an air of expectancy hung over the base, and rumors swirled through the huts and mess halls that the group would be stood down any time. Just recently they had seen in the station *Bulletin* that Harry Gregorian and Mel Rossman of the original crew had completed their tours. They were going home. Now maybe this was the end of the road for the rest of the crew, the end of their war. It seemed like a terrific birthday present for Dick Farrington, who turned twenty-two on the seventeenth.

But late in the afternoon they discovered that they were alerted for a mission, and on the eighteenth, a bright, clear spring morning with swallows dipping and soaring around the hardstands and runways, they took off on another long raid deep into southeastern Germany. Farrington again led the group. The marshaling yards at Passau, a small city on the Danube close to the prewar Austrian and Czech borders, were the target. The weather cooperated, and they bombed visually. Manners did a superb job. Strike photos showed that all three squadrons in the group had placed at least 70 percent of their bombs within five hundred feet of the aiming point and 100 percent within one thousand feet. That represented, they were later told, the most accurate bombing in the history of the Second Air Division. It was an excellent mission, but the crew, after almost nine hours in the air, staggered back to their bunks bone weary and ready for their pass.

The group stood down on the following day, and the crew attended ground classes. They convened for a meeting of lead crews in the morning and then split up, each man heading to his specific training exercises. Even with the war in Europe careening rapidly toward its conclusion there would be no break in the routine, no slackening of the pace or easing of the training regimen. "The war is still going on," Bob wrote that night, but "surely can't last too long now. I hope! We didn't have to fly today, but did have to go to school. Here it is the 19th and April nearing the end." Time had a curious quality in the ETO, Bob mused. "Some moments [slip by] fast and some just drag by. To say the least it is a very unnatural way to live."

The 466th did not fly on the twentieth, and the crew had no ground classes. They took it easy. They were looking forward to their three-day pass coming on the twenty-second. On Howard's recommendation Jerry was pressing everyone to go to the group's rest home at Mundesley, but Bob was planning another trip to the Red Cross in Norwich and Al and Jack were bound for London. Bob spent the day catching up on a week's worth of *Stars and Stripes* and a few back issues of *Yank*. He scanned the news from home, the coverage of Roosevelt's death and funeral, the stories about Ernie Pyle, killed by a Jap sniper on Okinawa. The guy had been on every front, seen more of the war than most, and now, with the war in its final stage, he got it. Didn't seem fair. In the late afternoon Brennan pulled him out of the top bunk and they walked through the mild spring weather to the PX. On the way back they stopped in to check the mail. Three of Marie's letters, two long airmails and a V-mail, had arrived, and Bob tore them open as they strolled beside the potato fields on the way back to the barracks. All around him the world had turned suddenly green. Even the scruffy shrubs in the

squadron area had sprouted a vibrant, yellow green growth and the tangle of
vines along the farmer's fences was dappled with clusters of pale white
blossoms. The whole flat expanse of AS 120 was bathed in milky sunlight,
and the breeze that blew steadily from the west, rustling the pages of Marie's
airmail, was mild and dry.

Reading and rereading the letters as they ambled along the narrow,
mud-spattered road to the WAAF site, Bob decided that Marie sounded a
little down. Her letters were almost always cheerful, relating the children's
latest achievements or offering her thoughts about houses, couples, families. But occasionally the tension and tedium of waiting day after day,
month after month weighed on her, and despite all her efforts to disguise it,
a tone of dark anxiety would slip like a shadow through her letters. When he
detected it, Bob would try to cheer her up as she did him. In the bleak days
of February, when Marie's spirits had sagged under the relentless burden of
loneliness and worry, Bob had written, "Right now there isn't much I can do
to help you for I have a mighty important job to do over here. It is much
easier for me to do it if I know all's well on the home front and you are all
happy and smiling and the home fire is burning brightly. Please, sweetheart, let's keep the chin up a little longer and smile—and pray—and
dream of tomorrow." So now, sensing the stress in the lines of her letters,
like a low-grade but lingering fever, he commiserated with her. "I realize
the strain you are under looking after a house and raising two boys. . . .
Being cooped up in a city doesn't help any [and] my being away doesn't
help either. I should soon be home."

Bob had reason to feel confident that afternoon. Each day the headlines
in *Stars and Stripes* trumpeted the rapid advance of the Allied armies, and
the long-anticipated linkup of Russian and American troops on the Elbe
was now only days away. The American Ninth Army was less than fifty
miles from Berlin, and dispatches from Marshal Zhukov's headquarters,
only twenty-three miles from the German capital, indicated that the Russians were preparing to launch their last great push toward Berlin. For days
the headlines proclaimed a steady stream of fallen German cities—
Hannover, Vienna, Bremen—and stories dealing with the postwar order in
Europe, the reorganization of Germany, and the future of the United Nations
filled the paper.

All afternoon on April 20 the radio in the barracks rang out a steady
stream of good news from the front. It was Hitler's birthday, but the führer
wouldn't be doing too much celebrating this year, the AFN announcers

commented dryly. The world news broadcast at 1800, just before *GI Supper Club*, confirmed that Leipzig had fallen and resistance in the Ruhr had at last collapsed. A late-breaking dispatch reported that the U.S. Seventh Army was approaching Nuremberg, and the Russians were confirming that forward elements of the Red Army were only eighteen miles away from Berlin. This was it, Bob thought, the big Soviet push everyone had been waiting for. With the fronts closing on the Third Reich like a vise, the end of the war in Europe—V-E Day, they were already calling it—was a matter of days, maybe hours.

Bob glanced around at the cluttered barracks. The windows were open and the blackout curtains were not drawn. Wavering shafts of sunlight, grainy with dust, slanted at regular intervals into the long barnlike hut. Outside, the evening twilight had turned a soft lilac, and above the distant droning from the hardstands he could hear laughter and shouting and the occasional twittering of the swallows. Howard and Jack and Bill Deal were playing a game of touch football, and their voices rang through the barren space between the huts like those of schoolboys on a playground. "I think that . . . after becoming a civilian again I will be ready to build a house of our own," he wrote. "I want a house where I can look out any window and not see a house closer than half a mile. I want air and open spaces." He would be on pass tomorrow afternoon. Who knows, he thought, maybe the war will be over before we're back. He could see that house. So real, so near, he could touch it. "Thinking of you and hoping to have you in my arms soon," he wrote in closing. "I love you."

They all grumbled as one by one they wandered into the barracks, back from the Aero Club or the PX or the USO show, and Bob relayed the news about the alert. Still, they might not go tomorrow. There was always the weather. By early evening rain had begun to fall steadily, the heavy, wind-driven drops rattling like gravel on the roof. And besides, it was not their turn in the normal rotation of lead crews. No lead crew had flown three consecutive missions in weeks. The odds, Jerry felt, were against their going. Still, everybody was glum.

Howard was weary but could not sleep. He lay on his bunk, hands clasped behind his head. The alert for tomorrow had been a jolt, not so much frightening as exhausting. There was a card game at the other end of the barracks. He listened to the subdued voices and the slapping of the cards. Occasionally someone from the row of bunks across from him would shout out, "Keep it down, for Chrissakes," and the voices would subside for several moments into a murmurous hum, then slowly rise again like the rumble of an approaching train on the London Underground. It was after midnight. If they were going to fly the CQ would probably be around in a couple of hours. He ought to sleep, but he could not. He decided to write a letter home.

He asked, as always, about his father's work, about James's school, and about his sisters. The usual formula, touching base. "The weather here is very nice and I guess it's quite okay at home, isn't it? I sure would like to get home this time of year," he paused, listening to the rain on the roof, "but I guess not." His old friend Buddy McLeod had already arrived back in the States, having completed a tour of duty in the Eighth. "I guess you all think it is funny that Buddy is home and I am still here, but I told you when we made lead crew that it would take longer to finish, so I guess that proves my point. I had eleven missions when he got on this side, so you can figure it out for yourself." He sighed. "Guess his crew was just lucky in finishing so fast. Hope he has a nice time at home, and, boy, who wouldn't?" The door of the barracks opened and someone staggered in—some lucky soul not alerted for tomorrow—and in an exaggerated effort to keep quiet stumbled with a clatter into a bunk bed across the way. A canteen cup rattled across the floor. From the opened door Howard could smell the rain. "Well, I guess I better hit the sack and get some sleep and get this war over. I'm fine so tell all hello." He sealed the envelope. He would mail it on the way to chow in the morning.

When the CQ stepped into the darkened barracks at 0200 Howard was already awake. He had wandered along the ragged fringes of slumber, never really relaxing into sleep, never rousing himself to full consciousness. It was always this way on the night before a mission, he realized wearily as he watched the dark figure of the CQ, his flashlight beaming on his clipboard, stop at Jack's bunk. "Brennan," he heard the CQ half whisper, "mission this morning. You're flying," and while Jack snorted, rolling groggily out of the sack, the CQ moved quietly down the aisle and paused at Jerry's bunk. "Barrett," he heard the voice begin, and without waiting Howard, next in the row, crawled out of bed and reached for his pants.

"Maybe they'll send us to France," Jack said hopefully. He was finishing Bob's scrambled eggs. The mess hall was almost deserted. Only the lead crews and a handful of men from operations sat in the enlisted men's combat mess.

"Could be," Jerry said. He held his pipe, unlit, between his teeth. Amazingly, small pockets of Germans continued to hold out in the south, bypassed by the Allied armies, and they were giving the French troops fits. "The group's gone there twice in the past week."

"That's right," Howard added, "on the Atlantic coast near Bordeaux— gun emplacements, I think—on the Gironde River." The coffee was working. He could feel the caffeine percolate through his veins.

"I like it," Jack said, "No flak, no fighters."

"It's possible," Howard said hopefully.

"Hey, Brooklyn," Jerry said suddenly, "what's that you got in your hand?"

"Nothin'," Al said sheepishly, slipping his hand back into his flight jacket.

"Looked like something to me," Jerry insisted.

"Nothin'," Al said, raising his coffee mug to his lips.

"Come on, come on, what gives?"

Reluctantly Al put his hand on the table, palm up, and slowly opened his fingers. They leaned over the coffee mugs and steaming trays of uneaten food and stared.

"Jeez," Jack said, "what is that? A diamond?"

"You got it," Al said.

Cupped in the folds of Al's palm, the small stone glittered in the bright lights of the mess hall.

"Where'd you get that?"

"Saved from my winnings," Al smiled proudly. "Got a good price on it from a guy down in London. A real deal! When we get back I'm gonna have it set, you know, in a ring."

"Ah," Jack said, "the girl he left behind."

"You're carrying it on a mission?" Howard asked incredulously.

"I didn't wanna leave it back in the barracks," Al said, "you know, stuff disappears around there all the time."

Howard shook his head in wonder.

"With your luck, Brooklyn," Jerry laughed, sipping the sweet syrup from the fruit cocktail, "you'll drop it out the bomb bay!"

"Might come in handy if we have to land in France," Jack smiled, raising his eyebrows comically, "a little French girl, a small hotel, champagne. . . ."

At prebriefing they learned they were not going to the south of France. The target would be Salzburg, another long, exhausting haul to southeastern Germany. The group intelligence officer explained the importance of the target. "Reports from ground sources state that the Germans are planning a last stand in the area south of our target. Reports state that leading party members are retiring into this region, assembling supplies, ordnance, and selected soldiers. Not only has recent cover shown much activity southward along the main line on which the target is located, but much activity has been seen in the area concerned. Excavations not associated with mining or quarrying, and tunneling have been noted. Also photos have revealed numerous mines in the area." They had all heard about what the brass was calling "the Alpine redoubt." They had listened to the briefings, heard the speculation about it on AFN broadcasts. Hitler was going to hold out in the Alps, near his Berchtesgaden retreat, dragging out the war for weeks, maybe months. "It is planned that the Second Air Division and the RAF will be making a coordinated attack . . . ," the officer continued. "The RAF will be attacking targets in the redoubt area, while we shall be attacking the main traffic center feeding this area. GH5530 is our first priority target."

GH5530, as the maps and aerial photographs revealed, was a railroad bridge in Salzburg. Manners groaned aloud when he heard this at prebriefing. Another railroad bridge, a viaduct, like the one at Bielefeld that the group had tried repeatedly to hit. For all he knew it was still there. Now they wanted a formation of heavy bombers, flying at twenty thousand feet, to hit a span of bridge less than fifteen yards wide. What happened to Spaatz's tactical bombing? Mustangs and Thunderbolts were swarming all over Germany, roaring in over airfields and railroads and bridges. This was a job for them. Who the hell thought these things up, anyway? Bombing would have to be visual—no radar—and the weather didn't look promising.

The meteorological report made clear that the ninety-sixth combat wing could expect "broken to overcast layered middle and high [clouds] between eight thousand and thirty thousand feet over England and the continent" north of the target area. A weather scouting force would be dispatched to fly in advance of the formation and would "check clouds in order to assist bombers in the avoiding of such clouds and assist in making the climb." On withdrawal the formation could expect "to encounter a cold front with 10/10 multilayered clouds in a frontal zone with thunderstorms possible." The group should be prepared to break up into squadrons to deal with the possible adverse weather conditions on the return trip. The weather report didn't sound very encouraging to Manners or the other bombardiers, who were surprised to hear the conclusion from division that "the possibility of visual targets is good. Scouts will fly ahead and check the target conditions to report to the bombers."

The briefing officer gave the usual presentation on flak and enemy air operations, noting the antiaircraft areas along the route. The number of ominous red circles on the briefing map had dwindled dramatically in the past weeks as Allied armies had seized city after city in Germany, but the southeast still bristled with flak. The group had flown missions to this area three times in the past ten days, and the navigators and pilots were familiar with the danger spots along the way. The red cord marking the route arced across Belgium and Germany just north of Schweinfurt, then turned southeast, following a course that would take the formation down a corridor between known flak batteries at Regensburg and Munich. "The channel from the IP [southwest of Regensburg] to the target is narrow, and this should be made good," the briefer cautioned. "Formations should . . . make their turn good after bombing as there are additional guns to the south. Formations will be within range of known defenses for approximately one and one-quarter minutes before bombs away and for approximately one and one-half minutes after bombs away."

As for expected enemy fighter activity, Second Air Division intelligence believed that the Luftwaffe had been concentrating fighters in the southeast and that a force of one hundred and fifty single-engine fighters could be operational there. That seemed unlikely, the briefing officer felt, but warned that there was a very real possibility that twenty to thirty Me 262s would attempt to intercept the formation in the target area. On the twelfth, the Eighth had lost twenty-five bombers, largely to the Me 262s, so the danger was always there.

Farrington would not be flying group lead this morning. The 466th was leading the 96th Combat Wing on this mission, and the wing would be broken into three groups, A, B, and C. Farrington would be flying lead of B group, consisting of a nine-plane squadron from the 466th and another from the 467th. It meant that they would be flying roughly in the middle of the formation, a slot they had not flown in weeks. The command pilot assigned to fly with them, Farrington discovered, was Louis Wieser. Farrington knew him from the lead crew briefings, but they had never flown together. Wieser

was a barrel-chested West Point man, barely twenty-five, who had already
flown a full combat tour and had served a stint in group operations before
becoming a command pilot in the spring. He was one of the very few career
army men in the group, a tough nut but well liked. At the Officers' Club,
Farrington remembered, they called him Bud. Studying the formation
diagram, Farrington noticed that Harold Read would be his right wingman,
flying deputy lead of B group. The Read crew had flown the mission to
Passau and had recorded the highest percentage of bombs within the target
area of any crew in 466th history.

As the men rose and began filing out of the briefing room, the navigators
and bombardiers to their special briefings, Earl Beitler studied their faces.
Since finishing his tour in early April he had worked in 787th operations,
and he had attended briefing on this morning as an authorized visitor.
Standing at the small sign-in table in the rear, he looked around the long
dusky room at the clots of intense, anxious men. Some edged toward the
exit, ready to claim their equipment, others stood at their chairs, making
last-minute notes on the handouts or conferring with others. There were a
lot of new faces in the room, he thought, replacements arriving all the time,
just starting a tour. Toward the front of the room a familiar face stood out,
framed against the wall map. Standing just beside the easel holding the
formation diagram Jack Perella, his old navigator, was talking with Farrington and Regan. God, they looked tired.

Just a week ago, he remembered, when his crew had finished up, they
celebrated together. The Beitler crew, which had begun its tour at the same
time as Farrington's, flew its thirty-fifth and final mission on April 10, and
they were ready to blow off some steam. They began the evening at the
Officers' Club, where the scotch was plentiful, but wandered finally into the
village beyond the gates to the pub, where the enlisted men joined them and
the party continued. Perella went along, elated that his old crew had made
it. They laughed and drank and sang and drank some more. Someone even
danced with the proprietor's wife. They recalled the practical jokes and
stunts from training, the close calls and the usual fuckups from the missions. They were happy. Their war was over, and the whole show would be
very soon. The Russians were knocking on the gates of Berlin. The Americans were racing toward the Elbe. Hell, some units of the Ninth Army were
in Czechoslovakia.

Seated at a table with his buddy and former copilot Neil Gobrecht, Jack,
glassy-eyed and grinning, matched his friends pint for pint. It was hot in the

snug little pub, and in their wool ODs they were awash in jubilant sweat. A new round of "Bless 'Em All" had begun when Jack leaned across the table, almost knocking over his glass, and grabbed Gobrecht's arm.

"Neil," he said, "I want you to do me a favor."

"Anything, buddy," Gobrecht answered, his eyes still bobbing with the rowdy dancers beyond his friend's perspiring forehead.

"Promise me," Jack insisted.

"Promise," Gobrecht smiled distractedly, trying to bring his friend into focus. He felt Jack's fingers close on his wrist. "Say, what is this?" he laughed. "You want my London telephone numbers? You got 'em."

"When you get back home," Jack said above the hubbub at the bar, his eyes suddenly clearing, his voice stone-cold sober, "I want you to go by and see my folks."

"Come on!" Gobrecht grinned, slapping Jack on the shoulder.

"In Joliet," Jack said with great deliberation.

"Get outta here," Gobrecht laughed, "The whole damn war is going to be over any day now. You'll be bouncing up the front steps yourself before long."

"Promise me," Jack repeated, his voice steady, and Gobrecht, blinking through the smoke and raucous laughter and singing, stopped short. Focusing his eyes with an effort, he realized that Perella was serious.

"Sure, sure," he answered. He studied his friend's earnest face, bathed in sweat, a trace of foam across his upper lip. "You bet, buddy."

"A promise?"

"A promise."

Someone, shot glass in his hand, was trying to climb onto a table close to the bar. He staggered upright, his arms windmilling. He was going to fall.

"All right, then," Jack grinned, leaning back in his chair. "Let's have another pint."

Beitler looked at Perella now, gathering his charts and navigational aids into his satchel in the cluttered briefing room. All business, Jack stepped past Farrington into the navigator's briefing. On his hip he wore his .45.

It was just after 0500 and the sky was still sullen and dark when the truck dropped them at revetment 58. It was not one of the older pan-shaped hardstands, but a larger concrete diamond just to the right of the control tower. On it, swaying in the cold rain that slanted in sheets across the field, crouched the *Black Cat*. From behind a fuel truck parked just off the right wing, its yellow eyes peered out at them, unblinking. One by one the crew dropped down from the 6×6, tossing their equipment bags onto the wet concrete. Threading their way between the iridescent pools of oil-stained water that pocked the rough surface of the hardstand, they stowed their gear in the aircraft. The crew chief wore a baseball cap, the bill pushed straight up. Hovering around the plane, the large wool collar of his jacket pulled up against the surprisingly cold breeze, he raised his hand in greeting as the crew filed past. He was talking to a man in grease-smeared overalls who crouched above the number two engine, topping off the tanks that filled the long, tapered wings with one-hundred-octane aviation fuel. The *Black Cat* had been in the hangar for repairs, having sustained some minor damage on the Passau raid three days before. It had been rolled out to its revetment late yesterday afternoon, the crew chief explained to Farrington. Everything was in good shape, the chief assured him, as they walked around for the preflight check. Farrington knew the aircraft. They had flown it to Berlin.

Takeoff was scheduled for 0630, but as they took their stations in the plane, running through the preflight routine, nobody really believed they would be going up. The weather was miserable, as bad as any they had seen. Dense, mountainous clouds, heavy with rain, scudded over the field, and the stiff breeze that flapped the canvas walls of the tent beside the plane was cold and raw. Watching the gray, lusterless clouds slide by in the black sky above him, Perella shook his head, wondering what the winds aloft would be, wondering how much they would alter their ground speed and all the calculations he had made at briefing. The winds and turbulence associated with the advancing cold front, not anticipated until the afternoon, had obviously arrived well ahead of schedule. He conferred with Manners, who was still complaining about the target. A visual target on a day like today, he grumbled, and a railway bridge at that. He was still grousing as he and Noe climbed up into the nose wheel well and took their positions.

Despite the weather the group's twenty-nine aircraft trundled from their hardstands on schedule and began the slow, lumbering procession around the perimeter track toward the main runway. At precisely 0631 Louis Wieser, riding in the copilot seat, saw over his right shoulder a two-pronged green flare rise in a slow, sputtering arc from the control tower and heard almost instantaneously the roar of the group's lead aircraft as it shot down the runway. Three minutes later the *Black Cat* was airborne, climbing into the dense cushion of cloud. The Farrington crew was on its twenty-third mission.

The ceiling was low but visibility at takeoff had been unexpectedly good—the field, the planes, the earth bathed in a monochromatic gray. The clouds hung in massive layers above East Anglia, and the group departed the English coast at low altitude, flying over the North Sea toward the wing assembly over the continent. Just before landfall Al climbed out of his turret, slipped past Brennan and Peterson in the waist, and edged his way toward the bomb bay. As he passed the retractable radar scanner, housed where the ball turret had been, he looked up and saw Howard in the small radio compartment that in this aircraft was situated on a small platform above the bomb bay and just aft of the left wing. Al pushed open the small folding door to the bomb bay and inched his way gingerly out onto the narrow catwalk to arm the bombs. They carried six 1,000-pounders. The giant gray bombs hung in their racks, three on either side of him.

Farrington hoped that the weather over the continent would improve, but as the formation rumbled over Belgium and then into western Germany the situation steadily deteriorated. Banks of leaden cloud, like mammoth slabs of concrete, stretched out in every direction. The weather ship flying in advance of the formation sent a steady stream of directions, leading the formation on a meandering course through the cloud banks. Like explorers crawling through the murky crevices of a cave, the formation twisted and turned as the ships climbed and dropped, swung to the left and right, seeking a gap in the mountainous clouds. Buffeted by strong winds and pockets of turbulence the formation formed and reformed, swinging at last to the southeast toward the IP. Maintaining a tight formation was out of the question. Holding to the briefed course was impossible.

In the 466th's three lead aircraft the navigators and mickey men worked desperately to determine the group's exact position, and as the formation approached the wing IP, less than an hour from the target, it was clear that their wandering through the clouds had put them off course to the left, east of the briefed route. The weather was abysmal and deteriorating by the moment. The meteorological boys had missed this one. A decision by the group's command pilot would have to be made any second now. Riding in the copilot's seat in the lead aircraft, he was in charge of the mission, responsible for leading the 96th Combat Wing to the target. Listening on the command frequency, Howard waited to hear the four-letter code for a recall. He had been expecting to hear it—M-A-L-T—tapped in Morse code, since they reached the continent. He had listened to Manners' complaining as they neared the IP and heard Perella, his voice tight with exasperation, calling out the coordinates of the formation's position. Unless the weather improved dramatically over the target, no visual bombing would be possible, and, Perella insisted, they were still off course left.

Just before 1030 the Second Air Division's scouting force reached the target area. They found Salzburg covered by a towering weather front— solid cloud, thunderstorms, and rime ice from fifteen thousand to twenty-five thousand feet. The weather ship's message to the group's command pilot crackled through the interference. "Recommend abandoning mission due to instrument conditions ahead and bad icing up to twenty-five thousand feet." The command pilot quickly examined the situation. The primary was out, but the secondary was not an option either. Unlike the narrow railroad bridge, the wing's secondary, the marshaling yards at Salzburg, could be bombed by radar, but, as the weather ship reconfirmed, conditions in the Salzburg area were utterly impossible. With the front lines so fluid and American troops streaming deeper into southeastern Germany, hitting a target of opportunity would be too dangerous. Speaking in the clear on the command frequency, the command pilot ordered a recall and a turn to the right for a return to base.

Relief swept through the aircraft. There would be no frenzied moments of terror over the target, no wading through a field of flak, suspended in time, no encounters with the Me 262s. They were close to American lines, they figured. In the nose Curly Manners turned away from the bombsight. No worrying now about speed and wind, no concern that the weather had made a hash of the figures fed into the sight before takeoff. In this aircraft the navigator sat on the flight deck, just behind the copilot, and so Manners had more leg room in the cramped nose than usual. He relaxed, stretching his feet into the closed wheel well. The plane banked right, heading for the base.

As Howard entered the recall in his log, noting the time at 10:32, he heard Perella's voice crackle on his headset. "Navigator to pilot, we can't make a right turn here," he said firmly, "we'll be going into a dangerous area." He gave coordinates. "As I calculate it a right turn will take us directly over Regensburg." They all knew about Regensburg. A major center for fighter aircraft production, it had been repeatedly attacked since 1943. Only ten days ago the 466th had raided an oil refinery in the city and several ships had straggled home with class A battle damage from flak over the target. Checking his scope, Murphy confirmed their position, and Howard listened as Wieser, after checking the mission map folded on his lap, warned the command pilot.

In all the lead aircraft throughout the formation navigators and mickey men had made the same calculation, and the command frequency buzzed with calls to the command pilot. In the CP's own plane the lead navigator for the mission had reached the same conclusion. So had the radar operator. Until recently he had been an instructor in navigation school in the States and in an effort to get into a combat unit had volunteered to go into radar. Riding with this veteran crew for the first time, he was flying only his eighth combat mission, but as he peered into his radarscope he could clearly see the bright, irregular image of Regensburg, split by the winding Danube, directly ahead. He wondered if the command pilot, sitting on the flight deck just in front of him, knew something he didn't know. After all, he was a combat veteran, a former fighter pilot, and a lieutenant colonel. He couldn't figure out why the lead navigator hadn't spoken up. Then, from the nose he heard the navigator's voice, giving a heading, a different heading. Almost simultaneously he echoed it, and the pilot, as if waiting for the signal, instantly swung the plane.

"Who ordered that?" the command pilot demanded.

"I did," the navigator and radar man blurted out.

"I'm in command of this mission," the CP barked. "We stay on this heading!"

"What the hell is going on?" the deputy lead of the group wondered, as he monitored the radio traffic from just off the command pilot's right wing. The whole formation was heading directly over Regensburg. The bright blotch of red on the briefing map rose up before him. This had to be a mistake. He radioed ahead to the lead plane, just below and ahead of him.

"Stay off the air," the command pilot snapped, "I'm leading this mission!"

"Jesus," the deputy lead heard someone mutter on the interphone. Then all was silent.

The formation began a sweeping turn to the right. In the *Black Cat* Jack Perella stretched to look over Jack Murphy's shoulder at the radar screen. As the images on the screen flickered he gave an angry, disgusted groan, and Murphy, glancing up, shook his head in agreement. At nineteen thousand feet George Noe, riding in the nose turret, could see through patchy clouds below a checkerboard of fields and villages. Out in front of the formation, rushing rapidly toward them, was the city of Regensburg.

The first burst of flak appeared just as the lead elements of the formation made the turn. Farrington saw it clearly. Four shells, distant black puffs, exploded about one-half mile out in front. "Flak," Noe called out from the nose turret. It was not intense. Maybe one four-gun battery.

The next salvo cut the distance in half. Four bursts.

A thunderous roar ripped through the ship. The impact hurled Murphy into the radarscope, and Barrett, riding in the top turret, slammed into the butt of his fifties. Perched on the jump seat between Farrington and Wieser, Jack Regan stumbled backward into Perella's table. Out of the corner of his eye Farrington saw the fire, not ten feet from him. A jet of bright orange flame shot back from the left wing, from a spot between the number one and two engines. A wave of stark terror swept through him. "Oh, God," he thought, "the fuel tanks!"

In the radio compartment Howard could see nothing. The concussion from the blast staggered him, knocking him backward off his stool. The walls of the ship seemed to swim suddenly upward. He slid backwards. Fumbling for his chute, he snapped it on and struggled to one knee. His head was throbbing. The noise, a ghastly metallic shrieking, was unbearable. He had to make it to the bomb bay to jump. He could hear nothing on the interphone, could see no one. He had to make it to the bomb bay.

Pulling himself to his feet, Bob looked out the waist window. The opaque gray sky was gone, blotted out by a gigantic sheet of flame. Behind it trailed a grim pall of smoke. A terrible whine whistled through the waist. The ship vibrated wildly, and the floor seemed to dip, then rise, lifting him off his feet, then slinging him backward. He pitched toward the radar scanner, almost fell, regained his balance, then swung around toward the escape hatch in the floor about three feet away. As he turned, he bumped into Brennan. Face to face they stared at each other, frozen for an instant, unable to see through the dark goggles into the other's eyes.

Al flipped backward out of the tail, ripping loose his oxygen mask and radio wires. Lying on the platform behind the turret, he grappled wildly for his parachute pack. Where was it? The plane was shuddering violently, convulsed by horrible wrenching spasms. An ammo box slid past him, and a large yellow oxygen tank broke free, crashing in front of him. He found it hard to move. His hand fell on the pack and he tried to snap it onto his chest, but his hands felt weighted with lead. The metal snaps seemed suddenly very complicated. Inching forward toward the escape hatch, a profound sense of weariness swept over him. He slumped. His sight grew dim. Through the smoke he could make out two forms in front of him. Peterson and Brennan stood a foot or so away from the escape hatch. They seemed miles away. He would never make it. His eyes closed. The world turned upside down. He was going to die.

Sprawled on the floor in the nose, his legs resting in the wheel well, Manners heard Noe call out the first flak. He sat bolt upright. His first instinct was to swing around and face forward, but before he could turn, the plane seemed to lurch upward and to the right, throwing him into the navigator's vacant fold-up stool. His head was ringing, and he could hear nothing on the interphone. He could not turn around, could not move. "Jesus," he realized, "I'm pinned to the floor." Lying almost flat on his back, the centrifugal force pressing on his chest like an anvil, he could see through the Plexiglas of the astrodome above him a blur of clouds, streamers of blue, patches of brown swirling by. In a flash he realized that he did not have on his chute, but it hardly seemed to matter. He was not going to be able to get out of the plane.

Flying just off Farrington's right wing Harold Read saw a plume of red orange flame gushing from the left side of the *Black Cat*. Almost instantly Farrington's ship heaved upward. Hurled up and to the right by the blast, it roared directly into Read's path. As he frantically swerved his own aircraft away, Read saw out of the corner of his eye Farrington's left wing fold and break away in an enormous, fluttering fireball. The ship listed over on its side and started down in a wide, flat spin.

As the plane flipped upside down and the sky shot by in a dizzying swirl, a dreadful roaring filled the aircraft. They were spiraling down, the wing had snapped off between the number one and two engines, and at any second the fuel tanks would blow. Farrington and Wieser struggled desperately for control, pulling savagely at the control columns, straining to right the aircraft. With the number one engine gone, the fire in the wing incredibly vanished. The nose nudged slowly upward, the spin seemed to widen into a great, lopsided circle, and the plane, shuddering through the wispy clouds, miraculously leveled out. Soaked with sweat, Farrington pulled back on the control columns, groaning with effort. He wondered if they could gain control, crash-land somewhere? Fields, villages, a swath of woods swam up through the clouds below them. Then, sickeningly, the controls went soft, the plane heaved a terrifying, metal-splintering shudder, and the nose swung buoyantly upward, weightless in the leaden sky.

"B-24 going down!"

Henry Hiter, flying copilot in the element just ahead of Farrington, heard his tail gunner shout. "Third squadron."

"Who is it?" the pilot asked.

"Lead plane, third squadron," the tail gunner said.

Hiter quickly studied his formation diagram. With a wrench in his stomach he saw that it was Farrington. They lived in the barracks together. He knew those guys. He had flown with them on the mission to Perleberg, had made the emergency landing with them in Brussels.

"Any chutes?" he asked.

"No," the tail gunner said, "no chutes."

"Top turret, any chutes?"

"Nothing."

Hiter strained to look around, but the formation was rumbling on. The flak had stopped. No more than eight bursts had come up. He shook his head in disgust.

"Wait," the waist gunner called out suddenly. "I see something." He paused. "Yeah, there's chutes coming out."

"How many?" Hiter barked.

"I see them, too," the tail gunner yelled.

Hiter cocked his head to one side, listening.

Above the whining of the engines the tail gunner began to count.

CHAPTER VIII

WHEN THE BOYS ARE HOME AGAIN

O n May 7 the radio announced that the Germans had surrendered. At 2507 Trunk Street the phone did not stop ringing. From the open windows Mildred could hear the blare of car horns and the ringing of church bells from Ocoee Street. She had been awake since before dawn, listening to the radio, to the reports crackling through the spring air from Washington, New York, and London. Was the war in Europe really over? For weeks she had anticipated this news, but there had been so many rumors, so many false alarms, that even now she could not comprehend fully that the war had come to an end. Tom, gone for almost two years, would be home soon, and Howard, too. She could hardly believe it. She tried to reach her mother in Knoxville, but the lines were tied up, as they had been all morning, and it was still too early to call Nancy, so she sat in the small parlor on the piano bench with her cup of coffee and tried to comprehend what the news meant.

The weekly newspaper, the *Herald*, was lying on the divan, and she picked it up. For weeks everyone had been anticipating V-E Day, and the paper was full of announcements of office closings and reminders that no beer would be sold. The chairman of the chamber of commerce announced that retail merchants had decided on closing hours for V-E Day. "If news comes before twelve noon," she read, "stores will close then and remain closed all afternoon; if news comes after noon, stores will close at the time the announcement is made and will remain closed for the remainder of the afternoon and all day the day following." She wondered if that meant the stores downtown were closing now. She checked the weekly ration calendar. She had several red stamps for meat and blue for processed foods. If she hurried, she had time to walk downtown to Calloway's Grocery. Maybe the post office would close too. She had her usual letters to mail. For nearly two years she had written a daily letter to Tom and every other day a letter to her brother Howard. Surely the post office wouldn't be closed too.

By the time she had cleared away the breakfast dishes, the radio was announcing that the news of a German surrender was premature, a false alarm. Supreme Allied Command had refused to confirm the earlier report. Still, the broadcaster emphasized, news of the war's end in Europe was imminent. Stay tuned. Mildred gathered up her letters, one V-mail and one airmail, slipped them into her pocketbook, and closed the door behind her. No need to lock it. She walked up Trunk Street under the canopy of maples, already brilliant green, turned onto Parker, and strolled up to the monument, her usual route downtown. For almost two years she had made this trek daily, wearing a path from the front porch to the yellow brick post office. Of course, the mailman would have picked up the letters for her right at the house if she had wanted, but she liked to take them herself. It seemed to make the connection with Tom and Howard more direct.

Everyone at the post office was talking about the surrender. They stood in clumps on the sidewalk and on the granite steps beneath the cast-iron lampposts with the frosted-glass globes. She mailed the letters, double-checking as she did every day the APO numbers, and then crossed over the courthouse lawn, slipping past the ornate bandbox and wooden benches, filled, even early on a weekday morning, with old men in from the country. The stores were still open and would be until at least noon, even if the V-E Day announcement came now. The ration coupons were in her pocketbook. She decided there was time to stop in at Central Drug Store for a Coke at the fountain before she went to Calloway's. It was already hot.

She walked in past the greeting cards and the magazine rack toward the soda fountain at the rear. The booths were full of merchants and lawyers from the courthouse across the street, already on their first coffee break.

Waving at the clerk from women's shoes at Parks Belk Department Store, she took a seat on a stool at the counter. Someone had left a copy of the county newspaper there, folded over to the serialized novel, John Hersey's *A Bell for Adano*. Her brother James—the young doctor, Howard liked to call him—was after her to read it, but she had missed the first several installments and never really got interested. She glanced absently at the first paragraph, ordered a Coke, stripped the paper off the straw, and waited. In the large mirror on the wall behind the counter she noticed that her hair looked a bit windblown. Small wisps swayed in the breeze from the overhead fan, and she discreetly patted them back into shape. Just the beginning of May, and the humidity was already bad.

She was still struggling with a bobby pin, slipping it up beneath the luxuriant pageboy roll that fell at the nape of her neck, when Margaret Ryden, her next-door neighbor, appeared, red-faced and panting, in the mirror behind her. Margaret's husband, Knox, was overseas too, and for months the two women had looked after one another, exchanging news, commiserating, talking in the mornings and evenings on the porch steps or across the hedge in the tiny backyards. Breathless, Margaret rushed toward Mildred, talking before she even stopped moving. She had ridden her bike, she blurted out, had been looking for Mildred at the post office.

"What is it?" Mildred asked, swiveling around on her stool.

Margaret patted her chest, trying to catch her breath. "It's Western Union," she almost gasped. "The truck stopped at your house just after you left."

Mildred's heart froze. She jumped down from the stool and rushed out onto Ocoee Street. Turning left, she raced past Merchant's Bank and the Cherokee Hotel and the bus station to the small Western Union office just across from the park. Her heart was pounding. Had something happened to Tom? To Howard? Maybe it was good news, the war really was over, Howard or Tom had gotten off a cable. A bell clanged as she flung open the glass door.

Mildred knew the clerk on duty. She had sent so many wires from this office in the days before Howard and Tom went overseas. "Miss Bielenberg," Mildred coughed, out of breath and fighting a surge of dread, "did we get a wire? I wasn't home. Margaret told me." The words didn't seem to want to come out right. Miss Bielenberg looked up at her, then down at some papers stacked neatly behind the counter in front of her. She was not smiling.

"Yes," she said, "there was a telegram, 2507 Trunk Street."

"That's right, that's right," Mildred gasped.

"Well, Mildred," Miss Bielenberg said, "the telegram," she paused, "the telegram was from the War Department."

"Oh no, oh no," Mildred muttered.

"It wasn't for you, dear," Miss Bielenberg continued softly. "It was for your mother."

Mildred's mind was reeling. Mother. That meant Howard.

"You know I can't reveal the contents of the telegram, Mildred," Miss Bielenberg said. "But this much I can say." Her voice seemed so far away, coming from another planet. "It's not the worst."

"Mother's not there," Mildred said. "She and Daddy have an apartment in Knoxville. He's working up there." The telegram would have to be rerouted. She gave the address on Morgan Street. Her father would still be at work and James at school. Her mother would be alone in the house. "Can you wait just a bit before you send it," she asked. "I want to call Mrs. Orr. She lives next door. She can go over and be with Mother." Miss Bielenberg nodded. "Of course, dear," she said, and Mildred was gone.

Racing home, hardly seeing the streets or stores, passing without speaking to people who waved to her along the way, Mildred tore into the house, got the operator on the line, and caught Mrs. Orr at home. Yes, she would be glad to go next door to Mrs. Goodner. Be brave, Mrs. Orr said. Have faith. Hope for the best. Mildred hung up. Standing at the open window, where the crape myrtle was just budding, she looked out at the pale green leaves. She began to pray.

The telegram did not reach Callie Goodner until late in the afternoon. She tried to call her husband Ernest at work after Mrs. Orr had knocked on the door and with a curious expression told her about the wire. But she could not reach him, and so the two women waited, barely speaking, barely breathing it seemed, for the telegram. They were standing on the red brick front porch when the familiar Western Union truck pulled up across the street and the driver darted across the trolley tracks with the telegram. Holding the envelope firmly in her left hand, Callie tore it open and unfolded the flimsy rectangle of yellowish paper. The neatly stenciled purple letters formed a message of only four lines, lines she would never forget:

THE SECRETARY OF WAR DESIRES ME TO EXPRESS HIS DEEP RE-
GRET THAT YOUR SON T/SGT GOODNER HOWARD G HAS BEEN
MISSING IN ACTION IN GERMANY SINCE 21 APR 45 IF FURTHER
DETAILS OR INFORMATION ARE RECEIVED YOU WILL BE
PROMPTLY NOTIFIED CONFIRMING LETTER FOLLOWS

Into the night in the small house on Morgan Street the Goodners talked about the possibilities. It couldn't be true. The war in Europe was over. The boys were coming home. It had to be a mistake. They had just received a letter from Howard two days ago. Callie went to the drawer where she kept all his letters. She opened the envelope. It was not a V-mail, but a letter of two pages, dated April 21, written apparently just as Howard was turning in for the night. How could he be missing in action on the twenty-first when he had clearly written a letter that very night? The telegram had to be a mistake. They decided to place a long-distance call to the Brennans in Cliffside Park, New Jersey. Howard had visited the Brennans when the crew was stationed at Mitchel Field, and the families had exchanged Christmas cards and other greetings since the boys had been overseas. The long-distance operator put them through. The Brennans were shocked at the news. They had received no telegram from the War Department, and they, too, had just heard from Jack. They would find his letter, check the date. It had to be a mistake.

The following morning at eight o'clock President Truman read a statement over the radio, announcing that the war in Europe was over. The Germans had surrendered. May eighth, he declared, in his flat Missouri twang, was V-E Day, the day they had looked forward to for so long. But on Morgan Street in Knoxville there was no celebrating. In the afternoon mail an official letter from the War Department arrived, confirming that the MIA telegram of May 7 had not been an error. The form letter offered no further information, no clue about what had happened. Signed by an officer in the adjutant general's office, it merely added, "I realize the distress caused by failure to receive more information or details," and assured them that any new information would be relayed as quickly as possible. "If no information is received in the meantime, I will communicate with you again in three months from the date of this letter." It explained that it was the policy of the commanding general of the army air forces to convey any details about missing airmen on receipt of the missing aircrew report but gave no indication of when such a report would be complete.

That night, in the midst of a euphoric broadcast from London, with wildly cheering crowds rumbling like a volcano behind the announcer's jubilant, giddy report, the phone rang, and when Callie picked up the receiver she instantly recognized the voice of Helen Brennan. They had received a telegram. Their son Jack was missing in action.

"I started to write you yesterday," Helen Brennan wrote to Callie on May 10, "but . . . I couldn't concentrate, so I hope I will be able to do better today. I was talking to Mrs. Barrett Tuesday evening and up until then she hadn't received any word, but she called me last night and said they received a telegram that afternoon. Her son was the engineer on the crew, and when Jackie wrote in his letter of April 6 (I don't know whether Howard mentioned anything to you about them coming down in Brussels, Belgium, about the third of April—when all the engines were conking out and they all had their parachutes on ready to jump) he said with the mercy of God and through the coolness of their engineer and pilot they came through safely. I write this in case you haven't heard about it before. It has given me courage insofar that I think they were a wonderful crew, that if there was any chance of being saved, they had the ability to do so. . . . I have a lot of faith in them. I certainly hope it won't be shattered.

"I wrote to the boy's mother who lives in Brooklyn, but up to now I haven't heard from her. I also wrote Mrs. Peterson, who lives in . . . Illinois. They are the only . . . addresses I have. . . . Well, dear Mrs. Goodner, I sincerely hope and pray that we shall receive some good news real soon, and please don't feel badly for calling me up because you helped me receive the news with less of a shock. The last letter I received from Jackie was written on the twentieth of April. I hope it is so that Howard's was written on the twenty-first and that this is all a mistake."

Helen Brennan sent the addresses of the Barretts and Seraydarians, and on the eleventh the Goodners called Ceceil Barrett in New York. She and her husband were separated, Helen Brennan had intimated. Ceceil Barrett lived at the Emerson Hotel on West Fifty-sixth Street, and her husband, Howard, resided in the Century Apartments on Central Park West. Howard Barrett was a prominent New York businessman, the owner of Barrett Amalgamated Industries, with offices at Rockefeller Center, and was well connected with members of the Roosevelt—now Truman— administration. They thought he might be able to gain access to information from the War Department, but Ceceil Barrett had no additional news. They, too, had received the telegram and confirming letter and were endeavoring to find out what they could and would be in touch immediately if they had anything to relate.

In the meantime another letter, this one bearing a Chicago postmark, arrived for the Goodners. "I am not acquainted with you but found name of H. Goodner on an English note my husband sent home for a souvenir," Marie Peterson wrote. Her husband, she explained, was a waist gunner on the crew. "We have two boys, one six years old and one fifteen months." She had received the War Department's telegram and was desperate for news. Did the Goodners know anything more? The last letter from her husband was written on 20 April and indicated that the crew had been in school and not flying. "The anxiety of not knowing their whereabouts is killing. I am hoping they are prisoners of war. Today's news says if servicemen who are liberated and returned to England request it, next of kin will be promptly notified, but not for us to correspond with them or War Department in the matter. If you can enlighten the situation, I will appreciate it greatly."

Callie wrote that afternoon, mentioning again Howard's April 21 letter and giving Marie the addresses of the Barretts, Seraydarians, and Brennans. "Our daughter's husband is also with the Eighth Air Force in England and is stationed only fifty miles from our son. They spent . . . their passes together and often talked together on the phone." Mildred had wired Tom at his base in Framlingham, giving him the news and asking him to see what he could find out from the 466th. "They kept in close contact," Callie continued, "so we feel sure that by now Tom has obtained all reports available, and we hope to hear from him soon. Just as soon as we receive any news, I will get it to you in the quickest possible way. . . . It may be that we will hear from some of the boys personally, even before we hear again from the War Department. We are praying for the safety of all the crew, and being God's will, they will come back to us."

In the aftermath of the telegram the Goodners decided to return to the house on Trunk Street. That address was Howard's official residence, and all communications from the War Department would come there. Callie wanted to be at home in the house where she had raised her family, surrounded by pictures of the children. Ernest would settle their affairs in Knoxville and join her as soon as possible. In the meantime, a letter arrived from Howard Barrett. Acknowledging that they had received an MIA telegram on May 9, he detailed the steps he was taking to get information on

the boys. "My very dear friend Senator Quinn immediately got in touch with
Mr. Basil O'Connor, who is head of the American Red Cross, and I know
they are working on it from every angle. I also immediately cabled Jerry's
fiancée in London, and she is also working to try and get some further
information. I have so many people working to try and get some information
that you may be sure that as soon as we hear anything we will immediately
contact you."

He concluded hopefully, "Jerry has told me time and time again what
a splendid bunch of boys he is with. The fact that they were the lead plane
shows that they were recognized as an unusually capable group, and we
feel, as you do, that they would be able to handle themselves in any
emergency. There is so much confusion over there just now that it is
almost impossible to get any information out. It may be that the boys were
forced to bail out over the mountainous country or even had to make a
forced landing. Communications are very bad there, and it may be that
they were captured and taken as prisoners, in which case there is just a
question of a few more days before they will all be released. We know
exactly how you feel, and I can only say to you to keep your courage up,
and I hope and pray that the boys will all come through okay. Jerry's
mother feels strongly that the boys are all okay, for just before Jerry left he
promised his mother he would be back and she says he has never broken
any promise he has ever made."

By the time Howard Barrett's letter reached Tennessee, the Goodners
were reeling from a second devastating jolt. On Thursday, May 17, Helen
Brennan phoned. Another telegram from the War Department had arrived
in the afternoon, she said tersely. It told them that their son Jack was dead,
killed in action in Germany on April 21. A wave of panic swept through
Callie. The Brennans had feverishly called the families of the other crew
members in the New York area and discovered that they alone had received
the second cable. Had the Goodners heard anything? No, no, nothing,
Callie stammered out. There were no details, Helen said, just the wire. A
confirming letter would follow, it stated.

All the next day Callie and Mildred waited in the house, afraid to leave,
afraid to answer the phone, afraid not to, afraid of every car that slowed or
stopped on the street, afraid of the mail, afraid of the small envelope from
Western Union. Mildred worried that they had not heard from Tom. Maybe
he couldn't wire. Maybe the air force wouldn't allow it. She had sent the
cable on the thirteenth. Maybe he didn't know anything yet. Then, in the

early evening, as she had done for two years, she sat down to write two letters, one to Tom and one to Howard.

She was still writing when the phone rang and Callie picked up the receiver. It was Helen Brennan, her voice breathless and taut. She had just received a phone call from Albert Seraydarian's family in Brooklyn. She had spoken with Albert's cousin only yesterday—Albert's mother had no phone—and the Seraydarians had heard nothing from the War Department since the MIA telegram. Today they had news, though, incredible news, good news! They had received a letter from Albert! He was alive! The whole crew was alive, the cousin insisted, liberated by the American army from a German prison camp! The Brennans were stunned. The letter was dated May 5, less than two weeks ago. Helen called her husband, and he picked up the downstairs phone. Together they listened breathlessly as Al's cousin read the short letter. He read it twice through. On the second reading, the letter seemed more ambiguous than Albert's cousin made it out, but he was adamant. The crew was safe. The Brennans should ignore the second telegram.

The Goodners were buoyant with relief. Their prayers had been answered. But their relief was short-lived. On May 21 Helen Brennan wrote again. "Enclosed please find a copy of the letter Albert Seraydarian wrote his mother," Helen began. "He was the tail gunner. The cousin who called us stated over the phone that *all* the crew was saved and all were well. Even after I questioned him and told him we received a telegram, 'killed in action,' he said disregard it as the letter said they were all saved and liberated. It sounded so good, I couldn't help but call you up and tell you the good news.

"Today to satisfy ourselves we drove over to Brooklyn to see the letter and copied same, so I am enclosing a copy."

The letter read:

My dearest Mom, I know by this time you have been crying and wondering where I am and if I am alive. Well, all I can say is that God scratched my name off and that I am alive and in one piece. It's quite a long and morbid story as to what happened to me, so I'll save it until I see you, which will be very very soon. I am thankful and grateful to God because He made it possible to see you folks again. Mom, please, for my crew's and my sake, light a few candles and have the priest say a few prayers for those living, and for those who gave their life away for the peace and safety of the world. I can't tell you much more, Mom, because every word brings tears and humbleness to my eyes and heart. I am not a prisoner anymore because our army captured the camp and we were liberated. I'll be home very soon. Please keep well, and tell everyone else that I am safe and will be home shortly. I know of no definite date as to my homecoming, but you can be well assured that it will be very soon. Your loving son, Albert

To Helen Brennan the letter gave little cause for renewed hope. "I don't know how you will interpret the letter," she wrote to Callie, "but it doesn't sound too good to me, especially after receiving the second telegram. Thus far I seem to be the only one to have received it, that is, of the four addresses I know." After the emotional roller coaster she had ridden for over a week, she was clearly shaken. "They promised to have Albert call and see us when he arrives home; so just as soon as we receive the correct story, I will pass it on to you—but I assure you it will have to come from an authentic source. I hope this doesn't let you down too much."

At approximately the same time George Manners in Pittsburgh opened his mail to discover a letter from his brother Christ. The bombardier was alive. He offered few details but indicated that he had been taken prisoner and then liberated by the American army. He had been transported to Camp Lucky Strike in France for processing and from there had flown back to Attlebridge. He was on his way home. His letter contained no information about the mission or about the fate of the crew, but news of his survival quickly passed among the families, igniting a renewed flare of hope. Since Manners had sat in the very front of the plane and Seraydarian in the tail, maybe others had been able to escape. So the tiny community of families, bound together in their anxiety, fear, and hope, continued to cling to the possibility that others had bailed out of the aircraft or that it had crash-landed successfully and the crew would still show up. In the great confusion in Germany at war's end that was certainly possible, and the stories of flyers appearing out of nowhere months after being reported lost were not uncommon.

Marie had been shopping on the morning of May 26. Bobby was in school, and she had taken Arthur down Hammond Street to the grocery to pick up some milk. With the baby balanced on her hip she slipped the bag of groceries down onto the step and opened the screen door. Fumbling with her key, she saw, propped against the house door, a small, bone-colored envelope. A telegram. They can't do that, she frowned indignantly as she stooped, reaching for the envelope. They can't just leave a telegram! It must be good news, she pleaded with herself. It has to be. They wouldn't just leave a telegram with something bad in it. No, it has to be good news, she reasoned. Please let it be good news.

Her fingers trembling, she ripped open the envelope and unfolded the sheet of paper. From the strips of stark black letters pasted unevenly onto the page a jumble of words leapt up at her, then settled in terrifying clarity.

THE SECRETARY OF WAR DESIRES ME TO EXPRESS HIS DEEP RE-GRET THAT YOUR HUSBAND S/SGT PETERSON ROBERT E WAS KILLED IN ACTION 21 APRIL 45 HE HAD PREVIOUSLY BEEN RE-PORTED MISSING IN ACTION CONFIRMING LETTER FOLLOWS

That day Western Union delivered the same devastating message to the Farringtons on Oriole Avenue in St. Louis, to the Regans on Ketcham Street in Queens, to John and Margaret Perella on Grant Street in Joliet, to Henrietta Noe in Detroit, and to the parents of John Murphy in West Chester, Pennsylvania. In the confirming letter that followed, the War Department provided the first fragmentary details of the mission. It disclosed that their son or husband was a crew member "on a B-24 Liberator bomber which departed from England on a bombardment mission to Salzburg Germany on 21 April 1945. The [missing aircrew report] reveals that during this mission about 10:35 A.M., while in the vicinity of Regensburg, Germany, [the] bomber was subjected to enemy antiaircraft fire and was seen to sustain damage. Three parachutes were observed from the damaged Liberator as it descended toward the earth. It is regretted that no other information has been received in this headquarters relating to the last mission of" Lieutenant Perella or Farrington or Regan or Murphy or Noe. The letter also included a list of the addresses of the next of kin of all crew members.

Sparse as those details were, they represented the first real information the families had. But the letter raised additional questions for everyone. Seraydarian and Manners were accounted for, but not the third chute. Six of the crew had been reported killed in action, but the Barretts and Goodners had received no KIA telegram at all. None of the boys had mentioned Louis

Wieser in their letters, and he did not appear in the crew picture. Maybe he was in the third chute.

"I wish that I could start this letter with good news or talk to you all myself," Tom began in his letter of May 20. "I received the news that Howard was missing from Mildred on Sunday, May 13. They brought me the cablegram to my barracks and after I had read it I went to the phone and tried to get through to his base. . . . I never could . . . but I made arrangements to take a jeep up there the next day. I called again at 0730 and finally got through at 1000. I talked to his adjutant and first sergeant and they said they had some news for me but they couldn't give it out over the phone. I left . . . and drove to his base, a distance of eighty-six miles by road, and went to his squadron. I talked to the first sergeant and adjutant. . . . Everything was being done that they could to find out the exact facts.

"The facts, as I can tell them, are these. They were shot down by flak. I talked to members of the other crews who flew on the same mission and read the reports from intelligence." But whatever he was able to find out about the *Black Cat* and its crew, he was forbidden to write home. "According to the rules of censorship and the army way," he wrote in resignation, "I can't tell you anything [more] until the War Department or his squadron officially notifies you. We still have the same censorship that we had when the war was going on and we will just have to wait. I call the squadron every day and they have my phone number, and they promised me the minute they get some more news they will immediately call me and I will then cable you." It was frustrating and nerve-racking, but he urged the Goodners not to give up hope. "When a person is listed 'missing' every effort is made to learn his true status, and a lot of mistakes are made. I've known a lot of boys who were listed missing and returned fourteen months later, so there is still hope." Yet despite his words of encouragement Tom's letter rang with an unmistakable tone of finality. "I hope in a few more days that I will be able to tell you all some good news about Howard, and help me hope and pray that he is all right. The last time we were together, we were planning on coming home and him going in the front door and I would come in the back. We had so many things to tell you all about Europe and where we had been and seen. Everyone here on the squadron was deeply shocked to hear the news, and they all join me in a prayer for his safety."

Tom's letter reached Trunk Street in the last week of May, at a time when all the families of the Richard Farrington crew were desperate for any inkling of news, any shred of hope to which they could cling. With no information coming from the War Department they turned to one another. Marie was certainly not ready to relinquish hope. "I, too, wanted to write in hopes of better news," she wrote to Mildred on May 31. After the second telegram, she had heard nothing. A letter from the chaplain and command-ing officer were to follow, but as yet she knew nothing. "I don't yet believe he is killed," she wrote. "I have a copy of Albert's letter and he relates 'what happened to me.' [He] presumably thought others of the crew were safe and heard from. He should be coming home soon if he was released on May 5."

In the first week of June Albert Seraydarian returned home to Brooklyn. He had finished his POW processing at Camp Lucky Strike in France and made the trans-Atlantic crossing to Boston. At Camp Miles Standish he completed the necessary paperwork for a furlough home, called his family, whose only communication with him had been his V-mail letter of May 5, and taken the train to New York. At Grand Central Station he decided not to go by subway to Borough Park but to splurge and take a cab directly to Fifty-first Street. As the cab rounded the old, familiar neighborhood corner he saw across the fence that separated the houses from the railroad tracks a large sign reading "Welcome Home, Albert" and another draped across the house just across the street. His sisters, his mother, now gravely ill, and his cousins had all gathered to welcome him home, and as he climbed from the cab, his duffel bag slung across his shoulder, Al Seraydarian was overcome with joy.

Yet in the great jubilation surrounding his homecoming he could not shed an almost crushing burden of sorrow and confusion. On June 11 Al went to visit Jack Brennan's parents. It would be the first of many visits and calls and letters to the families of his crewmates. That night Helen Brennan wrote the full story to the Goodners. "Today we had Albert Seraydarian over, and he told us the story of what happened. It appears as though the mission should have been scrubbed. The visibility was very poor over France, and over Germany it was still worse. Well, they finally were near their target, and the scrubbed signal was given, and they were returning home without dropping their bombs. The visibility was so poor that they were out of formation on a few occasions while going to their target.

"They were over Regensburg, altitude about 20,000 feet, when their left wing was hit with flak and burst into flames. In the meantime the pilot gave the signal to abandon ship. Albert was alone in the tail without his oxygen mask or parachute on. He started to come forward, and he saw Peterson and Brennan tugging at the hatch door to get out; he got groggy due to not having his mask on and fell.

"When he came to there was a big hole, and he realized the ship had cracked and he quickly grabbed his parachute and was trying to put it on. He only had it on the left side of him when it opened and dragged him out.

"The only thing he saw while he was going down was one parachute, which was the Manners boy, and the rest of the plane going down in a tailspin, and then an explosion. . . . Albert doesn't want to be quoted as saying they were all killed because he didn't see the bodies, but he said only something short of a miracle could have saved them."

On the following day Al told the same story to Howard Barrett, who relayed the gist of it to the Goodners. "The boys in the plane never had a chance," he related, "because it immediately went into a nosedive, and when it landed, naturally the bombs exploded. Albert says, however, not to give up because, just as he was saved by a miracle, some of the other boys may have been able to get out and might be hospitalized." About two things, however, he was quite certain. "He saw no other parachutes go down, for they searched the skies . . . [and] he definitely saw the plane land and explode. Albert feels that several of the other boys might also have gotten out, but the only two he is sure of are himself and Christ Manners."

While the Goodners were trying to cope with these grim details a letter arrived from the father of Louis Wieser. He explained his son's role on the plane, and revealed that they had not received the MIA telegram until May 21. He had spoken to Christ Manners in Pittsburgh, but had learned little from him. Mr. Wieser had also been in touch with all the families, but his own son was still listed as missing. "We are trying hard to find out what became of the rest of these unfortunate boys," he wrote. He had asked a close friend, a major stationed near Regensburg, "to investigate this mystery." He had also appealed to a local resident stationed at Red Cross headquarters in Brussels "to help . . . find these missing boys." He promised to forward any findings he received and urged the Goodners "to keep on hoping, as we are, for good news, in spite of everything that has happened."

Marie also wrote to Mildred in early June. "I haven't heard anything from Bob yet, but still hope to." She had read a copy of Albert's May 5 letter and had puzzled over its meaning. "Funny how words can make such opposite meanings. I had a copy Mrs. Brennan sent Bob's mother and read it 10,000 times or more trying to find a meaning that the crew was saved!" She went on to relate a news story about an air ace just returned to Chicago who was shot down, bailed out, was captured by the Germans, shot by SS troops, and left to die, but miraculously found his way to American lines. "Such tales give me hope that all of our crew who have been so brave and courageous will all return home." Her brother had also just returned from France, and he said that "all is so chaotic in Europe, and our boys might not be anywhere near where they could cable home, but he has hopes they are on the way home now."

As the days passed the families wavered precariously on the cusp of despair, buffeted by rumor and hearsay. In early June Mildred spoke with a man who had had a friend on the April 21 mission. The friend had assured him with great confidence that four or five chutes had been seen leaving the plane. Mildred quickly relayed this information to Howard Barrett via special delivery on June 15, hoping that Mr. Barrett would be able to unearth something more. After talking to several friends from the Eighth Air Force, Mildred had also been given another straw of hope. Since the mission had been recalled, perhaps the bombs had been disarmed, or perhaps the pins had never been pulled. If not, then they might be less likely to explode during a crash-landing and the boys in the plane might have survived. Manners should know if the pins had been pulled, and she wrote to Howard Barrett laying out the information and thoughts she had.

On June 17 Howard Barrett placed a call to Christ Manners, who was back home in Pittsburgh. In his phone conversation the bombardier essentially repeated Albert's story, but added a few new details. "Manners bailed out at about 20,000 feet, and his chute wasn't on properly and didn't open until he was very close to the ground. He was afraid his chute wouldn't open at all, and he went down in a spiral." Because of that "he was unable to see if any of the other boys outside of the Seraydarian boy and himself got out. He, of course, thinks that if any of the other boys got out it would be a miracle, but he definitely cannot say yes or no. He seems to agree with the Seraydarian boy on all other details."

Howard Barrett decided to see Al again the following day, hoping that he would "be in a better frame of mind" and could "discuss it a little more clearly." He promised to write Mildred again immediately after that conversation. It had not occurred to him to ask Manners if the pins had been pulled from the bombs, but he planned to ask Albert the next day. "The only encouraging thing I see here is that the boy you talked to is sure that he saw four or five chutes bail out. We all hope and pray that this is a fact, and it may be the Lord will spare a few of these boys. . . . I still do not know where the six boys who were reported killed were found," Mr. Barrett wrote. If Jerry and Howard and Louis Wieser were not found in the plane, maybe they had, indeed, succeeded in bailing out. Maybe *they* were the three chutes observed by the other planes in the formation. After all, Manners and Seraydarian both thought they had opened their chutes close to the ground. It would account for the discrepancy in the number of chutes.

Still, the conversation with Al did not give Howard Barrett much to hang on to. He wrote to Mildred that Albert had pulled the pins from the bombs when they got over their target, and "when the plane went down, he feels definitely certain that the bombs went off when the plane hit the ground. He also feels that there was an explosion of the gas tank in midair." Mr. Barrett had put all this in a letter to the War Department, emphasizing that "several of the families are anxious to get the details," but he had received no news from any official channels. "There is little else I can say at this time," he wrote, "but I certainly hope that the boy was right whose friend saw four or five boys bail out. Just keep on praying and hoping for some good news to come."

Several days later Marie wrote to Mildred. "I'm in the country at my mother-in-law's, temporarily visiting with the children. The Purple Heart was sent here, but I won't open the box to see it. I would prefer to return it to the president. Poor exchange, all these meaningless medals in place of my husband." The Catholic chaplain of the 466th had also written, and a letter from air force headquarters giving the already familiar details of the mission had arrived. Still, she could not give up. "It seems strange that the War Department lists them killed by Albert's word, yet letters state three chutes were seen to open. Where did Howard sit in the plane? . . . I hope yet to hear from Bob and can't believe he couldn't bail out somewhere before the plane crashed."

Throughout the last days of May, as one family after another received the KIA telegram, the Goodners waited with a combination of hope and horror. But no telegram arrived, and as the days passed they settled in for a long vigil, waiting for word from Howard. James was home from the university, Ernest had closed up the Knoxville apartment, and Mildred was still living in the house on Trunk Street. Nancy stopped by every day, and together they rehashed the various scenarios, the number of chutes, where Howard might be, why he had been unable to contact them. They dissected the statements from Albert and Christ Manners. They analyzed what little they knew from the War Department and from the others. They remained in contact with the other families, exchanging scraps of information and words of encouragement, bound to them in a tangle of desperate hopes. They continued to write to Howard daily, but by mid-June their letters began to return, MISSING stamped ominously across the envelopes. The first one had come to Nancy. Her mother, mistaking it for a letter *from* Howard, had called her excitedly at work, and for a brief moment there had been a new flurry of hope. Callie tried to sew, Ernest tried to listen to the fights on the radio, they tried to carry on, but the hours of the days drifted interminably by, borne on a sluggish current of dread.

June 24 was a Sunday, and Mildred and Callie were alone in the house when the man from Western Union knocked on the front door. He had a telegram for Mrs. Goodner, he said. In that moment so filled with terror and hope, so mingled with prayer and fear, Callie tore open the envelope. She read only as far as the opening words.

THE SECRETARY OF WAR DESIRES ME TO EXPRESS HIS DEEP REGRET

One look at her mother's stricken face told Mildred that her brother Howard would not be coming home.

On that desolate Sunday night Mildred called the Barretts in New York, asking if they had received the same telegram. The news about Howard came as a terrible blow to the Barretts. "I hope and pray that the telegram you got Sunday is an error, for somehow Mrs. Barrett and myself always felt that Howard and Jerry were two of the boys that got out. We feel this way in spite of my talks with the two boys who bailed out." The Barretts had not been notified, and on the following day Howard Barrett placed another telephone call to Washington. It produced absolutely nothing new. The War Department would not even confirm the report that three chutes had been reported emerging from the plane. Still, the Barretts urged the Goodners to hang on. "We know of nothing else to add at the moment, but I can only say to you to just keep hoping. The fact that several chutes were seen coming out of the plane and only two boys were accounted for would give you some hope of encouragement in spite of the notice you received from the War Department."

For days after Mildred's anguished call on the night of June 24, the Barretts waited with mounting dread, shuttling between relief that no telegram had arrived and the paralyzing terror that at that very moment the same bleak notification was winding its way through the military bureaucracy toward them. Using all of his connections, Howard Barrett was leaving no stone unturned in his efforts to find out what had happened, but even with the war in Europe over, military censorship and regulations proved an almost impenetrable barrier. Like all the stricken families of the crew, he found himself forced to pursue clues, rumors, and hunches with virtually no help from the War Department. Having spoken with numerous officials in Washington, he wrote to the commanding officer of the the 787th Squadron, still stationed in Britain. The letter he received in response, dated June 13, took weeks to reach New York and contained nothing. "I have not replied by cable as you suggested," the CO wrote, "because there has been no information from higher headquarters giving the status other than missing in action for your son." He offered no new details about the mission, nothing from within the squadron or group, nothing beyond what the War Department had already communicated. He did suggest that Mr. Barrett might wish to contact the bombardier of the crew who, according to his information, was now back in the States, and he provided Christ Manners's address in Pittsburgh. On July 5 Howard Barrett summed up his feelings to Mildred, reporting with frustration on his correspondence. "I hardly know what else I can say at this time, for we feel as you do that Jerry and Howard were two of the boys that were able to bail out. . . . Just keep on hoping and praying that the message you received was an error and some good news may be forthcoming."

On July 1 Howard's friend Buddy McLeod wrote to Callie from his air base in Texas. Word had reached him about Howard, and he was devastated. He recalled the old times growing up together, "being raised practically as brothers"—mowing lawns together, coaxing fifteen cents out of her for the movies or a swim at Fillauer Lake, playing sports together. "Just sitting here recalling a bit of our past together really brings back many, many of those . . . happy and beautiful days. What I wouldn't give for all that again!" He closed with a promise. "Although you have received the news I won't myself believe it, and I'll expect to get news soon that a certain buddy of mine has turned up someplace safe and sound. But until then both you and I will have to live on those sweet old memories and pray. Also, until we are all together again as before, I'll do all the football, basketball, tennis, and baseball playing for the two of us. Then on and on into the future I'll do whatever I might be doing for the two of us, always. Guess that will be a pretty big job, to do twice as much, especially his part, but I'll always be there trying until he shows up to take over the same old spot. In closing, let me say that I wouldn't want Goodner to read this so when he gets home make sure you have gotten rid of this bit of memory literature. And never give up hope," he wrote, "I haven't and won't."

In the meantime, army air forces headquarters wrote to Howard Goodner's family, stating with chilling finality that he had been killed in action on 21 April 1945 over Regensburg. The letter merely repeated the bare essentials concerning the mission, well-known by now to all the families of the crew, but it did note that three parachutes were seen emerging from the plane. The letter concluded by stating, "It is regretted that no other information has been received in this headquarters relating to the last mission of Sgt. Goodner." This line was particularly maddening, since the families themselves already had pieced together more than was revealed in this letter, and again, there was the question of the chutes. The letter also did not state explicitly that Howard's body had been found or where. Staggered with grief and yet unwilling, unable, to accept the War Department's terse communications as unequivocal, unalterable fact, the Goodners, like the Brennans, the Petersons, and the other families of the crew, found in the very vagueness of those grim messages enough to nourish a slim residue of hope. "They don't know what the fate of the crew or plane was," Marie wrote emphatically. All the War Department had, she believed, was Albert's testimony.

Marie had still heard nothing from Albert but was anxiously awaiting his letter. "Guess it's unpleasant for him to mention the facts and he's trying to forget as much as he can, I presume." The Goodners, however, continued to cling to the belief that Howard had managed to bail out, that the stories they had heard about four or five parachutes were accurate, and that Howard, despite the telegram from the War Department, was among them. Howard was so strong, so athletic, his brother James felt, that surely he could have jumped. If anyone could get out of that burning plane, surely it was Howard. "I guess we all feel the same way," Marie wrote to Mildred on July 10. "Just can't give up hope or figure out why more didn't jump when they were ready and capable of doing it. . . . I read where Group 466 had . . . movement plans for return to the USA. Wouldn't it be like heaven to have our fellows all turn up yet?"

The vast majority of Eighth Air Force bomb groups were returning to the States, including the 466th and the 390th. Tom would be home after two years in Europe, and perhaps he would bring more definitive news about Howard. For Mildred the emotions were very mixed. Her husband, gone for two years, would be home soon—perhaps as early as August—but her joy at the prospect of seeing him was tinged with the fear that Howard was lost. "I hope you enjoy seeing your husband," Marie wrote in late July. "You can't know how I feel after waiting three years for this war to end, and now when boys are returning he is not. . . . Each time the phone rings I jump, thinking it may be Bob. His mother thinks they are all dead, burned in the plane. . . . I don't believe it was the fate of all. Some, yes, but I do think more than two were able to jump somewhere. [But] where could the boys be this long without a word to home folks, unless a mental collapse could keep them in a hospital. . . . I, too, keep in mind those four chutes. They are the only thing that keeps me from a mental collapse." Even with the rising tide of discouraging news, Marie continued to pray that they would "hear something good soon."

When Al's letter arrived several days later it offered little cause for optimism. "I'm awfully glad you wrote to me," he began, "because I want to offer my services in any way possible. I'll admit it's a little hard for me to explain, but since I know how you feel, I will gladly try. . . . It's very hard to say just what his last few words were," Al wrote, "because we were all praying to survive. Then things happened so fast that my mind and I guess everyone else's . . . was all mixed up. Previous to that mission we used to sit and talk and Bob used to tell me about his children. Every time he wrote letters he'd have his family's picture in front of him. I can't explain his thoughts, but you should know he loved everyone.

"As for the amount of chutes leaving the plane, I myself can only account for two. Please don't hold me to this because I'm just as uncertain as you are yourself. I wouldn't swear to anything. . . . [but] I've been wishing and praying for the best.

"As for Jack and Bob not jumping, well, here's how I figure it. When we were hit, I was out of that turret, and when I turned around I saw [them] at the escape hatch, and then everything happened so fast that I couldn't keep track. When I got to my senses the tail was broken off and I was floating down nice and easy. Then I put on my chute and pulled the rip cord while I was still in the plane, and when the chute opened it pulled me out. I guess if they did the same they could have gotten out also. When I was floating down I looked for chutes, and I only saw two." Marie stared down at the letter, her eyes wide. Maybe he meant two *other* chutes, Manners and someone else, or maybe he was referring to his own. "I wouldn't swear to anything, Mrs. Peterson, because there's too much at stake to be sure of anything," Al continued. "If any of them were hospitalized, word would have reached everyone, unless they didn't wear dog tags."

Confused and anguished, Al's letter rambled to a conclusion. "I'm all mixed up and upset," he wrote. "That day was very sullen. Everything went wrong, but the mission had to be completed, and as for being lead crew, well, we all voted fairly . . . considering all the advantages and disadvantages. We were for it because it should have saved five extra missions. . . . I'm awfully sorry it happened the way it did. We were pretty lucky up to that mission, and then everything happened at once. If there's any more questions you have I'd be more than glad to try and answer them. I know every little detail would help to make things a lot more comforting. Believe me, Mrs. Peterson, I feel very bad about that because I feel just like the other half of my . . . life disintegrated with the losses of war. I guess I've talked long enough and haven't said anything to comfort you. . . . Please give my love and regards to the family and tell them I'm sorry."

Before Marie could absorb Al's letter the families of the Richard Farrington crew were jolted again. The news did not come from the War Department but through the initiative of one of the families. The father of John Murphy, the radar operator, discovered through unofficial channels that the members of the crew had been identified and were buried at Nuremberg. The news flashed through the beleaguered families from Philadelphia to New York to St. Louis to Tennessee to Chicago. Disconsolate, Marie wrote again to Mildred. "By now you may have heard the worst. . . . I still can't bring myself to believe that Bob is dead. . . . Now we are trying to figure out how they got so far from Regensburg, where the plane crashed, a distance of about fifty miles. It was a prison camp according to the newspapers. Did Albert ever know the name of the camp he was in? If our boys died in one, how come no reports, and if they were dead in the plane, the enemy surely *wouldn't* take them such a distance for burial! It all seems like a jigsaw puzzle, pieces everywhere but can't be put together, too many missing. . . . It really would be wonderful if some would pop up on a boat in New York but after [this most recent news], I don't hold out any hopes. . . .

Bobby, our six-year-old, says I should keep praying and maybe God will send our Daddy back yet. I haven't told him he's dead. All servicemen in khaki make me so blue when I see them."

On August 7 Marie wrote to Mildred. "Today our baby is one and a half years old. I sure wish Bob could see him now. Guess it will never be. I have given up hope." A local serviceman, she had learned, had been buried in Nuremberg in a U.S. military cemetery, a "beautiful place, surrounded by forest and kept neat with shrubbery and flowers. I can't bring myself to believe our boys are there and that we'll never again see them." Surrounded everywhere by returning servicemen and scenes of joyous reunion, it all seemed too much to comprehend, too much to bear. "I am like you. I see Bob in every khaki uniform. . . . I never dreamed he wouldn't return. Neither did he."

Writing in early August, John Regan responded with anguish to the Goodners' letter of July 24, which had informed him that Howard, too, was now listed as killed in action. "First, please accept my sincere sympathy. Like many thousands of parents, we know what it actually means not ever to be able to see our own again, in whom we have centered our thoughts, hopes, and plans; it just does not seem right or fair, yet it is a definite fact over which we have no control. It is a crime these exceptionally fine young men should have been sacrificed for *what* I would like to know. I am yet to receive the answer." Virtually everything he had learned, he added bitterly, came from two of Jack's buddies, one in England, who wrote a week after the crash, and another who had stopped by in Elmhurst on his way west with his unit. Still, his narrative did add to what the Goodners knew.

"It appears this particular mission was not a regular one but one hastily assembled, and consisted of thirty-seven planes. The weather was extremely bad, so bad, in fact, the planes could not hold their formations and the radio operators kept asking for instructions constantly from their own base, expecting to be recalled each time, but instead were instructed to continue, and the further they flew the worse flying conditions became. Many previous missions had been canceled due to weather not near so bad as this particular day." He then went on to recount the terrible and now familiar story of the flak over Regensburg, adding the new twist that "their plane was shot down, the only one in the thirty-seven." Also new to the Goodners was his observation, "if they had been flying their regular position of main lead plane this would not have occurred, but instead they were in about the center of the group, and if they used their chutes when first struck may have been saved, but instead they stayed with the plane until they had piloted it out of formation. Otherwise the disabled plane possibly would have caused several others to crash also."

He recounted the War Department's report concerning the three chutes and, of course, named the two known survivors, but included a new item. "Jack's friend who visited us several weeks ago stated he spoke to the chaplain and was informed he had flown to Regensburg, Germany, and attended the identification and burial at that place." In closing, Mr. Regan could restrain himself no longer. "I believe I am broad-minded enough to accept in good grace most of the adverse things that happen to us in life," he wrote, "but the loss of Jack I can never accept, because in my opinion it was caused by the stupidity of some one individual or group of individuals in charge of this particular mission. Also, to top matters off, all flying was stopped four days later."

The same mail brought a letter from Helen Brennan to Mildred. "We were in Philadelphia during the first week of July," she wrote, "and my husband stopped in to see Mr. Murphy. He had been to Pittsburgh and was talking to Manners. His story seems to be about the same as Albert's, only he doesn't say the plane exploded. They were flying at 180 degrees when they were hit. They had gone over to bomb a bridge in Salzburg, which was about three-quarters of a mile in length and two lanes [wide]. According to Mr. Murphy it was more for fighter planes or light bombers [than B-24s]. But such wasn't the case, and what can we do about it?"

The Brennans had also spoken again with Albert, specifically about Howard. Mildred persisted in hoping that since Howard had not been immediately identified as killed in action, he was not with the plane and hence had somehow parachuted to safety. Helen Brennan replied that she had raised this issue with Albert, who mentioned that Howard didn't always wear his dog tags, so perhaps that was the reason for the delayed message. Also, the many stories about downed flyers turning up months after [being] declared dead were largely from earlier in the war, she added with resignation. With the war in Europe over, recovery and identification of bodies was easier. If any of the boys were still alive, where, after all, could they be? "I really am at a loss as to what to say. And as time goes on, I agree with you, it is harder to bear. Why such a thing happened and in such a way, I will never be able to comprehend."

In the first days of August, as the war in the Pacific lurched toward its conclusion, the tide of bad news continued to rise like a swollen stream around the house on Trunk Street, washing away the last fragile timbers of hope to which the Goodners had clung for so long. A letter from Tom arrived. The 466th had confirmed to him that Howard was dead, buried in a military cemetery in Germany. The squadron had given him no details beyond what the family already knew, but the adjutant had spoken to him with grim certainty about Howard.

If the Goodners nursed a spark of hope after hearing from Tom, a letter from Richard Farrington's parents doused even that. "Like yourself," Mrs. Farrington wrote to Callie in late July, "I have been too upset and heartbroken to write." Her son had spoken often of Howard, and she noted that only recently, when he had sent the crew picture and commented on all the crew, he had described Howard as "his pet." Being young, she imagined, they had much in common. "Dick was just nineteen when he enlisted, and twenty-two days before their plane went down." What she knew of the events of April 21 she also had learned through unofficial channels. Her son was scheduled to meet his cousin in London on the evening of April 21. When Dick did not show up, his cousin called the 466th and was told that they had bad news but wouldn't relate it via telephone. He then went out to the base and contacted [the squadron commander] who told him that the group was going down to bomb Hitler's Alpine redoubt. When the mission was recalled because of weather, "they swung right over ack-ack battery at Regensburg. Six batteries cut loose at them. They were flying at 23,000 feet. The right wing was shot off. Two Mustangs tailed them down; *four* men bailed out and were machine-gunned from the ground. Two days later the Seventh Army took the town—Eighth Air Force ground observers found the ship—Dick was in it. It was the last mission the 787th flew." Dick's cousin did not report specifically about the other crew members, but he did say that he had quite a visit with their ground crew there at the base and he was left with the impression that they held out no hope of other survivors. "This is hard to write," she concluded, "but as you want to know all the facts I'm sure this has enlightened you some. I only wish we had some hope of Dick's return—[he was] our only son, and like all that fine group of boys it doesn't seem fair when it was so near the end."

While the Goodners continued to hope that somehow it was all an error, the War Department proceeded with remorseless administrative momentum to process Howard's death. On July 18, Henry L. Stimson, the secretary of war, notified the Goodners, "the president has requested me to inform you that the Purple Heart has been awarded posthumously to your son, Technical Sergeant Howard G. Goodner, Air Corps, who sacrificed his life in defense of his country. . . . Nothing the War Department can do or say will in any sense repair the loss of your loved one," the card stated. "He has gone, however, in honor and the goodly company of patriots. Let me, in communicating to you the country's deep sympathy, also express to you its gratitude for his valor and devotion."

Several days later a small box, its smooth, satin lining soft and shiny like the cushions of a coffin, arrived, containing the medal. Accompanying it was a scroll signed by the president. It read:

> In grateful memory of Technical Sergeant Howard G. Goodner, who died in the service of his country in the European area, April 21, 1945. He stands in the unbroken line of patriots who have dared to die that freedom might live, and grow, and increase its blessings. Freedom lives, and through it, he lives—in a way that humbles the undertakings of most men.

The formal condolences and patriotic tributes over, the families faced a flood of administrative communications. "Dear Sir or Madame:" the Veterans' Administration wrote with characteristic impersonal abstraction, "The VA has learned with regret of the death of the above-named veteran. Existing laws provide for the payment of a pension to the dependent mother or father, or both, of a veteran who dies . . . in the line of duty." The forms were enclosed. Shortly thereafter, Army Service Forces, Quartermaster Depot, Army Effects Bureau wrote to the Goodners, declaring, "I am enclosing two money orders in the total amount of $150 belonging to your son, T. SGT. Howard Glynn Goodner. No other property belonging to him has been received at the Army Effects Bureau to date. . . . Money ordinarily is sent from overseas by mail in advance of other effects; thereafter, it is probable that additional belongings of decedent will reach this bureau at a later date." Some time later another check, payable in the sum of $239.40, arrived from the General Accounting Office, "on account of pay due to decedent at date of receipt of evidence of death, May 5, 1945, as T SGT, Air Corps, serial No. 34, 726, 638." A month later another check for $20.18 arrived from the Army Effects Bureau. Callie placed them in the top drawer of the secretary in the parlor. She refused to cash them.

With no information coming from official sources Marie continued her quest to learn what had happened, "hoping," as she put it in one of her numerous letters to the War Department, "to find some comfort in the details." She also turned directly to the army air force. Noting that a chaplain from the 466th was "supposed to have been flown to Regensburg for identification and burial services" of the crew, she inquired whether "this man [can] be contacted to get the information we next of kin seek. It is the least comfort we can now have." The crashed plane and the bodies of the crew had been found when the American Seventh Army reached Regensburg, she explained, and she wanted to know "who were the men found in the ship and who were those who bailed out [and were] machine-gunned from the ground? Through crew members' families who have spoken to boys in that day's mission, this information has been passed on to me. I would like to know how my husband died and how he was buried. . . ." Months later a brief note arrived from the War Department, repeating only the well-known facts.

"We were thinking of you all," Helen Brennan wrote to Marie just after Christmas, "but couldn't get ourselves together to send out cards this year. We thought Christmas was bad last year, not having Jack with us, but this [year] was worse, knowing he would never be with us again. So Christmas was just another day." Writing to Marie in the last days of 1945, Phyllis Farrington sounded a similar note. "Yours, I know, was a sad Christmas," she wrote, "but there's nothing we can do—that is what makes it seem so terrible. . . . Your children are precious, Mrs. Peterson," Phyllis Farrington sighed, glancing at the small snapshot of the boys Marie had enclosed with her Christmas card. "You really have something to live for. May this new year bring you contentment and joy to your children—surely there's a reason, although it's hard for us to understand. Sometimes I can hardly stand it. But," she wrote in closing, "what else can we do?"

While most families of the Farrington crew struggled to cope with their loss, the Wiesers and Barretts confronted another form of excruciating anguish. Weeks passed, then months, and no telegram arrived. The War Department forwarded no information. At Christmas, 1945, Louis Wieser and Jerry Barrett were still officially listed as missing in action, and no additional facts, no new details, no explanation about their status was forthcoming. The possibilities seemed terrifyingly limitless. Perhaps they had somehow managed to bail out. Perhaps they were lost in Europe. In September Howard Barrett, responding to a note from Marie, lamented, "I have not received any further news about Jerry, except that he and Captain Wieser are still reported missing. . . . I spoke to Captain Wieser's father some time ago, and he told me he had a friend who is a major in the army and a former West Point man who is making a thorough search, and he would communicate with me as soon as he heard anything, but so far we have received no information. . . . Naturally we are terribly broken up by the prolonged time in waiting to get information of any kind. . . . The whole thing seems like a horrible nightmare."

In Hammond, Indiana, the family of Louis Wieser was no more successful in wrenching information from the War Department or the air force. Repeated inquiries and appeals to different offices had brought no new information, and as the new year approached their son was still officially listed as missing in action. In desperation Mr. Wieser decided to make an extraordinary proposal. He determined to use his son's West Point connections to gain permission to go to Germany himself. He had emigrated from Austria on the eve of the First World War, spoke German, and even had relatives living in the area. If the army couldn't find out what had happened to his son, he would.

To bring pressure to bear on the appropriate officials in the War Department, Mr. Wieser appealed to a family friend whose son was a colonel at West Point. That friend, an attorney in Chicago, contacted a major general in the judge adjutant's office, informing him that he was writing at the request of a United States district judge for the Northern District of Indiana, who had become interested in Mr. Wieser's case. But January turned to February and the Wiesers, like the Barretts, continued their tortured vigil. While Mr. Wieser made plans for a trip to Washington to press his case in person, the adjutant general's office at last provided the family with some of the information they had sought for so long. It was not what they wanted to hear. Without offering a comment or any details about the mission, the letter stated simply, "A report has been received which discloses that the remains of Captain Wieser are interred in Grave 258, Row 11, Plot B, in the United States Military Cemetery, Nuremberg, Germany."

Shortly thereafter a telegram arrived at the Wiesers' house on Lawndale Street in Hammond and at the Barretts' apartment on Central Park West. Their sons, it informed them, had been killed in action in Germany on 21 April 1945. No further details were ever offered.

"I intended answering your last letter," Phyllis Farrington wrote to Marie in April 1946, "but after I heard from you, we received Dick's effects, and that upset me about as much as the bad news last spring. I got a footlocker full and a corrugated box . . . all in perfect condition. He had a beautiful battle jacket that I have hanging in the closet where I can look at it most every day. Just seems to keep him closer. You know Dick loved new clothes and he had told me he'd had the jacket made in London—the wings and arm insignia are in metallic thread and the lining is red silk. He must have looked fine in it, as *I* think he was quite handsome. [In] the crew picture he looks tired and old, but he was so young—he would have been twenty-three yesterday—just four days over twenty-two when they went down."

A year after the mission the Farringtons, like all the families, remained haunted by the shadowy details of that day. "I don't remember if I told you about a boy who came to see me who had been stationed at Attlebridge where our boys were. He . . . knew Dick well—had flown with him he said. He told me that on this mission . . . the CO directed them in one direction and the navigator on our boys' plane insisted, even argued should they follow his directions they would encounter flak. Well, they had to obey orders and they did and we all know what happened. . . . He said Wieser, Dick, and the whole crew were so well liked that when that group returned to base the boys were so bitter toward the [command pilot] none wanted to talk to him at all. . . . Didn't tell before for fear it might upset you, but you are curious, just as I am, to know the details, so I guess after all we can stand most anything now."

"I think of you and your children very often. . . . I love children so and were we not so old I would take one to raise. We are fifty and fifty-two so at that age I'm afraid we'd be too attached and, well, it just wouldn't work out. . . . I've decided to work in the yard—planted rosebushes and some flower beds—and when I can't stand it I go outside. Seems nature has a way of helping in such situations. Well, my dear, if I get any more information, I will write you immediately. . . . We can't do a thing but go on as best we know how, and we know they wouldn't have us grieve. So keep your chin up—you have those dear babies and I have my husband, so there you are. Kiss them for me and love to you. . . ."

CHAPTER IX

I'LL BE
SEEING YOU

H oward came home on December 10, 1948. An honor guard from the
local American Legion met the train and escorted the flag-draped
coffin to the house on Trunk Street. The family was waiting there—my
grandparents, Ernest and Callie, my aunt Sibyle with Elizabeth Ann and
Charles from Carthage, my parents Mildred and Tom, and Uncle James.
The hearse stopped in front under the black, leafless maples where Howard
had waved good-bye four years before, and the men carried the coffin
through the front door. Inside, the living room was a sea of flowers. Wreaths
and floral arrangements flooded the room from the floor to the ceiling,
blotting out the windows and doorway into the dining room. It was a room
filled with color, and while the adults whispered and sobbed I stood
transfixed, staring at the enormous flag and the oil portrait of my uncle
Howard that hovered above the casket. It was my second birthday and, as I
discovered in my grandmother's house three years ago, that room filled with
color has lingered with me through the years, a dim but indelible image just
beyond memory's grasp.

I never knew Howard. They talked about him of course, about Nancy, about Buddy McLeod, and on occasion about what happened on April 21, 1945, about Albert Seraydarian, the boy from Brooklyn who miraculously escaped from the plane on that day. I do not remember the details of any actual conversation, but the shadow of that nightmarish day lingered on and on, haunting the family for years after the war. Standing at the edge of the kitchen table or playing on the porch while they went over the events of that day, discussing various scenarios, trying desperately to tease some new perspective from the meager information they had been given, I would watch and listen, never fully comprehending the questions. Only the grief was real.

Among the papers I found on that night three years ago was a copy of a letter from my grandfather written in November 1945. Resigned and despondent, he had appealed to the adjutant general in Washington for information, posing the same questions that had tormented the families since May. "We have had very little information from your office in regards to how my son met his death or where he is buried," the letter read. "We have talked to several members of the 466th Bomb Group who were on the mission, and they have differed on the number of chutes that were seen coming from the ship. According to records that you sent me, he was killed in action over Regensburg, Germany, on April 21, 1945. Could you tell me whether my son was found in the ship or did he parachute out? I would also like to know what means . . . [were] used to identify him." In a final plea he added, "I know you have thousands of letters like this and that your office is a very busy place, but please try and understand my position as a parent and that I want to know every detail regarding my son for the sacrifice that . he made for our country. I feel sure his country will give me all the details they have on my beloved son."

In a letter dated July 1, 1946, the adjutant general had at last responded, but after providing the exact location of Howard's grave the officer concluded, "no information as to the circumstances surrounding your son's death, in addition to that previously furnished, has been received." It was the last official communication they received about Howard's final mission.

In the summer of 1946 Mildred and Tom and James drove to New York to talk to Albert Seraydarian. They stopped in Cliffside Park to visit Jack Brennan's family and then found their way across the Hudson to the Borough Park section of Brooklyn. From Albert's house they were directed to a neighborhood candy store where he was playing cards, and when he came out to the curb they instantly recognized him from the crew photo. He stood uneasily beside the car, shifting his weight from one leg to another. Shy and obviously uncomfortable, he struggled with the questions they put to him. They were the same questions that he had tried to answer for the Barretts and Brennans, for the Regans and Marie Peterson, and he had nothing new to add. After only a few minutes the conversation stumbled to an awkward close, and they stood quietly looking at one another, unable to think of anything to say.

From New York they drove west to Pittsburgh, but Christ Manners would speak with them only over the phone. He had nothing to tell them, he insisted, beyond what they already knew. Like Albert, he had recounted the story over and over again since coming home, to his own family and to the families of his crewmates who had phoned or visited. It was obvious that he did not feel like talking. He did not want to relive that day again, and they did not press him.

Later in the spring Tom traveled to Washington, determined to get some answers. After a day of trudging doggedly from orderly to orderly and building to building, he was finally directed to an office where a bored young clerk produced a folder marked TSGT Goodner, Howard G., from a bank of filing cabinets behind him. Shuffling through the papers, the clerk extracted two forms, both carrying a restricted classification, which he reluctantly allowed Tom to see. Glancing quickly over the battle casualty report and report of burial, Tom found no new details about the time and place of Howard's death, but under Cause he read, "multiple skull fractures." Just beneath that entry the burial report also indicated that Howard had been identified "by fingerprints submitted by the FBI in August 1945" and that "name on crew list checks with clothing marks." Sparse as this information was, it suggested to Tom that his brother-in-law had *not* been burned and had therefore probably not been found in the crashed plane. This could mean that he had bailed out and died somehow in the process.

When Tom returned home Mildred relayed this information to Marie Peterson, who in June turned once again to air force headquarters. "I have written to your office several times in a *vain* attempt to get the details of my husband's death over Germany 21 April 1945," she began, but the "replies have been *very* unsatisfactory." She demanded that the air force supply her with information from Bob's file. "I have two small children and cannot take off for Washington to read that record, but there are plenty in your office who are paid to do such work and it is very little to ask one's countrymen to perform such a duty, in comparison to the horrible death my husband and many more faced for their country. Circumstances following or prior to a civilian's death are right at hand, [but] when death occurs in foreign lands on battlefields, we next of kin are . . . anxious to know what we can, if it is available. Your letters contained nothing so far and I do realize the details were slow in coming in, but they are in the air force office now and can be sent to me, with only some book work involved. Hoping to hear from you soon . . ."

In early September Marie received a letter from the quartermaster general assuring her that her husband had been "properly identified," but offering no comment on cause of death or where his body had been recovered. His initials and serial number had been found on his clothing, which seemed to indicate that he had not been burned in the crashed plane, but the letter provided no additional details. He might have been able to bail out after all, she thought. He might have been in the third chute. Like Mildred, Marie continued to write to the War Department, to the air force, to other men from the 466th, searching, she could not even say exactly for what, as if some new piece of information, one last detail, would complete the puzzle and make the whole terrible ordeal somehow comprehensible. But the details never came.

For several years after the war the families of the Richard Farrington crew remained in contact. They exchanged bits of information, things they had heard about the mission and about the crew. They sent photographs. At Christmas and Easter and Mother's Day cards arrived at Trunk Street from the Barretts, from Marie Peterson, whom Mildred had met briefly in the train station in Chicago, and from the Brennans, who had come to Tennessee to visit on their way to a Florida vacation. In 1948, when James took a job in New York—he became a banker and not a doctor—Howard Barrett invited him to dinner at his apartment, and he spoke on the phone several times with Alice, although they never met. The cards and occasional letters intensified briefly in the course of 1948, when the War Department informed them that it was at last able to return the remains of servicemen killed in Europe to the United States if the families so desired. The families wrote as one by one the members of the crew began to return to Joliet and Queens and Manhattan and New Jersey. By the close of the year only Richard Farrington, George Noe, and Bob Peterson remained at the American Military Cemetery at St. Avold, France, where the crew had been moved in late 1945. They are still there today.

As the years passed the Goodners and the other families of the Richard Farrington crew picked up the pieces, coped as best they could, and got on with life. But questions about that day lingered, like fault lines far beneath the placid surface, hidden but never healed. Then, from the open drawer of my grandmother's secretary on that night three years ago, the aftershocks of a crashed aircraft reverberated across the decades and that terrible time rose again, released from the vaults of memory. That night and into the following day I read through the anguished letters from the Barretts and the Brennans, from Marie Peterson, Phyllis Farrington, and the others. I found and read more than three hundred letters from Howard, the last one dated April 21, 1945, and as I did the pull of a past I had imbibed since childhood drew me irresistibly into its powerful grip and I knew what I would do. Nothing could change the losses of that day or erase the grief. But I could follow the trail of the Richard Farrington crew to discover what I could about an uncle I had never known, but whose presence had hovered over me from my earliest memories, and I would find answers to the questions that had haunted my family and the others since the spring of 1945.

After making some preliminary inquiries I discovered that the records of the 466th Bomb Group were housed at the Air Force Center for Historical Research at Maxwell Field in Montgomery, Alabama, and I decided to drive there. The large, dust-coated cartons, wheeled out to me in the brightly lit, air-conditioned readers' room, contained individual files for all of the 466th's combat missions. Each mission folder contained a copy of the briefing notes, maps of the routes in and out, strike photos, and a final summary of the mission. Turning nervously to the folder for the recalled mission to Salzburg, I studied the briefing map, folded perhaps since that day in 1945. A thick red line traced the planned route to the target, a route that should have taken the formation well to the west of Regensburg. The folder also contained a formation flight diagram, a copy of which was given to each pilot at briefing. In the midst of the formation, in the lead of B Group, the names Farrington–Wieser stood out in bold lettering. They were flying aircraft number T9-592-OU, the *Black Cat*. Stapled to the back of the folder was a brief report from Air Station 120 to Second Air Division HQ. Filed late in the afternoon on April 21, 1945, it stated, "Flak at Regensburg meager and accurate. One A/C lost by this group. Lost by flak at Regensburg. Crews report one to four chutes observed." One to four! I was stunned.

Thumbing through the other files, I located the group's secret operational diary—a narrative account of each of the 466th's 231 missions. Turning quickly to its account of the April 21 mission, I found a slightly different entry. "One A/C (Farrington) was shot down near Regensburg, Germany. Four chutes were seen in the vicinity before the ship was seen to explode just before it hit the ground." Four chutes! Then maybe the story Mrs. Farrington heard was possible, that others had gotten out of the plane and were shot by the Germans as they drifted down in their chutes. And if two others had gotten out, who were they? Could it have been Barrett and Wieser? If one to four chutes were seen, how did the War Department arrive at the number three? Rather than clarify, the files only clouded the issue.

Studying the thin mimeographed sheets of the 466th's operations diary, I was staggered by the cruel ironies of the mission. The recalled raid to Salzburg was the group's 230th mission. The 466th, as the ops diary revealed, flew only one more combat mission. On April 25 the 466th returned to southeastern Germany to attack Traunstein. The formation encountered no fighters and no flak, and the group suffered no casualties. A day later the bombers of the Eighth Air Force stood down, their war in Europe over. The *Black Cat*, the only aircraft in the entire formation to be hit over Regensburg—an area far from the planned route—was the last plane lost by the 466th Bomb Group. Later I would discover that it was the last American bomber shot down over Germany in the war, and the men of the Farrington crew were the last combat casualties from the entire Second Air Division.*

Nor was this all. Another file on the Salzburg mission contained the report of the weather scouting force. The scout planes had reached the target area in advance of the 96th Combat Wing and discovered "solid cloud with rime ice from fifteen thousand to twenty-five thousand feet." It was their radio message that convinced the command pilot of the 466th to recall the mission at approximately 10:30 on April 21. The report concluded that "the bomber force made every effort to attack the target and their determination was highly commendable." But my eyes were drawn to the final sentences of the report. "The weather was as briefed. It is believed that this mission never should have been dispatched in view of the forecast and the actual conditions."

Before leaving Maxwell I was told that the Washington National Rec-

* On April 25, five B-17s were shot down over Czechoslovakia in the Eighth's last raid of the war.

ords Center, a branch of the National Archives located in Suitland, Maryland, held additional records from the 466th, including the missing aircrew report, MACR, a form filled out "within forty-eight hours of the time an aircrew member is officially reported missing." This report was the official basis for all communications concerning missing aircrews for the War Department.

Two weeks later, seated at a microfilm reader in the users' room at the National Records Center, I strained to decipher the cloudy lines of the MACR for the Richard Farrington crew. In addition to information on the type and unit of the aircraft lost and a list of the missing crew members, the report noted under "Weather conditions and visibility at the time of crash or when last reported" that there was "no cloud cover below the aircraft (scattered middle clouds; visibility down—twenty—thirty miles)." The two pilots who signed the report were from the lead and trailing squadrons, and as a final entry on the form they had added, "three chutes reported at interrogation." This, then, was the source of the War Department's communications with the families, but just how they had arrived at the number three remained unclear.

Attached to the missing aircrew report was a typed statement by Christ Manners, written in October 1945, after he had returned home to Pittsburgh. It was his account of what he saw on April 21, 1945. "Our plane," he wrote, "was hit by flak over Regensburg . . . [and] within ten seconds the plane was on fire and starting into a spin. The left wing was torn off by the shell. All interphone communications failed, and I was unable to determine the disposition of my fellow crew members. Due to the fact that I was seated on the floor with my legs extended into the nose wheel well, I was able to drag myself out. After escaping from the ship I dropped several thousand feet in a free fall. I opened my chute at ten thousand feet. I saw the wings and rudders of the ship floating down to earth. I saw the wreckage burning on the ground about three miles from my position. I saw one chute besides mine; that was the chute of S/Sgt. Albert Seraydarian, my tail gunner. No other chutes were seen. Sgt. Seraydarian and I were taken prisoner immediately after reaching the ground. It is my belief that all other crew members were killed in the crash. Sgt. Seraydarian was caught in the spin, and remained motionless in the ship. Only when the fuselage broke behind the camera hatch was he able to fall out. He later told me that he had seen Sergeants Brennan and Peterson, the waist gunners, making a futile effort to reach the rear hatch exit." At the time Manners wrote this report for AAF headquarters, Louis Wieser and Jerry Barrett were still officially listed as missing in action and the air force was attempting to determine definitely who might have been in the alleged third chute. Hence the concluding line of Manners's statement. "At the time of the above incident, Capt. Wieser was in the copilot seat, which in my estimation made his chances for escape almost impossible."

The details of the mission had begun to crystallize, but the vexing question of chutes remained a puzzle. Unfortunately, the 466th had not kept the interrogation sheets from the April 21 mission, and so I had reached the end of the line with official documents. In Suitland I sifted through the 466th's operations folders, searching for the Farrington crew's missions. The crew, Howard's letters had made clear, had arrived in England in October 1944, and I began checking the mission folders until I found them. By my count the Salzburg raid was their twenty-third. As I perused the mission maps, read the briefing notes, and examined the loading lists for their missions, I wondered, as I had often since that night in my grand-mother's house, if Manners and Seraydarian were still alive and if I could find them.

Directory assistance in Pittsburgh had no number for Christ Manners, but in 1945 the War Department had listed his brother George as the next of kin. After checking again the operator affirmed that she did have a number for a George Manners, and I called. Christ Manners, I discovered, had died of a stroke in 1960. He was forty-one years old. His brother told me a bit about the family, about the bombardier's military experiences, but could add nothing to what was already known about the crew's last mission. Christ had never wanted to talk about it much. That left Albert Seraydarian.

The New York telephone directory listed no Seraydarians, and the surrounding area codes in New Jersey, Connecticut, and even Pennsylvania yielded nothing. I wrote to the Veterans' Administration in St. Louis, where all such queries must be addressed, but weeks passed with no word. In the meantime it occurred to me that the Eighth Air Force Historical Society, a veterans' organization with a large and active membership, might be able to help. Almost every one of the Eighth's units had its own association affiliated with the society, and the organization's quarterly newsletter pro-vided the names and addresses of contact men. The secretary of the 466th's association confirmed that he had a roster of the group's vets containing over a thousand names. No Albert Seraydarian appeared on the list, but there was an Albert Seraydar, living not in Brooklyn but in Coconut Creek, Florida.

I immediately called information, got the number, and that evening, after thinking for hours about what I would say, how I would explain myself, I dialed the number in Coconut Creek. I was nervous. Maybe he would not speak to me. Maybe he would not want to revisit that past, relive that day. He might feel I had no right to intrude on him now, dredging up wrenching memories from almost fifty years ago. After all, I knew from my family's trip to visit him in Brooklyn in 1946 that he had found the relentless questions impossible to answer and excruciatingly hard to bear.

The phone rang and rang until at last the receiver clicked and a man's voice, thick with the unmistakable tones of Flatbush Avenue, carried over the wire. Stumbling over my words, hardly daring to pause for breath, I blurted out my name and explained, none too clearly, that I was calling about the 466th Bomb Group.

After what seemed an eternity the voice responded warily, "That's my group."

"Well," I continued, gaining a measure of control over my voice, "actually, I'm really interested in the Richard Farrington crew."

Another pause, longer than the first. I could hear his breathing at the other end of the line.

"That was my crew," he said at last.

"My uncle's name," I stammered simply, "was Howard Goodner."

Without even a second's hesitation he heaved a sigh, and, his voice cracking, he muttered, "The most beautiful guy I ever knew."

We were off and running.

Within days a letter arrived from Albert Seraydarian. "Your phone call to me . . . was like I was struck by lightning. My head hasn't stopped spinning. My past keeps popping in and out on me." In the months that followed that call we spoke often on the phone and exchanged letters, and I made two extended trips to Florida to visit Albert Seraydar. He had changed his name after the war, he explained, when the engravers' union in New York refused him membership. They already had too many Armenians, they advised him, and so he dropped the "ian." During these visits we spent hours on end discussing the crew, their training, their missions—anything he could remember—and in the process we became very close. "It's good that you're doing this," Al's wife, Grace, whispered to me during a lull in our conversation one hot October afternoon. "Not a day has passed since I met Al that he doesn't think about what happened with his crew. It's always with him."

He had been confused and traumatized when he returned to the States in 1945 and was confronted by the Brennans and Barretts and Regans—by all the families who wanted to know what had happened on that day, looking at him, the survivor, and wondering, he always thought, why he had come back and their son or brother or husband had not. For years after the war he was tormented by nightmares about the crash, about being trapped in the fluttering tail. At dances or out with buddies he would drink too much and without warning would slip back in time. While his date or friends stood in stunned silence, he would throw himself to the ground and thrash about in a frenzy. The wing was on fire and he was groping for his chute, struggling to get out of the turret. The Barretts invited him to their apartment for dinner and to Barrett Amalgamated's offices in Rockefeller Center. Mr. Barrett wanted to give him a job, but every time Al saw them the conversation turned to Jerry and they dissolved in tears. In the end he just couldn't face it. He turned down the offer, and contact between them lapsed.

As the years passed the crew and the events of April 21 slipped beneath the surface, but they were always there, never far away, and our conversations always, inevitably, returned to them. We went over what had happened, what he had seen, the various possibilities. He wrote his recollections of that mission in his first letter to me, and although he would later add details, the account never changed. "The only two of my crew I saw was Peterson and Brennan when I threw myself out of the turret," that first letter read. "When I came to, I realized that the tail section was torn off from the rest of the airplane. I was terrified. I didn't know how I was going to get out. Millions of thoughts raced through my head in seconds. My crew, my family, etc. I had the sense enough to realize that I was floating down in the tail. I put my chute on and in the excitement . . . was only able to hook my left side on. I pulled the ripcord and the chute blossomed out and pulled me free of the tail section. But . . . the chute was badly torn by sliding past the jagged and torn metal of the fuselage and all the other jagged pieces of metal.

"I was floating down in my chute. I didn't see any other chutes or any smoke. It was a very hazy day. When I got about five or six thousand feet off the ground I heard whistling noises and looked down behind me and saw two soldiers on a motorcycle shooting at me. I could see flashes from their rifles. I took my .45 . . . and threw it away. When I hit the ground I was at a very steep angle and hit hard. I hurt my back and my right ankle. I couldn't move. The soldiers grabbed me and searched me. I didn't know the language so I pointed to my injuries. They understood and lifted me up and put me in the sidecar of the motorcycle. They let me straddle my arms over their shoulders and they carried me toward this large building. As I was approaching about the second step I felt a sharp, burning pain in my back. I screamed and looked around. This German woman who came from nowhere poked me with [a] red-hot poker, clear through my flying clothes. They hurriedly carried me inside, and to my astonishment I saw Lt. Manners there. He was already stripped of his flying clothes. He was soaking wet. I later learned that he had just missed the corner of the building that we were in and landed in the creek. I also learned that he had to put his chute on in midair because he fell through the nose wheel door. He grabbed his chute on the way out.

"I'm jumping around a bit, but to clarify the question of how many chutes, I didn't see any. You have to realize that the tail section was great deal lighter than the rest of the plane. . . . That part of the plane went toward the ground much faster than the tail, so while I was floating down in the tail unconscious, the fuselage must have hit the ground before I even gained my senses. Being that it was hazy I didn't see anything. . . . I didn't even see Lt. Manners's chute."

As I read the letter and during our various discussions I was puzzled by the inconsistency between this account and the version he had related to Howard Barrett and Marie Peterson in 1945. He told them that he *had* seen another chute and *had* seen the plane explode and burn maybe a mile away. Now he claimed to have seen nothing—no chutes, no burning plane. We talked about this, but Al had no explanation. He and Manners were marched from the village where they landed to the gigantic POW camp at Moosburg, and on the road they talked about what they had seen. His story in 1945 sounded very much like the account given by Manners in the MACR, and maybe, we speculated, he had merged the two. It was also possible that in the trauma that settled over him after the war, he had simply blotted things from his memory.

In the meantime I had begun to locate other members of the 466th who were on the April 21 mission to Salzburg. The files in Suitland contained a flight diagram and loading lists for each plane in the formation. Checking the loading lists, which provided the names of each crew member in each plane, against the roster of the 466th's veterans' association, I was able to find more than a dozen men, including the formation's lead pilot, lead navigator, lead mickey man, deputy lead pilot, and many others, who flew that day. I spoke to the pilot flying off Farrington's right wing, the copilot in the plane to his left, and gunners in the planes in the squadron just in front of them. They all remembered the mission, sometimes with great clarity, and although details varied they told essentially the same story. They recalled the horrible weather, the massive layers of lead-gray clouds and high winds that threw them off course and made holding formation impossible. They remembered the order recalling the formation, and they recalled bringing their bombs back across the continent. But above all they remembered with deep bitterness that a decision by the command pilot—against the pleas of his own navigator and mickey man and others throughout the formation—took them directly over Regensburg. They remembered that the flak was light, no more than eight or nine bursts, and they remembered the one plane, hit in the left wing, spinning out of control into the haze below. Some saw two chutes, some three. Others couldn't believe that anyone got out.

Despite months of examining the records and talking to men who flew the mission, the question of the chutes remained mysterious. Documents that disclosed where the bodies were recovered might provide the answer, but such records might not exist. The Veterans' Administration in St. Louis had already informed me that thousands of personnel files, almost all from the Second World War, were lost in a fire, Howard's among them. The only remaining hope was the Graves Registration Service, and after numerous inquiries in Washington I was directed to the agency responsible for GRS records. There a clerk confirmed that his office did possess such papers and I might order not only Howard's files but those of the entire crew. Since the plane went down so near the end of the war, he said, the files might indeed have information on where the bodies were found. I ordered them and waited. I was not prepared for what they brought.

On a dreary, sunless February afternoon a thick package arrived from Washington. It contained files for each of the crew members, and some were far more extensive and detailed than I had dared hope. The house was empty as I sat in the living room and began to read. Jerry Barrett's file was on top, and I discovered, to my astonishment, that it contained a narrative account of how the plane was found. Elements of the American Seventh Army had entered the region one week after the plane went down, and a report written by the Graves Registration Service of the Sixty-fifth Infantry Division revealed what they encountered. "GRS personnel were directed by Twentieth Corps to remove the remains of bodies from a wrecked four-motored plane of the Army Air Corps. Before reaching the scene of the disaster they stopped at a . . . headquarters of one of the battalions of the Sixty-fifth Infantry Division in the town Oberhinkofen, Germany, for information pertaining to the exact location of said airplane.

"Upon speaking to a major of this battalion . . . the GRS personnel learned that three American Air Corps men were supposed to have parachuted out of the said plane on . . . 21 April 1945. The three men who jumped from the plane were taken prisoner by the Germans it was said. All this information was received from . . . two English PWs . . . who were at that time liberated by the American soldiers. . . . The town of their internment camp was Piesenkofen, Germany, very close to where this plane crash took place. . . . The nearest town to the plane crash was Scharmassing, Germany."

An additional report elaborated. "GRS personnel arriving at the scene found the following: Tail assembly found in due north position from grid coordinates (U218506). It was the rear assembly consisting of rear fin, two tail flaps, and tail fin. Just above what appeared to be the tail gunner's section, markings of T9 were visible. One other structure from the tail assembly that lay to the right of the main part of the rear assembly had markings of 295592. . . . Main part of airplane (wreckage) found about fifteen hundred yards due west of tail assembly. Contained the whole outline, except the tail assembly, of a four-motored plane. Impossible to identify plane other than of four motors because airplane was burned beyond recognition. The plane faced in a due westerly position. GRS personnel evacuated from the center portion of the fuselage where the wings bisect the fuselage the remains of bodies, how many cannot actually or definitely be determined because there was no complete torso intact."

Did this mean then that none of them had gotten out of the plane after all, that they were all found inside the wreckage, that all the agony of the families, all the days and weeks of desperate wondering about the three or four chutes, had been for nothing? Identification of some of the bodies had been difficult—no dog tags were ever found for Jerry Barrett and Louis Wieser, delaying for months their positive identification—but then how could one explain the three or four chutes reported at interrogation in the 466th?

In Jack Brennan's file another brutal shock awaited me. A report written by a Medical Corps captain and signed on May 8 was appended to the other forms. It read, "I certify that on or about 29 April 1945, I inspected the remains found in an airplane wreck near Obertraubling, Germany. Two of the bodies were intact and lying clear of the plane. Both men had apparently died instantly upon hitting the ground. One man had a dog tag on his chest reading: John C. Brennan 12206828. This man had a severe compound fracture of his right thigh, multiple fractures of the skull, and a fracture of the jaw. The second man had no dog tags, but . . . on his pants was the laundry mark G-6638. This man had a compound fracture of the left elbow, a simple fracture of the left humerus, a compound fracture of the right thigh, a broken jaw, a broken nose, and multiple contusions. In a nearby farmhouse infantry troops found a dog tag with the name Peterson on it and an identification bracelet with [the] name Brennan on it."

I took a deep breath. G-6638, I realized, referred not to Bob Peterson but to Howard. As grim as the description of the wounds was, it was clear that Howard and Jack Brennan had *not* been in the plane. Tearing open Howard's file, I read quickly through the various forms until I came upon a short note in the file that sent me reeling. "Information obtained from G2 (Twentieth Corps): One plane . . . shot down by En AA about noon 21 April vic (U 213502) and vic (218504). Russian PW reported two men escaped alive from the plane, were captured by the Germans and taken to a town and paraded through streets, where they were beaten to death and then taken and placed in wreckage of plane. Serial numbers of clothes on deceased were as follows: G 6638 and B 6828." The report was filed by CIC [Counter Intelligence Corps], Sixty-fifth Infantry Division. In Howard's file another note, written at the American cemetery in Nuremberg, concluded with the chilling line, "Body evacuated [for burial] following investigation as an atrocity case."

Stupefied, I stared at the sentence, "paraded through streets . . . beaten." My head swam, and my eyes flooded with tears. What had begun as an effort to close a circle in my family had turned instead into a nightmare.

As I sat and read the reports over and over again, hoping that I had made a mistake, that I had misunderstood, a ghastly scenario began to take shape. It seemed possible that the three chutes might have been Christ Manners, Jack Brennan, and Howard. After all, Al thought he was trapped in the tail for some time—just how long he could not even estimate—and he saw no other chutes. In that case, Jack and Howard may have managed to get out immediately after the plane was hit. Al saw Brennan and Peterson in the waist just as he passed out and assumed that they had been unable to jump. And yet Al lost consciousness and lost sight of the plane until several moments later. The radio compartment in the *Black Cat* was above and aft of the bomb bay, and Howard was strong and athletic. He might have been able to jump down from the radio compartment, open the bomb-bay doors, and get free of the burning plane before it went out of control. If the first three chutes had drifted far away by the time Al freed himself from the tail, this might account for the differing numbers of chutes seen in the formation—one to four.

The files referred to an investigation, but none was enclosed, and the conclusions of the reports present were maddeningly contradictory. The Medical Corps captain, Edward N. Snyder, Jr., was convinced that Howard and Jack had died on impact with the ground. Was his report part of the investigation? Was it the final conclusion reached by the investigation, or was the Russian POW's allegation confirmed? Snyder described the bodies as "lying clear of the plane," wording that suggested that they were found close to the wreckage. But if they had been thrown out of the plane as it fell, would their bodies have been found together and as near the wreckage as the statement implied? It certainly seemed suspicious.

That night I called Al in Florida. The thought crossed my mind that he might have known about this all these years but had sought to shield the families, making his encounters with them all the more unbearable. But when I stammered out what I had read, he was clearly in shock. He knew nothing about it, and neither, he assured me, had Christ Manners. Both had believed that they were the only ones to escape from the *Black Cat*. He seemed devastated.

As soon as I could get away I took the train to Washington. The National Archives held records for all war crimes cases, and if an investigation had been undertaken its paper trail would begin there. The files were stored at Suitland, and the number of war crimes cases ran into the thousands. The records were filed under personal or place names, but after a day of searching they yielded nothing under Goodner, Brennan, or Peterson. Nor did any village or town in the area appear. The GRS report had stated that the nearest village to the crash was Scharmassing, and it had also mentioned Oberhinkofen; the English prisoners who had reported three captured Americans were in Piesenkofen, and the CIC was headquartered in

Obertraubling. A map of the area revealed that these villages formed a rectangle just to the west of Regensburg, but the files contained nothing.

During the spring I made repeated trips to Washington, sorting through war crimes records, 65th Infantry records, 466th records, exploring every conceivable avenue. I weeded through the files of the fighter groups that accompanied the 466th on April 21, searching for some hint of the story related to Mrs. Farrington about four men being shot by the Germans. The medical examination of the bodies at the crash site seemed to exclude that possibility, but I needed to check. It was one more piece of a puzzle that eluded me.

In the process of searching, I began to find the families of the Richard Farrington crew. Marie Peterson had written to Al only a few years earlier, reestablishing contact after almost forty years. She had been to St. Avold in France to visit her husband's grave, and that visit prompted her to write. I traveled to Illinois to see her. I visited Joliet, where I met Jack Perella's brothers, and to Hammond, Indiana, where I spent an afternoon with Louis Wieser's sister. I located Jack Regan's younger brother on Long Island and Jack Brennan's sisters in New Jersey and Florida. The Farringtons and the Barretts were no longer alive, and I could find no living relative.

Everywhere I saw reflected back at me the same tableau of love and pain that I had known in my own family—the same snapshots from the last visit home, the scrapbooks full of yellowing newspaper clippings and curling photographs, the boxes of V-mails, the same heartbreaking tele-grams, kept neatly in their torn envelopes. Everywhere we had the same aching, bittersweet conversations I had had with my mother and uncle, as I asked them to open old wounds, to rip away the scar tissue of decades, to remember. In Joliet, Mel Perella produced a thick album on whose cover the words *Our Jack* were engraved, an album so familiar it could have been Howard's. As we talked about Jack and turned the pages of the scrapbook, Mel Perella rose from his chair, and while his wife and brother Al and I continued to talk, he wandered into a small den. Out of the corner of my eye I could see him, breathing deeply, staring out the window. He had seen Jack for the last time at an El station in Chicago, he told me, on his way to a Cubs game in the summer of 1944, and he was at home with his parents when the War Department telegram arrived. It was the first time he had spoken about it in years. I had tapped a vein of sorrow so deep and abiding that the years could obscure but not efface, and still we kept on talking. And as we talked and wrote and visited in the months that followed, the crew came alive again, one by one, borne on the wings of memory, and we found ourselves bound together in a chain of love and loss that passed beyond the generations.

In the spring I decided to go to Germany. I had known since that terrible afternoon when the GRS reports arrived that I would be drawn inexorably to Regensburg, to the villages outside the city where the plane came down. I have spent a great deal of time in Germany over the years studying and doing research. I speak the language, and I know my way around. I would conduct my own investigation.

En route I stopped in England. The 466th Bomb Group Association was holding a reunion in Norwich to dedicate a monument at the old air base at Attlebridge, and I decided to attend. For three days in June I talked to men from the group and prowled the streets of Norwich with them searching for pubs, dance halls, and other old haunts. I visited the market, still cluttered with canvas-covered stalls, the train station, the castle, and Blackfriars' Hall, where Howard and Jack Regan had played basketball. I stepped into the Bishop's Palace, now a prestigious school for boys on the cathedral grounds, and stopped in for a drink at the Maid's Head Hotel. Across the square stood the dance hall the men had frequented, its portals still supported by the hulking figures of Sampson and Hercules.

Then, on an unusually hot, muggy afternoon, we went by chartered bus to AS 120. A handful of dilapidated armaments sheds, Nissen huts, and hangars dotted the fields, specters shimmering in the moist sunshine. The WAAF site, where Howard and the other enlisted men had lived, was overgrown with thistles and hawthorns, and the huts had long vanished. But amid the dense underbrush a mosaic of weathered concrete floors, with raised triangular slabs where the tiny stoves had perched, could still be seen. The main briefing building and the control tower were still there, and the long silent runways, and, amid the high, wind-whipped weeds, spaced at regular intervals, the pan-shaped hardstands. Pushing through the weeds to the right of the control tower, I came upon hardstand 58. I stood on its crumbling concrete surface, flooded with emotion. It was here, on the morning of April 21, 1945, that Howard and Jack and Al and the others had clambered into the *Black Cat*, bound for Germany.

I left East Anglia in early July, following the trail of the *Black Cat*. Rather than go directly to Regensburg, I decided to begin the search in Freiburg, where all German military records were housed. Every flak battery that shot down an Allied plane was required to submit a report, an *Abschussmeldung*, that recorded the time of the action, the type of plane hit, and, for me the most important part of the form, "the fate of the crew: (1) dead, (2) parachuted, and (3) prisoners." But, as I had feared, no reports existed for so late in the war. From Freiburg I traveled to Munich, where I spent several days poring over reports from the Nazi officials in the Regensburg area. Local authorities were required to report any air activity and any downed aircraft in their area to the state government in Munich, but, as with the military records, the steady stream of dispatches came to an abrupt halt in mid-April 1945. I had reached a dead end with official documents. It was time to go to Regensburg.

I had explained my search to a senior archivist on the staff in Munich, and although he had little to offer me in the way of documents, he stopped one afternoon at my desk in the readers' room. He had remembered that a man from a small town near Regensburg was in the archives a few weeks earlier. The man—his name was Peter Schmoll—was not a professional historian, the archivist emphasized, but a firefighter and a local history buff who was researching the American air attacks on Regensburg. The archivist recalled Herr Schmoll mentioning that, as a hobby, he liked to investigate air crashes in the Regensburg area, and he gave me the address and telephone number.

I reached Regensburg on a cool, rainy Friday afternoon in early July. The train carried me on a northeasterly route beyond the sprawling suburbs of Munich and Freising, through Moosburg, where Manners and Al were taken to a POW camp, to Landshut, a town the 466th had bombed on the crew's twenty-first mission. The crew flew lead that day. At Landshut the train headed north, crawling through a landscape of green rolling hills and dense stands of black firs and yellow fields thick with sunflowers and rapeseed. We passed through clumps of neat whitewashed houses with orange tile roofs and brightly painted churches whose onion-shaped steeple domes lent the tidy villages an exotic Turkish aspect.

After settling into a hotel near the cathedral I dialed the number I had been given in Munich, and Peter Schmoll answered the phone. Rapidly I explained that I understood that he was researching the American air war in the Regensburg area, and so was I. He listened politely while I rambled nervously on, but when I mentioned that I was searching for information about a crashed aircraft, he perked up. Encouraged, I told him that I was trying to find out about an American plane, a B-24, that went down near Scharmassing in April 1945, and I had been told by archival authorities in Munich that he might be able to help. Yes, he said, he and a friend did make searches for planes—they had found dozens—and he was definitely interested in seeing me.

We met at the main entrance to the train station early the next morning. I had hardly slept. A tall, slender man, born, I later discovered, in 1952, Peter Schmoll spoke little English, but he could read the documents I brought. We took a table at the station restaurant and ordered coffee. Spreading his materials out on the table, he explained that for years he and a friend had been investigating downed aircraft in and around Regensburg. Most were American. They had made a map of all the known crash sites in the area, had ordered the MACRs from Washington to find out about the crews, and had accumulated as much material as they could about each. After listening to him and examining the map he brought, I showed him the documents I had collected in Washington and explained what I was investigating. He listened attentively, studied the GRS reports, and asked thoughtful, knowledgeable questions. Neither he nor his friend had heard of a B-24 shot down near Scharmassing in April 1945, and he eagerly examined the map and sketch I had brought. To the critical question of whether the Russian's story could be true, he thought that it might certainly be. Things like that happened, he knew, even in the last days of the war. But he was equally certain that if two American flyers had been paraded through a village and beaten, the Americans would have discovered it when they arrived a week later. People in small villages talk, he said, and those responsible would certainly have been denounced to the arriving Americans, possibly by other Germans themselves, and, if not, certainly by the Russian and Polish laborers—prisoners of war—who worked in the villages. At any rate, he seemed confident that we would find out.

As he read the documents and studied the crew picture I could see that he was hooked. During the weeks and months that followed I would come to appreciate the full measure of Peter Schmoll's judgment and dedication to finding the truth, but even on that first morning something in his eyes, his manner, his speech told me that I could trust him, that he would help.

Within an hour we were in his red BMW heading for the villages just west of the city.

After studying the map we agreed to start our search in Scharmassing. Weaving through the mid-morning city traffic, we drove west, past the new university and the *Bundeswehr* base, past a cluster of home and garden centers, furniture discount houses, and shopping plazas that seemed more appropriate to the Philadelphia suburbs than Bavaria. But just beyond the Autobahn that swept toward Nuremberg and Passau, both targets of the Farrington crew, the urban sprawl of Regensburg halted abruptly and a countryside of green hills and black firs appeared, and I realized that I was nervous.

The early morning rain had stopped and the sky had turned a bright, cloudless blue when we pulled into Scharmassing and parked. Typical of German farm villages, the neat stucco houses, their windowsills accented with potted geraniums, were clustered around a single street, with the fields spreading out from them in all directions. It was possible to leave the car at the edge of the village and stroll along the street, knocking on door after door.

We had discussed strategy before we left the train station. In the villages we would simply ask if anyone remembered a plane coming down in the last days of the war. We would volunteer no information, say nothing at the outset about the Russian's story, but simply allow the people to talk. After hearing what they had to say we would ask if they had ever seen or heard any rumors about Americans bailing out and being taken through a village in the area. After that we would play it by ear. We agreed that Peter would do most of the talking. Over the next few days we developed a routine, knowing when to ask questions, which ones the other would pose, always proceeding cautiously, never asking leading questions or giving anything away. If it seemed appropriate to raise the Russian allegations directly, we did, although we always used a euphemistic term—had they ever heard any rumor, any story, about *Misshandlung* (mistreatment) of American flyers? In Munich a German historian at the Institute for Contemporary History who had conducted hundreds of interviews with Bavarians about their experiences in the last year of the war assured me that people in these villages would speak quite openly. Enough time had passed, most of those directly involved were dead, and any reluctance to talk—characteristic of the immediate postwar years—was gone. He believed that if people in the area had information about the *Black Cat* or had heard any rumors about a beating they would speak up. After the first day of talking to people, I agreed.

Finding a group of farmers chatting behind a tractor on the roadside, we stopped, and Peter, speaking even more heavily in the local Upper Palatinate dialect, explained that we were seeking information about a crashed aircraft from the last days of the war. He asked if they knew anyone who was living in the village in the spring of 1945. They directed us to a man whose father had run the local pub during the war. If anything had happened in Scharmassing or the area, he would know.

We found Anton Feigl at home in the center of the village. He confirmed that his parents had owned the village pub during the war, and, yes, he remembered hearing about the plane crash at the very end of the war. He was not in the village at the time, he said—he was a POW in Virginia, having been captured by the Americans in Normandy—but his father saw a plane crash in April or May, he wasn't sure which. His father had described a large four-motored plane—an American bomber with one wing blown away—spiraling down over the village. As an afterthought he added that the plane tore in half as it fell. Peter glanced at me. It had to be the *Black Cat*. Feigl continued. Everyone was afraid that it was going to come down right in the middle of the village, but it crashed beyond the high ridge of trees just to the east, beyond Ebenteuer's farm. His father and brother were among the first on the crash site. It was still burning when they got there, and a small crowd had gathered. His father never mentioned seeing parachutes, but he said they found the bodies of Americans in the field—he thought it was two—who had been unable to open their chutes. We should talk to his younger brother, the one who went to the crash site with his father.

Georg Feigl lived in another village close by, and we arrived at his farm in a matter of minutes. He ambled out to greet us as we pulled into the barnyard at the side of the house. He was happy to talk to us, and he certainly remembered the plane crash, he said. Although Regensburg was attacked repeatedly during the war, only one plane was shot down around Scharmassing. Straining to follow the conversation through the almost incomprehensible dialect, I did understand that he did *not* go to the crash site that day. His father and two soldiers who were quartered in the house rushed off just after the explosion, but he went the next day. The plane was completely burned, a mere shell, and there were bodies in the wreckage—how many he could not say. Two others, though, were in the field, and he saw them. Peter asked if they were close to the plane. No, he said, they were several hundred meters away, the first maybe three hundred meters from the crash, the other several hundred meters farther east. Three hundred to five hundred meters! The Medical Corps captain who examined Howard and Jack in the field described them as lying "clear of the plane," implying to me—and Peter agreed—that they were close by the wreckage and near one another. I interrupted, pressing Feigl about the distances. Yes, he was sure that the first man was several hundred meters—three hundred, approximately—away and the other well beyond, another hundred, maybe two hundred meters. His father speculated at the time that their chutes had not opened or that they had been thrown from the plane after it broke apart and began to plummet.

When, a bit later, Peter asked if he had heard any rumors in the village about *Misshandlung*, he told us without hesitation about an American pilot who had bailed out over Unterisling, a nearby village. The flyer had landed in a tree, and an irate farmer tried to kill him with an ax. The arrival of German soldiers saved the flyer, and the farmer was arrested and tried after the war. Feigl hadn't heard anything about mistreatment in this case, but he volunteered to call some of his old classmates who were in the village at the time. They were all thirteen or fourteen years old at war's end, and aside from old men and the foreigners—Poles, Russians, Serbs, and others—who worked as forced laborers on the farms, there were no civilian men in the village at that time.

Driving back to Scharmassing, we stopped at the farm of one of Feigl's classmates, who he believed might also have seen the crash. We found the man standing in his barnyard just beside the road. He instantly remembered the plane crash. He had gone immediately to the site above Ebenteuer's farm, climbing the path up the steep wooded hill and into the fields that slope down toward the villages of Piesenkofen and Obertraubling to the east. The plane was still burning, and he saw three, not two, bodies lying in a line that stretched over an area of maybe five hundred meters. One was very close to the plane and badly charred. Another, he distinctly remembered, seemed to have been driven into the ground by the force of his fall. The third man lay far out in the field toward the second part of the plane, which had crashed near the flak battery at Piesenkofen. Had he ever heard anything about *Misshandlung*, his friend asked him, and he also told us the Unterisling story.

Both men suggested that we talk to Maria Wittig, the daughter of

Heinrich Ebenteuer. Her father was dead, but she lived in the big farm at the edge of the village, the closest to the crash. She was in Scharmassing at the end of the war and, they thought, had gone up the hill to see the burning plane. We took names of other people we should talk to in Oberhinkofen, including the burgomaster and his wife, who were youngsters at the end of the war.

It was about six o'clock when we pulled into Oberhinkofen. We had stopped at the Ebenteuer farm along the way, but no one was home. Hans Gattinger, the burgomaster, was out fishing, his wife told us from the front door, but when we explained our business she invited us in. She had been nine years old at the end of the war, but she vividly remembered the crash. It was a cloudy day, a Saturday, and she was not in school. She was playing in the garden when she first heard the flak. She had run inside when almost immediately her father shouted, "Come out, they've hit one." She rushed back into the garden with her brothers and sisters and saw a plane "tumbling down." As it flipped over and over she saw one wing rip off, then another, until the sky seemed filled with bits of the doomed aircraft. She saw no chutes. Within an hour they had gone up the hill to the crash site. The wreckage was still smoking, and the soldiers wouldn't let them get too close. Without prompting she said she had seen three bodies scattered over several hundred meters in the field. She was afraid of the dead soldiers and would not look closely at them, but one was lying in the field belonging to her father. Her husband saw the crash, too, she confirmed, and he could tell us all about it. We arranged to come back on the following day.

The next morning Peter picked me up again at the train station. He had been mulling over the things we had heard and had decided to take a few vacation days. He would devote the next week to the *Black Cat*. We looked up several possible witnesses in Obertraubling and Piesenkofen, but none had seen the plane or heard anything about it. In the early afternoon we returned to Scharmassing to talk to the daughter of Heinrich Ebenteuer. The farm was a very large, U-shaped *Bauernhof*, and Maria Wittig, a sprightly, almost girlish-looking woman of around sixty, welcomed us into a cavernous rustic kitchen, then took us to the living room. She had no trouble remembering the crash. She was a young woman, nineteen, at the time. She did not see the plane come down but remembered the air-raid alarm and the flak and the tremendous concussion from the crash and exploding bombs. The Russians who worked on the farm—there were dozens of them—were afraid that the plane would land right on top of them, but it crashed just beyond the trees on the hill behind the farm. The shock waves from the crash blew out the windows of the small chapel behind the barn. Within thirty or forty minutes she was at the crash site. She believed that there were four men in the wreckage. The charred remains of the pilot were still at the controls, she said with a shudder, and two others lay in a line over several hundred meters from the plane. One of the two bodies in the field she would never forget. The soldier was a healthy, athletic-looking man, fair skinned and handsome, with delicate features and long, graceful fingers. She was struck by his good looks—and by the fact that he had hit the ground so hard that a mold several centimeters deep was made in the ground around his body.

She would remember the young man's face as long as she lived, she said wistfully. "I can still see him before me." Taking the crew picture from my jacket pocket, I placed it on the table between us. These, I explained, were the men in the plane. "So many," she said sadly, "so many." I asked her if she recognized anyone from the photograph. Leaning over the table, she studied it carefully. As her finger followed along the two rows, she paused first at Farrington, frowned, and said it could have been him, but no, no, it was not him. Then her eyes widened and she looked up at me. "There he is," she mumbled, her voice actually quaking with astonishment. She was pointing at Howard.

While I sat trembling, unable to speak, Peter asked her if she remembered any problems when the Americans arrived. She recalled that they had come to her father to ask questions, and Prince Johannes of Thurn und Taxis had accompanied them to act as translator. The prince's father was a well-known anti-Nazi, and the family's country estate, Höfling, was close by—in fact, very near the crash site. She could not remember exactly what the Americans were after but seemed to think it had something to do with the Russians who worked on the farm. Dozens of Russians and Poles had been quartered in the village after the bombing of Regensburg, and feeding them had put a great strain on everyone. The Russians, she thought, had complained to the Americans about bad care. The Russians had also told the Americans that they wanted to bury the dead flyers on the hill but the Germans prevented them from doing so.

Before leaving we asked if she knew of anyone else who might have seen the crash or might know anything about the Russians in the village. It was too bad, she said, we couldn't speak to a Pole—Petro Lawrynec—who worked on the farm. He certainly knew the other foreign laborers in the village, and he had rushed to the scene of the crash. He worked on the farm for years after arriving with other foreign workers from the east. He left Germany after the war and moved, we were astonished to hear, to the United States. Rummaging in a desk drawer, she produced a letter, ten years old, with an address and a photograph. In 1982 Petro Lawrynec celebrated his eightieth birthday, the letter said, in Cleveland, Ohio. It didn't seem likely that he would still be alive, but I planned to call Cleveland information as soon as I reached the hotel.

Later in the afternoon we returned to Oberhinkofen. Georg Gattinger and his wife welcomed us into their kitchen. He had been working in the fields; his sleeves were rolled up, and his flannel shirt was open at the neck revealing a triangle of sunburned chest. Yes, he remembered the plane shot down at the end of the war, the one that came down in three pieces. He was fourteen at the time and was in the church tower when the flak began firing. When he looked up he realized that they had hit one, and he watched as the silver plane, one wing on fire, started down in a spin. He saw the wing snap off and the tail of the plane tear away and begin to flutter down in the direction of Piesenkofen. We asked if he saw any chutes. "I can't say for certain," he replied, "but it may have been three or four." He was the first person who remembered seeing any chutes. "They were drifting down in the distance," he added, "to the east, toward Obertraubling or Burgweinting."

He had rushed down from the tower, through the village streets, and across the fields to the burning plane. Within thirty minutes he was at the scene. A crowd of around twenty people gathered in the field while the plane burned. He could not get close to the wreckage, but he did see two bodies scattered at a great distance. The first man, the one closest to the plane, was lying on his back, and, most striking to Gattinger, the man's body had made an indentation in the ground twenty to thirty centimeters—about eight inches—deep.

We asked about the Russian's story, and it was clear that they were hearing it for the first time. Shaking his head vigorously, Herr Gattinger acknowledged that anything was possible in those last days of the war, but neither he nor his wife believed that it could be true. They had never heard the story or anything like it, and they both agreed that in such small communities as Oberhinkofen, Piesenkofen, Scharmassing, or Obertraubling anything of that nature would have been impossible to keep quiet. People would know about it, talk about it. Besides, with the war lost and the American army only days away, it made no sense. Someone would have informed the Americans, someone would have been arrested, but neither had ever heard of any such thing. Both were troubled and excited as we left, and both were eager to help. Herr Gattinger offered to take us to the crash site and suggested other people in the area who might know something about the plane.

The next day Herr Gattinger led us to the field where the *Black Cat* came down. We drove in Peter's car out of the village, up the hill, and along a narrow tractor path through gently rolling fields until Herr Gattinger motioned for Peter to stop. There, he said, pointing to a deep, broad trough in the wheat along the tree line to the left, was the *Absturzstelle*, the place where the plane had smashed into the earth. Even from one hundred meters away we could see that the wheat all around was not as high as in the rest of the field, and Herr Gattinger told us that nothing would grow on that spot for years after the war. To the east the fields dropped away in a gentle incline toward Obertraubling and Piesenkofen, perhaps a mile away. To the north, hidden by a copse of trees, was Castle Höfling, and beyond, in the distance, the twin spires of the Regensburg cathedral rose through the morning haze. Looking down across the fields, I could see the stand of oak trees, vaguely triangular in shape, sketched by GRS personnel in 1945, and beyond, the church steeple at Obertraubling. Herr Gattinger motioned toward the fields to the east, planted now with sugar beets and rapeseed. He had seen the two dead soldiers there, he said, the first about fifty or sixty meters from where we stood, the other well beyond, toward Obertraubling.

While Peter and Herr Gattinger began walking through the waist-high wheat toward the *Absturzstelle*, I stared out in the other direction at the field where Howard and Jack were found. Thousands of miles from Tennessee and New Jersey, they died here.

I turned and made my way down toward the tree line, where Peter was probing the hard, dry soil with a small trowel. Every year at planting time, Herr Gattinger told us, plowing brought bits of the plane up to the surface and shards of metal and glass lay scattered among the furrows. The larger metal items were removed after the war, first by people who wanted to sell them and then by farmers who wanted to clear their fields, but the smaller pieces continued to emerge year after year. The trowel hit something hard, and Herr Gattinger bent down to examine what Peter had found. Wiping the dirt away with his handkerchief, Peter looked up at me and slowly raised his hand. In his fingers he held the casing of an exploded fifty-caliber cartridge.

Later we drove down through the fields over the tractor paths into Piesenkofen. We had the name of an elderly lady who lived in the village all through the war, and we found her at home. Now in her eighties, she remembered the crash. She didn't actually see it, but she had heard that two men had bailed out. One landed in the creek in Obertraubling near the church, and one landed at the edge of the Burgweintinger Forest. She didn't know what happened to them, she had heard no rumors, but it seemed clear that one of them was Christ Manners. Al had told us that Manners landed in a creek, barely missing the building where they were taken for interrogation. That building, we later determined, was the old school in the center of the village, just beside the creek. She also suggested that we speak to Herr Ramsauer across the street. He was a young boy at the time serving as a flak helper on the Piesenkofen battery. He would know something.

We were just in time to catch Herr Ramsauer as he came in from the fields on his tractor, pulling a wagon loaded with hay. He confirmed that he was on the flak battery at Piesenkofen, not far from where we stood and, yes, he remembered the plane shot down at the very end of the war. "It came down in three parts," he said briskly, adding, while my heart stopped, "and four chutes." We listened as he described the wing and tail breaking off the plane and four fully opened chutes drifting down. One of the men landed in the creek, and one in the trees in the Burgweintinger Forest. Two of the men were brought into Obertraubling, but he did not know what happened to the others. One of the men, he said with conviction, landed in a tree and was threatened by a farmer who wanted to kill him with an ax, but was saved by soldiers. Where did the other two men land? "There," he said, pointing to a knoll at the edge of Obertraubling covered with a new housing development. That would have placed them exactly between Manners and the crash site. If Ramsauer was correct, then Manners should have seen them. After all, he described seeing the wings floating down and the plane burning on the ground. Yet he saw only one chute, presumably Al's.

Peter asked if the plane was hit during a raid. Again with great certainty Ramsauer answered yes, the planes had dropped many bombs on the airfield or the Messerschmitt factory. Since the 466th had dropped no bombs on the raid, and certainly none over Regensburg, and since the story about the farmer was a variant of the familiar Unterisling story, Ramsauer appeared to be confusing two different incidents. Yet his recollection of some details was striking and, we knew, accurate. Numb with dread, I asked him about the Russian's story. He had never heard anything like that, he said, nor had his wife, who listened to our conversation from the doorway.

On a subsequent visit Ramsauer changed his mind about the number of chutes, saying that it was, after all, three. A Russian who worked as a helper in the flak battery and a German soldier who was billeted with his family went out to capture the flyers, but neither ever said anything about what happened. A day or so later he went up to the burned-out husk of the plane and saw the bodies, how many he could not say, lying close to the plane, covered by a tarp.

For days we searched for witnesses, asking questions and going from village to village, lead to lead, but we turned up nothing new. A call to Cleveland information also yielded nothing. No Lawrynec was listed in the city or the surrounding area codes. He had been close to eighty when he had written to Maria Wittig ten years earlier, and, I feared, was probably now dead.

Each day Peter and I sifted the information we had, and as we did, the Russian's story appeared increasingly inconsistent with the evidence. By all descriptions the plane came almost straight down, and Howard and Jack were found several hundred meters apart and in a line between the tail compartment and the main section of the ship. Several days later their bodies were apparently moved up to the wreckage. Frau Gattinger had remarked that after a day or so the body in her father's field was gone, buried, she assumed, but in fact it was moved close to the wreckage. When the Americans arrived on April 27 they found a highly suspicious scene: a charred aircraft and two badly bruised bodies lying nearby. That lent the Russian's story a certain plausibility. Yet several people who rushed to the scene on April 21 reported independently of one another that one or both bodies (some looked at only one of the men) were buried six to eight inches deep in the ground, as if they had fallen or been thrown with great force from the plane as it plummeted out of the sky. This description suggested that both died, as the Medical Corps officer assumed, on impact with the ground.

Another aspect of the Russian's story didn't make sense. If two American flyers had been paraded through a village and killed in public, it seemed odd that those responsible would bother to make it appear as though they had fallen to their deaths by distributing the bodies over a distance of several hundred meters in the middle of a vast field, far from the tractor paths. Such a plan would also have taken time, and within minutes of the crash people had begun to arrive in the field and had seen the bodies.

We were also struck by the fact that not one person had heard the Russian story or any variant of it. We gave them every opportunity, asking about rumors and innuendos. After days of listening I was convinced that at least the people with whom we had spoken were telling the truth, that they were hearing the story for the first time. We had interviewed people in the four villages surrounding the crash site, and they had not been in the least reluctant to tell us what they knew about the Unterisling incident, to volunteer information about local Nazis, and to suggest others we might interview. It was, of course, possible that everyone was lying, but this seemed increasingly implausible. The people with whom we spoke were thirteen or fourteen years old in 1945, and covering up a crime of this nature would have been almost impossible. It was also obvious that in these tiny villages—hamlets, really—nothing could be kept a secret. Everyone would know if an atrocity had been committed, and someone would certainly have talked. Maybe someone had. Maybe testimony had been taken in the "investigation" referred to in Howard's file. Yet only Maria Wittig remembered the Americans asking questions about the crash on the hill.

Then again, the puzzle of the chutes would simply not go away. Gattinger wasn't certain, but believed there might have been three or four, and Ramsauer, though he was clearly confused and initially said four, thought he had seen three chutes. It could be that one or two chutes had partially opened and then collapsed. The *Black Cat* was on fire, and the air was filled with flying debris as it broke apart and began spiraling downward. It was a thought I did not like to entertain, but it could account for the different numbers of chutes reported.

At the end of each day Peter dropped me off at the train station and I made my way back toward the hotel on the Tandlergasse. I walked along the muddy Danube or wandered through the meandering cobbled alleys of the old city, going over the day's events, sifting what we knew, what we needed to do. Sleep was impossible, and I came to dread my room at the hotel. It was modern and narrow, with high ceilings, and I lay awake until two or three in the morning, drifting in and out of consciousness. I dreamed about the crash, about the Russian's story, about collapsed parachutes. I startled, sat up. Haunted by a nagging fear that somewhere, someone knew something that would unravel the mystery of that day, that somehow we were missing one critical piece of the puzzle, I paced the narrow room, washed my face, stared at myself in the mirror, and finally went back to bed. By five I was up again, dressed, and ready to begin anew.

I left Germany in late July. Peter would continue to gather information and follow leads in the Regensburg area, and I would renew my efforts in the United States, looking for new avenues to follow. I thought the investigation might be filed somewhere in Washington under some agency or office that had simply eluded me. Back in Philadelphia I read through my notes from the interviews. I studied the map. For maybe the hundredth time I scoured the various entries in Howard's file, trying to tease a new of shade of meaning, a new clue, out of them. As I read through Edward N. Snyder, Jr.'s report once again, it struck me that, of course, this Medical Corps captain must have been a physician. His description of the wounds was professional, his anatomical terminology technical. If he was not a doctor in 1945 maybe he was a medical student and had finished his studies after the war. He might still be alive.

The American Medical Association in Chicago, I learned, maintained a roster of all its members, and after a long chat with the woman in charge of the master file, I learned that, in fact, three Edward N. Snyder, Jr.'s were currently practicing medicine in the United States. I explained to her that I was interested only in a man who would have been old enough to practice medicine in 1945, and, while insisting that she could give me no more information, she acknowledged that only one of them fit that description. She couldn't give me the address, she emphasized, but at last she relented enough to hint that he might practice in Pasadena.

In the afternoon a receptionist in Edward Snyder's office in Pasadena explained that the doctor would not be in at all during the day but would be on duty at Huntington Hospital in the trauma unit all night. I could reach him there. At two in the morning Philadelphia time I dialed the hospital pager number, and after an interminable pause Dr. Snyder was on the line. Was this, I asked nervously, the Edward N. Snyder, Jr., who had been company commander of C Company, 261st Medical Battalion, 65th Infantry, in 1945? He was a bit nonplussed, but after a short pause, he replied that yes, he was the man. "I have a report you wrote in May of 1945," I told him, "a report about bodies found in a crashed American aircraft." Before I could finish, he interrupted, saying, "yes, the one outside Regensburg."

I had not yet read him his report when he launched into a vivid description of what he had seen. Examining the bodies inside the burned wreckage was impossible, but there were two men, clad in their green flying fatigues and jackets, who were not in the plane. Because of the lingering cold, their features were still clear and the bodies were well preserved. Though he wouldn't hazard a guess about distances, the bodies were lying together and close by the wreckage, certainly not two to five hundred meters away. They had died in a fall, he volunteered, no doubt about that. I had not identified myself as a relative of one of the men, and he spared me no detail. Virtually every bone in their bodies was broken, he thought, and an autopsy would have revealed damage to every major organ. The two men were so broken up, their internal injuries so extensive, GRS personnel had had difficulty picking them up for burial.

At this juncture I related the Russian's story, and although he conceded that it was possible, he didn't put too much stock in it. A beating—and he had seen his share in the trauma unit—would be unlikely to produce wounds as extensive as those he had found on the bodies, especially the lower-body injuries. Both Jack and Howard had suffered compound fractures of the thigh, and that, he was convinced, would hardly be the result of a beating. He thought it possible that their chutes opened too late or only partially deployed or that they were flung out of the falling plane. All were more likely, in his estimation, than a beating. He did not recall how he happened to go to the crash site or why he was asked to write a report on May 7, but writing such a report was highly unusual, he said. I wondered if he wasn't asked to submit it as part of an investigation into an alleged atrocity, but he could not remember any such investigation and he had never heard the atrocity story.

A few days later a letter arrived from Ed Snyder. He was a member of the 65th Infantry Division veterans' association, and a recent newsletter contained a list of men from E Company, 261st Infantry regiment, the unit that found the plane in April 1945. Maybe they could tell me more. The list contained a half-dozen names, and I began to call. One of the company's platoon leaders, Francis Brown, lived in Philadelphia, and he not only remembered seeing the crashed airplane and the bodies in the field, he had written about it to his parents in 1945. He had recently unearthed his wartime letters and was astonished about the timing of my call. Later that night he phoned back and read excerpts from two letters. The first, dated July 8, 1945, described his company moving out of Regensburg on April 27 into a small village just to the west of the city. "We landed in a *Gasthaus* and drank beer. The regiment rounded up hundreds of POWs in the woods." On a hill just outside the village they found what they believed to be a crashed B-17 and bodies and "guarded them until the air force people arrived. Stayed in the village of Scharmassing until May 1." He returned to the incident in a letter of August 25, 1945. "When we moved to a small town outside Regensburg called Scharmassing we stayed there for a few days. I believe I mentioned a B-17 which had crashed on a hill near there. Some Poles in the town said the flyers had been beaten and whipped in the town. I saw the bodies, which were up by the wreck, and they sure were bruised."

He suggested that I contact John Massey, another platoon leader in E Company. Massey lived in Louisburg, Kansas, and I called him that same night. Massey also vividly remembered seeing the plane and the bodies. The company was in Regensburg, hoping for a few days rest before the next big push, when they were sent into the countryside to set up a perimeter defense. They were on their way to secure a castle—Castle Höfling, the estate of Thurn und Taxis, I assumed—when they came across the charred wreckage of the plane and found the bodies close beside it. He told me that in the village the men heard stories from the Poles that the American flyers had been tortured and beaten. He did not recall an investigation at the time, but remembered being visited by a CIC man in Vienna around January 1946 and being shown photographs of the bodies in the field. He then put me in touch with two other men from E Company, who also recalled hearing the stories in the village and finding the bodies in the field fifteen yards or so away from the plane.

Although everything the men of E Company related to me was based on hearsay, their recollections sent me plunging again into uncertainty. Maybe I had been misled in Germany. Maybe Peter and I were wrong. If Massey was questioned by the CIC, then an investigation had indeed been mounted, but where was it and what were its conclusions? I needed to find that investigation and I needed testimony from the Poles or Russians who seemed to have been everywhere around the Regensburg area. After almost a year of searching, the likelihood of either seemed remote.

Then we found Petro Lawrynec.

Richard Sloane, a college student working with me, spent weeks in the fall making inquiries of Polish-American organizations in the Cleveland area, searching for Petro Lawrynec. We knew that he had lived in Parma at one time and that he had a brother in Cleveland, but we could find no trace

of either. Then, one afternoon in early December while we were going
through old Ohio telephone directories, a librarian commented that the
name didn't actually sound Polish. Maybe, she said, it was Ukrainian.
Within days we traced Lawrynec to the rolls of St. Pokrova Ukrainian
Catholic Church in Parma, and when I called, Father Michael Krupka
confirmed that not only was Petro Lawrynec alive, but he lived in a room on
the grounds of the church. I explained why I wanted to speak with him, and
Father Michael agreed to talk to Lawrynec about the incident.

Three days later Father Krupka called. He had spoken with Lawrynec,
who was very old and whose memory was spotty, but he had agreed to talk to
me. Father Krupka would bring Lawrynec, who did not speak English very
well, and a translator to the rectory at eight o'clock, just after mass, and we
could talk. His phone could be rigged as a speaker, so both Lawrynec and
the translator would be able to hear my voice. At eight o'clock sharp I
called. As I posed my questions I could hear the translator's booming voice
and then a weak, gravelly response as Lawrynec spoke to the men in the
room. He remembered the crash. He saw a fire in the sky and the plane
coming down in a flat spin. At first it looked almost as if the pilot was trying
to find a place to land, and the people at the farm were terrified, certain that
it was going to come down on top of them. Looking up as he ran, he saw the
wings and tail rip free. Then the plane disappeared behind the trees at the
top of the hill. One explosion followed another, and a great plume of smoke
rose from beyond the firs.

Contrary to Maria Wittig's recollection, Lawrynec did not go up to the
crash site until the next day. He remembered seeing one body in the plane
and two or three close by, maybe ten meters away. He saw no parachutes
and heard nothing about any. When I asked him directly if he had heard the
Russian's story, he knew nothing about it, had never heard it. During the
course of our conversation I repeatedly rephrased the question, changing
the wording, shifting the emphasis, approaching it from different directions,
but always he reiterated that he knew nothing about any Americans para-
chuting into the village and being beaten. I asked him if he thought it was
possible that something like that could have happened without his knowledge. On this he was quite adamant. No, he said, that was impossible.
Besides, he volunteered, in April of 1945 the Germans there were looking
forward to the coming of the Americans because it would mean the end of
the war. Asked if he remembered the Americans raising questions when
they arrived several days later, he said yes. The Americans came to the

farm and spoke with Heinrich Ebenteuer. They wrote things down, took notes, but he did not know what it was about.

Later, after our conversation ended and Lawrynec left for his room, Father Krupka said that he had known Lawrynec for more than fourteen years. Lawrynec was a forced laborer, captured by the Germans in 1942, and he stayed on in Germany until 1949, when his brother helped to bring him to the United States. Father Krupka knew Lawrynec when he was more vigorous and remembered more, and the priest believed that if Lawrynec knew anything about an incident of this sort, he would have talked about it. Petro Lawrynec was a good man, Father Krupka insisted, an honest man. He would tell the truth.

In early January I returned to Suitland, determined to check the war crimes files once again in case I had missed something. There I had a conversation with the chief archivist, who suggested one more possibility. The records center held an enormous group of files for *untried* war crimes. Only a very crude index existed, listing more than eight thousand cases. The index was a large ledger book, and the entries were by country, but the individual cases might be listed by name of locale, witness, or victim. Taking the ledger back to my table in the users' room, I opened it to the three thousand cases from Germany. I began by looking for Goodner, Brennan, or Peterson, but found nothing. Meanwhile I jotted down every Polish or Ukrainian name that appeared, since the case might be entered under the witness's name. Then I went back through the index, slowly running my finger over the handwritten entries, searching for the towns and villages in the Regensburg area. The process consumed an entire day.

After thumbing through the long ledger pages for hours, I had virtually given up hope. It was another dead end, like so many others. Then the name Schar*l*massing materialized on the page. It was misspelled, but there it was—case 12-1882. With shaking hands I grabbed the case reference book that accompanied the index and turned to case 12-1882, where a brief typewritten description stared up at me: "Alleged killing of two American flyers by unknown German soldiers or civilians after they had jumped from bomber near Scharlmassing Germany on/about 21 April 1945."

Springing from my chair with the ledger in my hands, I rushed to the archivist, who examined the entry. He did not make me wait to order the file. "Let's go have a look," he said, and we took the large elevator down into the stacks of the records center. The size of two football fields, the basement was filled from floor to ceiling with crates, boxes, and files. The fluorescent lighting cast the endless rows of documents in a dim, yellowish hue, and as we marched between the rows I was so nervous I could barely breathe. At last we stood shoulder to shoulder in the narrow aisle where the file was stored, boxes rising above us on both sides. We located the file, opened it up, and there, on top, was a folder marked War Crimes Group, case 12-1882. The search had taken almost a full year, but at last I had found it. With the file in my trembling hands, I took the elevator back to the brightly lit users' room to read.

A large map of the area above Scharmassing was enclosed. On it the crash site was marked, exactly where Herr Gattinger had taken us, as well as the position of the tail section and the bodies of Jack Brennan and an unidentified American soldier, G-6638, almost exactly where Peter and I had been. I began to read.

On May 3, 1945, the commanding officer of the 609th QM Graves Registration Company filed a report with Third Army headquarters about the crash. It stated flatly that "two members of the crew, John C. Brennan and one unidentified individual with clothes marking G-6638 are reported to have escaped initially. It is alleged that they were captured, killed, and their bodies placed on the wreckage. One identification tag, that of Robert E. Peterson, was recovered from civilians and may belong to the individual who was killed with John C. Brennan. Neither of these bodies was burned."

After this report was filed a team from the special War Crimes Group arrived in Scharmassing to conduct an investigation. Lieutenant Dwight McKay was in charge, and he quickly discovered that the Russian who made the original claim had vanished and could not be found. "The CIC had no record of the supposed witness's name, and to their knowledge he had disappeared from the scene of the crash." Nor could he find other Russians or Poles in the villages who had actually *seen* the alleged beating. He interrogated Heinrich Ebenteuer, and his testimony was recorded in the file. With Prince Johannes of Thurn und Taxis serving as translator, Ebenteuer stated under oath, "on April 21, 1945, about 1200 hours [11:00 British time], I saw an American bomber hit by flak. It broke in half and fell to the ground. I went up to the field and saw five bodies in the burning plane and two others lying about five hundred meters from the oak woods. I did not see any parachutes come out of the falling plane. I went to the field about forty minutes after the plane fell." He was shown photographs of Howard and Jack and identified them as the two men in the field. He "did not see any parachutes in the field," adding, "the bodies of the soldiers were lying about twenty centimeters in the ground. I would say that their fall had caused them to make such a hole. . . . I was one of the first persons to see the two soldiers in the field, and I am sure they died as a result of their fall. . . ."

McKay also interrogated a young Polish worker in Scharmassing who had seen the plane come down but also knew nothing about a beating. "The Germans near Regensburg had been shooting flak at [the plane]," he said. "I saw them hit the wing once. The plane came over the town at about three thousand meters; it was burning and began to wobble; then I saw three men parachute when the plane began to fall. I saw three parachutes open, but I didn't see them land, since they drifted into the distance. I could not get near the wrecked aircraft because it was burning and ammunition was exploding. The next day when I went up to the airplane, it was still burning. I saw one burned man in the wreckage. I saw two men lying in the field about one thousand yards from the wreck. Their clothing was all ripped. I recognize the men in the photographs. Brennan was lying about one hundred yards east of the other soldier."

A third statement was taken from Prince Johannes. The prince declared, "I was in my home on 21 April 1945 about 1200 hours when about fifty American four-motor bombers [were] flying above my house. They were flying [at] about four thousand meters, one of them had been hit by flak and fell into the field southeast of my home. About half past twelve two German flak soldiers brought an unopened American parachute to my house. [One] told me that he had taken it from the body of a dead American soldier. About one o'clock I went to the field and saw the aircraft and two dead Americans. I have seen photographs of two dead Americans, and I recognize one of them as the soldier I saw lying in the field. The airplane was burning while I was there. Coming to the two American soldiers I saw that one of them made a hole in the earth about thirty centimeters deep in the form of his body."

McKay also "interrogated six other persons in the vicinity of Scharmassing. Two of the persons were Catholic priests. They did not witness the plane crash but saw the bodies of the two dead soldiers shortly after the witness Heinrich Ebenteuer did. Their statements as to the place and condition of the two soldiers were in agreement with Ebenteuer's statement."

Summarizing his investigation, McKay emphasized that the two bodies "were found in the field about halfway between the burning forward part of the plane and the rear section" and that "civilian witnesses, on the scene about forty minutes after the crash, saw the bodies of the two dead American soldiers. The bodies had not been removed from the field and were sunken into the ground about four to six inches. The impression made in the ground was in the form of the body." McKay concluded, "the American soldiers mentioned above died as a result of the fall of the wrecked aircraft. . . . There is evidence of one unopened parachute. The indentations in the ground where the bodies were found lying indicate that they fell with great force. No tangible evidence has been found indicating a war crime, and the report of the Graves Registration Officer was merely hearsay and unsupported conclusion of fact."

A second round of interrogations was conducted in August by a different investigating officer, but the questions raised at that time concerned the identity of the men in the field. Louis Wieser and Jerry Barrett were still officially listed as missing, and with the men buried, the army was clearly trying to make certain that the two bodies in the field had been properly identified. Those questions may have continued on into January of 1946, when John Massey was shown photographs of bodies in the field, but the investigation into the alleged beating was already closed. On September 11, 1945, a final report on the case was submitted to Third Army headquarters. It concluded, "there is no evidence of the commission of a war crime. The report of the investigation reveals that death occurred as a result of the fall of the airmen without the use of parachutes. No further action is required. It is recommended that this case be closed administratively."

In the spring of 1993 the Regensburg newpaper, *Mittelbayerische Zeitung*, ran a full-page story about the *Black Cat* and its crew. It called for eyewitnesses to come forward, and several did. Many saw two parachutes on that day in 1945, but only one man, standing in a nearby village on that morning, thought he had seen three chutes open, although he was certain about only two. Another witness said he and a friend saw the ship break apart, then watched as first one, then another chute appeared. They thought for an instant they saw a third one, but their attention was riveted on the plane careening from the sky and they lost sight of the chutes. When they looked again they could see only two drifting down in the direction of Obertraubling. No one saw four, and no one saw any American fighters following the chutes down. All agreed that the chutes appeared only when the plane broke apart, and although Al thought he had blacked out for some time, the sequence of events was probably much faster, a matter of a few seconds.

After the tail broke off and the chutes appeared the plane reared almost straight up in the sky, hung for a moment, then flipped over and began to tumble over and over toward the earth. As it did the right wing broke off and bombs, oxygen tanks, and other bits of the aircraft showered down. I have come to believe that three parachutes opened in that instant, but one, perhaps burned or ripped or snagged by flying debris, collapsed. Howard's position in the ship made it unlikely that he was able to bail out, and his body was found closest to the main part of the wreckage. It seems probable that he was thrown from the plane close to the ground. If a third chute opened, it would most likely have been Jack Brennan's.

The Russian's story, which tormented me for more than a year, may have been a pure fabrication, told to the Americans to cause trouble for the Germans. Some of the Russians and Poles in Scharmassing did complain of bad treatment and may have wished to settle scores. Yet there may be another explanation. One witness who came forward after the newspaper story was in Obertraubling as the plane came down. It was a market day, and the streets were crowded. He had just come into the center of the village when he saw an angry crowd gathered around an American flyer who had landed in the creek. The crowd was surly and taunted the flyer, but two German soldiers pulled him out of the creek and took him away through the jeering crowd. When Al arrived on the scene moments later, he was set upon by an irate villager with a hot poker. It may be that the Russian who reported that two Americans had been paraded through a village and then beaten was in Obertraubling. Perhaps he saw Manners and then Al being taken through the streets and later heard from other Russians in Scharmassing that two badly bruised Americans were lying dead in the field. He may have come to the conclusion that the two he had seen—or even just heard about—in the village were killed by the Germans. In either case, the man vanished before the investigation became serious, and no other witnesses were ever found.

Shortly after the newspaper story appeared I returned to Germany. Albert Seraydar flew with me. As we entered German air space en route to Frankfurt he turned to me and whispered, "You know, Tom, the last time I flew into Germany Howard was with me." We went to Regensburg, to the crash site, to the building where he was interrogated, to Moosburg, where he was taken as a POW. We met people who had seen him in his parachute almost fifty years before, and he was interviewed by the newspapers and filmed for a Bavarian television program. We learned that they had erected a marker on the crash site, a simple cross made of birch. The marker is dedicated to all the casualties of war, but at its base a small bronze plaque lists the names of the men who died there on April 21, 1945, a reminder to all who pass that even in triumph there is heartbreak.

On our last morning there Peter Schmoll drove us again to the crash site. We walked out through the flowing green wheat, and in the declivity where the *Black Cat* had come to rest we placed eight red roses. I thought of each of them—Farrington, Regan, Wieser, Barrett, Noe, Murphy, Peterson, and Perella—men whom I had never met but whom I would never forget. We crossed the tractor path at the crest of the hill and passed into the field where Howard and Jack Brennan died. All around us fragile shoots of green had burst through the soil, and as I knelt to place two roses there Al laid his hand on my shoulder. I thought of my grandfather's anguished letter from November 1945, of the room filled with color, of the path stretching across the decades that had led me to this strange, haunted place. Looking across the wide expanse of tilled soil that ebbed away toward Piesenkofen and Obertraubling, across a field we had come to see for the last time and yet knew we would never leave behind, I realized that I had reached the end of my search. The circle had been closed, and the time had come, at last, to let go. As we drove slowly along the path toward the road I turned for one last look. It was springtime, and they were plowing in the fields above Scharmassing. Tractors moved across the rolling swells of the rich, dark earth, and in their wake, as happens each April, shattered bits of Plexiglas and twisted metal—mute reminders of the *Black Cat* and the men who died here—were rising in the furrows.

AUTHOR'S NOTE

Wings of Morning is a work of nonfiction based primarily on three
extraordinary collections of correspondence. More than two hundred
letters written by Howard Goodner between the fall of 1942 and the spring
of 1945 and approximately three hundred letters written by Robert Peterson
to his wife Marie during the same period form the documentary core of the
book. Both men wrote almost daily, and together their letters offer a
remarkable guide to an American air crew's day-to-day experience in
training and combat. Another set of roughly one hundred letters written by
various members of the Richard Farrington crew and their families comple-
ment those. I was also able to conduct interviews with dozens of 466th
veterans who knew one or more members of the Farrington crew and could
recall, sometimes in striking clarity, events and conversations from 1944
and 1945. The recollections of Albert Seraydarian (Al Seraydar) whose
recall of small details about his crew mates—their conversations, their
habits, their activities, their likes and dislikes, and their reactions to
events, both great and small—were indispensable. Three diaries written by
men who were at Air Station 120 during the same period as the Farrington
crew—one by a radio operator (Frank Spurlock), one by a navigator on a
lead crew (Joseph Edwards), and one by a 785th veteran (James H. Lorenz)
who flew many of the same missions as the Farrington crew, provided
valuable insights into the life of men who flew combat in the 466th between
the autumn of 1944 and war's end.

The records of the 466th Bomb Group (H) are housed at the National
Archives, the Washington National Records Center, The Center for Air
Force History at Bolling Air Force Base, The Albert F. Simpson Center for
Historical Research at Maxwell Air Force Base, and the Second Air
Division Archive in Norwich, England. The history of the 466th's Medical
Department, the files of its Special Services Section, and the *Daily Bulletin*
of AS 120 offer up a rich portrait of day-by-day life on the ground, while the

mission folders, with their maps, photographs, mission summaries, and the hand-written notes of the briefers, yielded detailed accounts of the crews' missions.

In researching the book, I employed methods normally used by professional historians, but in telling the story I have turned to narrative techniques usually associated with fiction. All the incidents depicted in the book happened—were recounted to me in interviews or were described in the letters or in the official documents—and the quotations from the letters are rendered as they stand in the original except for corrections to grammar and spelling. I have used the device of dialogue to present some scenes. The sentiments, impressions, and ideas expressed in them are those of the individuals themselves, derived from the letters or interviews, but the wording is naturally mine.

I am deeply indebted to many people for help in researching and writing this book. I owe a special debt of gratitude to the men of the 466th Bomb Group Association, who shared their experiences and memories with me, particularly Barky Hovsepian and Louis Loevsky who helped me locate other veterans who knew the Farrington crew. So many 466th veterans answered so many questions and offered so many of their own recollections that to single out any seems almost arbitrary, but Robert Moore, Henry Hiter, Bill Deal, Harold Read, Richard Baynes, Earl Wassom, and Earl Beitler deserve special thanks. I am also particularly grateful to Dr. Edward N. Snyder, Jr., who volunteered not only his memories but professional guidance in evaluating important medical evidence.

In England, Ted Clarke, who worked briefly on AS 120 and at the Bishop's Palace Red Cross Club during the war, was tireless in guiding me not only around the old air field but the familiar haunts of the American flyers in Norwich. Peter Schmoll's role in tracing the fate of the *Black Cat* and its crew is described at length in the text, but I can never adequately express my thanks to him. Without his help, honesty, and friendship, the investigation in Germany might never have gotten off the ground. Barbara Blake, Elizabeth Block, Bruce Kuklick, Walter McDougall, and Jonathan Steinberg followed the sometimes agonizing progress of the research and each gave the finished manuscript constructive readings, as did Gerard McCauley.

Above all, I wish to express my gratitude to the families of the Richard Farrington crew—to Mel and Al Perella, to James Regan, to Jeanette Sketo and Winnifried Hordych, Jack Brennan's sisters, to Josephine Graegin, the sister of Louis Wieser, to Ronald Rossman, Steve Manners, Henrietta and Judy Noe, and especially to Mrs. Marie Peterson Dennis and Art Peterson, who granted me access to Bob Peterson's letters. All of them opened old wounds to speak to a complete stranger, trusted me with treasured family photographs and letters, and waited patiently for the book to appear. My mother, Mildred Childers, my Aunt Sibyle G. Sadler, and my Uncle James E. Goodner, bore with questions that forced them to revive painful memories, and I owe them debts I can never repay. A final word of thanks and deep affection is also due to my friend Al Seraydar, the luckiest guy I know. All of these people supported and sustained me through four years of research and writing. But ultimately this book belongs to my father, Tom Childers, who inspired it and who did not live to see it completed, and to my late grandparents, Ernest and Callie Goodner, who preserved Howard's letters and his memory and who always believed, as the old wartime song went, that they would meet again.

BIBLIOGRAPHY OF
SELECTED ARCHIVAL SOURCES

Washington National Records Center (National Archives)

Record Group 18
Mission Reports for the 466th Bomb Group (H), the 96th Combat Wing, the
Second Air Division, 1944–1945, Cartons 1737–1743.

Record Group 92, Missing Air Crew Reports

Record Group 94, World War II Reports, XX Corps, December 1944 to
April 1945, Box 5125, G-2 Journals File

Record Group 153, Judge Advocate, War Crimes

Record Group 338, Headquarters, U.S. Army Europe, War Crimes Branch,
Cases Not Tried

Record Group 407, 65th Infantry Division
65th Inf. Div., G/S-2 Periodic Reports 16 April–June 1945
365 Inf. Reg., After Action Reports, March–April 1945, (261) -0.3, 15104.

Office of Air Force History, Bolling Air Force Base, Washington, D.C.

2nd Bombardment Division Mission Folders, 1944–1945. 526.332
Daily Bulletin, 466th Narrative History, Medical History, Operations Diary,
Reel Boxes 618–620

Albert F. Simpson Historical Research Center, Maxwell Air Force Base

History of the 787th Bomb Squadron, April–May 1945
History and Mission Reports, 466th Bomb Group, 1944–1945
Operations Diary, Station Bulletin

Bayerisches Hauptstaatsarchiv, Munich

MA 106 674, RPB Monatsberichte des Regierungspräsidiums. Nordbayern und Oberpfalz, November 1943–February 1945;
MA 106 696 Monatsberichte Regensburg, January–April 1945

Militärarchiv Bundesarchiv, Freiburg

RL 5 Luftwaffe-Personalamt/Abschussanerkenntnisse

Militärgeschichtliches Forschungsamt, Freiburg

"Regensburg in den letzten Kriegstagen des Jahres 1945, berichtet von Robert Burger damals stellvertretender Kampfkommandant"

Second Air Division Archive, Norwich Central Library

Lt. James H. Lorenz, Diary, September 1944–April 1945
Lt. James H. Lorenz, "Story of a Typical Mission"